A Judge's Advice

Also by Ruggero J. Aldisert

Opinion Writing: Second Edition
(AuthorHouse 2d ed. 2009)

Road to the Robes: A Federal Judge Recollects Young Years & Early Times
(AuthorHouse 2005)

Winning on Appeal: Better Briefs and Oral Arguments
(NITA 2d ed. 2003)

Logic for Lawyers: A Guide to Clear Legal Thinking
(NITA 3d ed. 1997)

The Judicial Process: Text, Materials and Cases
(West 2d ed. 1996)

A Judge's Advice

50 Years on the Bench

Ruggero J. Aldisert

SENIOR UNITED STATES CIRCUIT JUDGE,
CHIEF JUDGE EMERITUS,
UNITED STATES COURT OF APPEALS FOR THE THIRD CIRCUIT

CAROLINA ACADEMIC PRESS
Durham, North Carolina

Library of Congress Cataloging-in-Publication Data

Aldisert, Ruggero J.
A judge's advice : 50 years on the bench / Ruggero J. Aldisert.
  p. cm.
Includes bibliographical references.
ISBN 978-1-61163-052-7 (alk. paper)
1. Law--United States. I. Title.
KF213.A52 2011
349.73--dc23
                    2011020193

Editorial cartoons copyright © 2011, Russell Hodin.

CAROLINA ACADEMIC PRESS
700 Kent Street
Durham, North Carolina 27701
Telephone (919) 489-7486
Fax (919) 493-5668
www.cap-press.com

Printed in the United States of America

DEDICATION

This book is dedicated to my colleagues on the Court of Common Pleas of Allegheny County (Pittsburgh), Pennsylvania, all of whom are now deceased, and to my colleagues on the United States Court of Appeals for the Third Circuit, including those appointed by Presidents Franklin Delano Roosevelt and Harry S. Truman and who are no longer with us, as well as the outstanding men and women serving with great distinction today in active and senior status.

CONTENTS

FOREWORD

David W. Burcham

The Honorable Ruggero J. Aldisert is the consummate teacher. I have first-hand knowledge of this fact inasmuch as I served under his tutelage 27 years ago as his law clerk. At the time, he was the Chief Judge of the United States Court of Appeals for the Third Circuit. The lessons learned in his chambers have formed the foundation of my professional life. He emphasized that nothing refines thinking better than writing, but that there is no such thing as good writing, only good rewriting. He taught his clerks to work quickly and proficiently and to approach each task with painstaking thoroughness. He instilled in us enormous respect for the law and for the judicial process. And all of this was on the first day of our clerkship. The ensuing two years were professionally rigorous, enlightening and transformational.

This latest book is a treasure and the reader is in for a treat. Distilled between these covers lie the lessons and wisdom of Judge Aldisert discerned over the course of his amazing legal career. The breadth of his experience is astonishing—he has served his community and country with distinction as a judge for over 50 years, and at 91 years of age he continues his extraordinary service as Senior Judge for the United States Court of Appeals for the Third Circuit. He is the author of over fifty scholarly articles in legal publications and he has written five books. He has been an adjunct law professor and has lectured widely to judges and lawyers across the nation and abroad.

This book represents, if you will, a sort of "best of Aldisert." He has compiled into one volume his teachings and insights generated by his previous writings, lectures and judging. This book provides each reader—whether judge, lawyer or student—the opportunity to benefit from the teachings of this remarkable jurist and scholar.

David W. Burcham, President
Loyola Marymount University, Los Angeles

ACKNOWLEDGMENTS

As I have written elsewhere, the word "acknowledge" has two meanings. I invoke both of them here. To the extent that it means to recognize or confess, I represent that what I say in these pages is as authentic as it was when the various chapters were first published. The selection from my books and articles was made to supply a proper answer to the questions I raise in the introduction.

To the extent that to acknowledge means to express gratitude or obligation for I do so freely in thanking friends who offered advice. I am indebted to Prof. Paul Lomio, Librarian of the Stanford Law School Library, for his generous and gracious advice. Former law clerks now in academia shared their profound wisdom in my efforts. They include David W. Burcham, president of Loyola Marymount University in Los Angeles, Prof. Edward L. Carter of Brigham Young University, and Prof. Thomas O. Main of McGeorge School of Law, Pacific University. Judicial colleagues were generous with their advice—retired California Superior Court of Santa Barbara County James Slater, retired Pennsylvania Superior Court Judge and Supreme Court historian Patrick R. Tamilia of Pittsburgh, and Senior U.S. Circuit Judges Joseph F. Weis, Jr., of Pittsburgh and Leonard I. Garth of Newark of the U.S. Court of Appeals for the Third Circuit.

Former law clerks, now with prominent law firms, government units or as corporate counsel throughout the country, offered excellent suggestions, include Matthew Bartlett, Robert J. Cindrich, Erin Campbell Framke, Staff Counsel, U.S. Court of Appeals for the 10th Circuit; Rita Lomio, Michael A. Mugmun, Meehan Rasch, James R. Stevens III and Anika Stucky. Candace Jackman and Leslie Goemaat, my 2009–2010 law clerks, were in Dean Acheson's words, "Present at The Creation"; in their free hours they assisted in organizing materials in a first attempt at a rough draft. I freely acknowledge the profound assistance of Patrick C. Bageant and Joseph C. Hansen, my 2010–2011 clerks, in reducing the size of early drafts and generously contributing superb editing skills during their personal time. I acknowledge with appreciation the dedicated assistance of my career law clerk and judicial assistant Grace W. Liu.

Other friends who offered valuable advice include Michael T. Reagan, Esq. of Ottawa, Ill. and Kay Bruce, Esq. of Santa Barbara. In original publications of the text I noted with gratitude contributions of the law clerks then serving in various periods. An expression of appreciation to them is reiterated. I thank Russell Hodin for his imaginative editorial cartoon contributions.

A special word to members of my family who have been very supportive in this effort—daughter Lisa M. Aldisert of New York City, president of Pharos Alliance, Inc.; sons Robert L. Aldisert, Esq. partner in Portland, Ore. law firm of Perkins Coie, and Gregory J. Aldisert, partner of the Santa Monica, Cal. law firm of Kinsella Weitzman Iser Kump & Aldisert; and my brother-in law, James E. Brophy III, Esq., and his son (and my godson) Joseph Brophy, Esq., both of Phoenix, Ariz.

Although technically I retired in 1987, since that time I continue to be a very active "senior" federal judge, and in addition, have written five serious books on the law together with four supplemental editions. This has involved incredible demands, expending valuable time that drastically intrudes on the retirement time of Agatha and me. As in the case of the other books, my fantastic wife has soldiered on with me and my writing, and thanks to her patience and encouragement, as well as excellent literary advice, our almost 60 years together have been extraordinarily happy, loving and rewarding. For making so many good things in my life happen, I can only reiterate overflowing gratitude over so many decades of our deepest love.

A Judge's Advice

"BACK IN 1941 WHEN I STARTED LAW SCHOOL..."

INTRODUCTION

This book is ambitious. It seeks to offer a special intellectual stimulation to lawyers and law students by adding to their tools of advocacy a selected number of observations accumulated by a judge who slipped into his black robes in 1961 and is still wearing them as a rather frisky senior judge of the United States Court of Appeals for the Third Circuit. These pages flesh out the instruments and implements of lawyers with a far-ranging "view from above" with one objective in mind: to enrich the skills of these men and women so that each may bear—to borrow from Izaak Walton's *The Compleat Angler*—the noble title of "compleat lawyer."

It seeks to do this by allowing the reader to figuratively open the Chambers door of a veteran member of the state and federal judiciary, who then invites the reader to sit down with him to have an informal conversation. The voice is a nonagenarian who has rolled up his sleeves, sat back in his chair and says he is willing to share observations on the law, both its anatomy and philosophical purposes, based on a rather prodigious and extensive experience. He says he is willing to share reflections from one who has been active in the law for an extraordinary period of almost 70 years; ever since entering law school in September, 1941 (with the exception of four years with the Marine Corps during World War II in the Pacific between his 1L and 2L years at law school). He begins by explaining the thesis of his presentation—to become a truly compleat lawyer, he or she must learn "*Why am I doing what I do?*"

I have translated those imaginary conversations to the pages of this book. The content is selective reflections from my books, lectures and essays over my many years as a lawyer, judge, teacher and author. My service on the bench, past and present, gives me the inspiration and opportunity to reflect on the law. In this single volume I distilled from my writings—from 1966 to date—observations that I have contributed to the body of American legal scholarship; writings that have spanned a number of topics and have been set forth in five books, most with multiple editions, and over 50 scholarly articles in legal publications here and in Europe.

Five major themes have commanded my special interest over the years, with my preoccupation evidenced by these themes recurring or resurfacing in my books, articles and lectures. Lawyers and law students are now afforded an answer to the essential query mentioned before: *"Why* am I doing what I do?" And in so doing, answers are furnished to subordinate questions: *What* is the bedrock of our common law system and *how* can I use that knowledge to better advocate? *What* are trial and appellate judges *really* looking for? *How* can I create a writing structure that will persuade? *What* logical configuration is absolutely necessary in any legal argument? *What* practical challenges do judges face when deciding my case? *What* is the difference between *the* philosophy of law and *a* philosophy of law? *What* is the difference between a judge making a decision and a judge justifying it, and why does that difference matter to me? *How* do I convince a judge to decide my way when no precedent controls and the law is not clear? The following five themes are designed as a reply to these questions:

- The Common Law Is Still Alive and Kicking
- Logic and Law
- Avoiding Assembly Line Justice
- The "Write Stuff"
- How Judges Decide Cases

To reflect my academic emphases I have designed discrete portions of the book, labeled as "Parts," to each of these themes. Part A through Part E each has its own perspective, with its concomitant Chapters containing excerpts from what I have written and lectures I have delivered. These observations remain as relevant today as they ever have been.

And that's what this book is all about.

In formal legal writing the text is punctuated with citations to cases, statutes and secondary references. Although a paean to authenticity, the references constitute a hiccup to easy reading. To make these pages more reader friendly you will not find them in the text. At the end of the book, however, I have prepared an Appendix, chapter by chapter, where authorities may be located.

Santa Barbara, CA

RUGGERO J. ALDISERT
Senior Circuit Judge,
Chief Judge Emeritus,
U.S. Court of Appeals for the Third Circuit

THE COMMON LAW IS STILL
ALIVE AND KICKING

The professional who wants to be the compleat lawyer must understand that "the Law" in the courts in this second decade of the 21st Century is merely the living edge of centuries of tradition. He or she must not only know what we do but also why we do it. The starting block is an examination of our house of law, which has been built on five supereminent principles for centuries. In recent times, however, its longstanding foundations have received haphazard additions and modifications, some sensible and durable, others ill-advised and fleeting. This Part contains the state of our "house" of law, the role of courts in contemporary society and a careful examination of the doctrine of precedent.

What then does the lawyer who seeks to be compleat absorb from Part A? Each of the Chapters seemingly address three separate and facially different subjects. Upon careful analysis, however, the reader will see that they are all intimately related. The role of courts in contemporary American society has undergone a metamorphosis from applying legal precepts to drily logical extremes regardless of consequences, to a recognition that the effect on society of a court's decision is a legitimate tool in decision-making. Nonetheless, as this change has come about, the five super-eminent legal precepts—truly wonderful basic concepts that originated in centuries past and form the foundation of our house of law—are still with us and, with a tweak or two or ten or twenty, are still the major tenants in the house of the law. And all this has come about because through the doctrine of precedent and *stare decisis*, ancient concepts, precepts and experiences live and breathe today. Advocates who possess this careful yet basic understanding of the riverbed of our legal system will be able to effectively navigate the currents swirling above, regardless of the bend of the river upon which they find themselves.

CHAPTER ONE

THE HOUSE OF THE LAW

Author's Note: With only slight modification, these passages are taken from remarks delivered to the faculty of Loyola Law School, Los Angeles, on February 24, 1986, and of the State of the Circuit Address delivered October 7, 1985, at the 48th Annual Judicial Conference of the Court of Appeals for the Third Circuit at Hershey, Pennsylvania. It was subsequently published in 19 Loy. L.A. L. Rev. 755 (1986).

———————

The time is ripe to take a critical look at what federal courts are doing to our house of the law. My view will be that of an insider; it will be through a jaundiced eye. It will be the focus of one who is in his fiftieth year as a judge, a judge on both the state and federal benches. It is through the eyes of a student of the judicial process, of one who concentrates not so much on the nuances of substantive or procedural law, but on the tools of decision-making. What these eyes see, in short, is this: a system in which there is too much pettifogging about gingerbread and encrustation in the trimmings of our house, and too little attention paid to its basic structures—to the fundamental precepts upon which the house of the law is built.

The Structure of the Law Obscured

In observing the house of the law today, I have extreme difficulty in recognizing the eclectic components of its architecture. Surely, there is a Georgian front and a Queen Anne behind, but the design tinkering just starts with that. We have added porches, screened them in and, finally, expanded them, helter skelter, into a series of rooms. Perched on top we see a hip roof, a gable or two, and a mansard, along with a generous sprinkling of skylights. Originally, the house was clapboard; then someone added a touch of brick here and there. At spots there is aluminum siding and you can see countless layers of paint in a rainbow of colors in various stages of adhesion and peeling. Parts of the house of law seem firmly grounded and appear able to withstand the challenges of changing judicial winds; other parts are quite fragile.

What Henry Maine once said of the infiltration of Roman law into Western thought also may describe our house: "nearly buried in a parasitical overgrowth of modern speculative doctrine." The architect of the finished product resembles not so much Thomas Jefferson at Monticello but Rube Goldberg. Yet we know that because ninety-five percent of federal court work is interpreting statutes and constitutional clauses, and because this interpretation proceeds in the common law tradition of lawyers and judges, we cannot expect a Palladio as an architect. We cannot follow the common law tradition and still guarantee clean lines and symmetry as we develop the law. "We have thought less of symmetry than of the advancement of knowledge," Maitland told us. Under the case-by-case method, we cannot expect the *elegantia juris* of the original Twelve Tables of Rome or the unannotated Ten Commandments of Moses. We cannot look for the crisp order we see in the Napoleonic Code or the clean statutes prepared by the Commissioners of Uniform State Laws or the American Law Institute. We cannot expect this because we know that the common law tradition is a "byzantine beauty," a method, in the words of John Ely, "of reaching what instinctively seems the right results in a series of cases, and only later (if at all) enunciating the principle that explains the pattern—a sort of connect-the-dots exercise."

We know that a gulf will always exist between the scientific theory of law and the practical doing of it. As Emerson said, "[w]e boil at different degrees." The lawyer has to be more than a historian. The lawyer's knowledge is an inversion of "real" or "scientific" history. The lawyer seeks authority, and the newer the authority the better, because that is what the courts seek. By comparison, the historian seeks evidence—the older the evidence, the closer it is to the event, the better.

Notwithstanding the common law tradition, and notwithstanding the absence of pristine pure lines in our house of law, it was still possible, until the recent era, to identify familiar disciplines of the law as we looked upon its house. Fundamental foundations and structures were always there to see. Although we constantly modified and tinkered with its profile, a physiognomy of the law was there to recognize.

These fundamental legal precepts were either immediately recognizable or reasonably retrievable. There was much of what Oliver Wendell Holmes described as "predictability," of what Karl Llewellyn called "reckonability," to the law. Dean Roscoe Pound summed it up for us:

> What we are talking about, then, is the body of authoritative materials, and the authoritative gradation of the materials, wherein judges

are to find the grounds of decision, counsellors the basis of assured prediction as to the course of decision, and individuals reasonable guidance toward conducting themselves in accordance with the demands
of the social order. This point of view assumes a developed social and
economic order and a corresponding development of the legal order,
with an organized judicial and administrative hierarchy, definite law
giving and law declaring agencies, and above all a developed profession of advisors upon the legal conduct of affairs.

We were able to possess what Hugo Grotius described in the seventeenth century as "a power of discrimination which enables [us] to decide what things are
agreeable or harmful as to both things present and things to come."

We knew that a court's expression had the force of law, yet we knew that
this force was proficient and efficient only to the extent that its expression was
clear and its reasoning persuasive. We knew that public acceptance of judicial
expression was directly proportionate to an understanding of what was said
and done and why; that this was but a paraphrase of *lex plus laudatur quando
ratione probatur* (the law is most praiseworthy when it is consonant with reason). But we also knew that there may be a conflict between justice according
to law and the *aequum et bonum* (that which is fair and good). We also knew
that the good judge always has an unquenchable thirst for justice.

Have things changed? I think so.

I have an abiding concern that most briefs from lawyers and many opinions from judges seem to have lost their way. Many no longer appear as instruments of persuasion or explanation; rather, they appear as instruments of
commentary, resembling more a ritualistic exercise than a decision-making
tool.

A promiscuous uttering of citations has replaced the crisply stated, clean
lines of legal reasoning. In judicial opinions, especially those of the United
States Supreme Court, we see a mishmash of citation in text and footnote.
Spewing case after case has replaced a tidy explanation of what is important in
the case and a clean description of why it is important. It is not too unkind to
suggest that often what poses as a work of scholarship is actually a work of
journalism. As Fred Rodell remarked, "a pennyworth of content is most frequently concealed beneath a pound of so-called style."

The great author Barbara W. Tuchman sounded a call for "clear, easy-read-
ing prose" in today's writing community. She asked all writers to avoid "the
Latinized language of academics with their endless succession of polysyllables,
their deaf ear for sentence structure, and unconcern for clarity." Over sixty
years ago, Benjamin Cardozo warned that

precedents [should not be] ultimate sources of the law, supplying the sole equipment that is needed for the legal armory, the sole tools, to borrow Maitland's phrase, "in the legal smithy." Back of precedents are the basic juridical concepts that are the postulants of judicial reasoning, and farther back are the habits of life, the institutions of society, in which those conceptions had their origin, and which, by process of interaction they have modified in turn.

Cardozo condemned, and properly so, the color matching process. He warned against a process of search, comparison and little more, stating:

Some judges seldom get beyond that process in any case. Their notion of their duty is to match the colors of the case at hand against the colors of many sample cases spread out upon the desk. The sample nearest in shade supplies the applicable rule. But, of course, no system of living law can be evolved from such a process, and no judge of a high court, worthy of his office, views the function of his place so narrowly.

A stuffy style and fluffy padding in appellate court opinions (and I sadly include myself among the participants and perpetrators) shows that we suffer from acute pedantry. We seem to forget that all lawyers and judges are professional writers. Professional writers are aware that prose, like any other art, calls for frequent compromise among desirable aims—sound and sense, force and fluidity, clearness and precision, emphasis and nuance, wit and truth. The very need for balance rules out consistency in the use of any component of writing. Each sentence and paragraph is a special case. Yet all of us—judges and lawyers alike—are guilty of bombastic propositions and legal dialectics in long sentences, awkward constructions and fuzzy-wuzzy words that seem to apologize for daring to venture an opinion.

I say all this not to suggest that effective legal writing should be graded for literary style for the sake of style. Rather, I emphasize this problem because the purpose of all legal writing is persuasion. Without clear writing, communication is lessened, and to the extent communication is diminished, the powers of persuasion decline. The common law tradition demands no more than a clear statement of reasons. The judicial process expects no more; the brief reader or the opinion reader deserves no less.

Let me return to the house of the law. We must be able to identify its architectural lines. We should know front, rear and side elevations, and floor plans of each component. If each legal decision builds on another, deft hands must stack each building block in its proper place. Our house must appear as a majestic cathedral and not as a frazzled parcel for urban renewal.

The time has come for the legal profession to simplify, rather than to complicate, current legal issues. The time has come to identify exactly what fundamentals underlie the controversy in each case, and to isolate which is the governing branch of the law's family tree. Our first step in any legal argument must be to look at the tree's trunk and main branches, rather than to concentrate on new twigs that continually sprout in all directions.

This analysis must be made because the starting point of every judicial decision must be a recognition of the controlling dogma, doctrine and fundamental principles. Only this recognition will permit our decisions to be both consistent and coherent. This call for more simplicity and more order in briefs and opinions will cause us not to regress, but to progress. This call will create better communication between lawyer and judge and between judge and community. This call will seek to remove from judicial decisions that which is idiosyncratic, and in its place will attempt to establish predictability and reckonability.

The Five Supereminent Legal Principles

The law explosion—reflected by statute or case law, by the new causes of action churned out by Congress, by the nuances of specialized government regulation or by the geometric expansion of law school curricula—has *not* spawned a corresponding increase in bedrock concepts upon which modern law and modern litigation rest. Fundamentals of law remain. They still loom large and foreboding, but will be more easily seen once we blow away mists that surround them.

I am prepared to defend the thesis that all substantive law including constitutional law, is but a spin-off of five fundamentals taught in the first year of law school:

1. Creating and protecting property interests;
2. Creating and protecting liberty interests;
3. Fulfilling promises;
4. Redressing losses caused by breach or fault;
5. Punishing those who wrong the public.

To deserve the accolade of "supereminence," the principles must demonstrate two critical characteristics: their presence must be vigorously felt and clearly recognized in most current federal litigation, and they must prove a philosophical kinship to some hefty ancestors. In these two very important aspects, I think that the "big five" pass with flying colors. Let me turn now to the first of these.

A. Creating and Protecting Property Interests

Although the earliest acquisitions of property rights are shrouded in unrecorded or fragmented history, we are treated to several interesting theories. First, Blackstone suggested that property rights are originally based upon possession, hypothesizing that "the ground was in common, and no part of it was the permanent property of any man in particular; yet whoever was in the occupation of any determined spot of it, for rest, for shade, or the like, acquired for the time a sort of ownership." Yet others would simplify the quality of acts necessary for primitive ownership in the far away dawn of property law. Their theory begins with the concept that everything ought to have an owner and that under Roman law there was a concept known as *res nullius,* an object which is not, or had never been, reduced to dominion. Therefore, the possessor is permitted to become the proprietor from a feeling that all valuable things are naturally the subjects of exclusive enjoyment. The occupant, in short, becomes the owner, not through adverse possession or prescription, but because all things are presumed to be somebody's property and because no one can be pointed out as having a better right than he to the proprietorship of this particular thing. Hence, the popular American lay expression: "Possession is nine-tenths of the law!"

Property law is probably the most ancient method of protecting recorded legal rights. In most societal forms, including the present as well as the very old, property law concerns rights of possession, use, alienation and succession. In America most of these attributes are governed by state law and, by far, most property litigation takes place in state courts. But the federal courts also find themselves deeply immersed in this most ancient legal discipline, especially in the recent era. It therefore deserves its rank as one of the five supereminent principles.

The definition of legally protected property rights evolved largely from the regulation of property ownership and use. In ancient societies, it focused most generally on the rules of succession to, or transfer of, real and personal property. In the Western world there is a large body of written property law, recorded from the promulgation of the Justinian *Institutes* in the year 533 through Blackstone's *Commentaries* in the eighteenth century. As legal systems became more sophisticated over the centuries, however, the nature of legally cognizable interests expanded dramatically. Thus, today property may be an object of physical existence or an intangible, such as a patent right, a chose in action, a right to retain a driver's license or a right to retain a position in a university tenure stream. In a broader sense a personal right to property goes even further and includes concepts of not causing injury to a person's good reputation, fireside and shelter, spouse, child, cow, Ferrari or copyright. As the Supreme Court observed in *Goldberg v. Kelly*:

> Much of the existing wealth in this country takes the form of rights that do not fall within traditional common-law concepts of property. It has been aptly noted that "[s]ociety today is built around entitlement. The automobile dealer has his franchise, the doctor and lawyer their professional licenses, the worker his union membership, contract, and pension rights, the executive his contract and stock options; all are devices to aid security and independence. Many of the most important of these entitlements now flow from government: subsidies to farmers and businessmen, routes for airlines and channels for television stations; long term contracts for defense, space, and education; social security pensions for individuals. Such sources of security, whether private or public, are no longer regarded as luxuries or gratuities; to the recipients they are essentials, fully deserved, and in no sense a form of charity."

So viewed, there exists more architectural uniformity in our house of the law than a cursory examination might reveal. Within the confines of this first supereminent principle, many federal judiciary efforts can be characterized as providing the vehicle by which persons can seek to protect those property interests that have been created through positive law.

B. Creating and Protecting Liberty Interests

It was Benjamin Franklin who said, "[w]here liberty dwells, there is my country." Liberty does dwell in our house of the law, and from the perspective of a federal house of the law, or, if you will, a house of federal law, it boasts a favored dweller status. It rates this special status because, whether viewed as a jurisprudential concept or as a highly treasured private interest, liberty is the spirit in our Nation's law that makes freedom ring.

The private liberty interest that is protectable by the federal courts is a freedom on the part of one as against another or the state to do or not to do a given act. It is the right to be left alone. Justice Douglas defined it as "the autonomous control over the development and expression of one's intellect, interests, tastes and personality." Unlike many other private interests, liberty to act may be presumed, unless restricted by custom, tradition or positive law. This basic presumption may be traceable to Roman law, especially to the ringing phrases of *The Institutes* of Justinian: "Liberty, from which the expression free men is derived, is the natural ability to do anything one pleases unless it be prohibited by force or law." In a more modern era, Eugene V. Rostow makes the point that "[t]he root idea of the Constitution is that man can be free because the state is not."

No less than the exhortatory opening statement of the Constitution catapults the individual liberty interest to the level of our supereminent principles:

> We the People of the United States, in Order to form a more perfect Union, establish Justice, insure domestic Tranquility, provide for the common defense, promote the general Welfare, *and secure the Blessings of Liberty to ourselves and our Posterity*, do ordain and establish this Constitution for the United States of America.

Constitutional case law has now precisely identified certain liberty interests, for example: freedom of communication and religion, freedom of the individual, embracing many particulars, such as freedom from slavery or peonage, freedom to travel, freedom of enterprise and contract, freedom to follow a chosen profession, freedom for individuals in the expression of their personalities and freedom from an establishment of religion.

In sum, whether viewed from the Justinian notions that everyone has "the natural ability to do anything one pleases unless it be prohibited by force or law," or from the notion of custom or traditions, or by constitutional clause or statute, the liberty interest has to be construed as one of the premier federal law principles. Yet, as I have emphasized elsewhere,

> drawing the line between individual liberties and rights, on the one hand, and those of government action for the larger good, is still the perpetual question of constitutional law. And about two thousand years before the Constitution, the same problem bothered an ancient social order which spoke through Heraclitus: "The major problem of human society is to combine that degree of liberty without which law is tyranny, with that degree of law without which liberty becomes license."

C. Fulfilling Promises

Any house needs housekeeping rules. Our house of the law is no exception. Prominent among our rules is that once the formalities of making a binding promise are made, we will enforce that promise. This housekeeping rule was not very important in primitive society, whether pre-Roman in the Mediterranean area, or post-Roman in the Dark Ages in England and on the European continent. But to the extent that societies confer upon their members the abundant accoutrements of better living and the fruits of expansive commercial intercourse, this rule becomes not only important, but essential. So it is in today's *la dolce vita.*

The increase in the quality of our social environment has bestowed upon society members great benefits, comforts and conveniences. We ride high in an era of rampant "plastic money," the credit-card vehicle of buy now, pay later. In an era not too dimly past, the legal niceties of contract law did not affect the average citizen and primarily attracted the attention of those engaged in mercantile or commercial pursuits. But rapid escalation of sophisticated consumer purchases, in quantity and quality, has increased the number and amount of contractual relations in the retail and wholesale levels as well as in distributing and manufacturing. This effect is seen today in the federal courts, where thirty-five percent of all civil filings sound in contract. Because of its formidable effect on our economy, the concept of fulfilling promises easily deserves our attention as a supereminent principle.

Of course, federal statutes have also contributed to the proliferation of federal cases arising under the concept of fulfilling promises. During the past century we have seen federalization of employment relationships and contracts under the labor laws, providing federal court protection to practically all aspects of an employment contract, from the initial stages of employee collectivization through bargaining for, executing and enforcing the contract. Added to these bodies of specialized contract law are the employment features of the Civil Rights Act of 1964. No less revolutionary in this field have been the antitrust laws, wherein certain types of contracts are completely outlawed. Such agreements are challenged in thousands of cases each year. Finally, federal programs create essentially fiscal promises, or contracts, between taxpayers and the federal government. Normally, because of the intricate hurdles posed by standing requirements, a taxpayer cannot challenge an expenditure of tax funds by the government. Yet there are exceptions, and these exceptions have spawned a plethora of lawsuits. Under the Social Security Act, for example, a covered employee may agree to pay money to the government for a certain number of years or to perform certain services for the government, with the understanding that by doing so he will be repaid in money or services at a certain time as specified by the program. Although some courts may regard these programs as creating quasi-property interests, the overall quid pro quo aspect gives these programs a contractual flavor. Each year, tens of thousands of Social Security actions are filed in United States district courts.

Although the spectrum of these actions is rather vast, the starting point for analyzing these problems is still the law of contracts, whether at the common law, or, in the federal scheme, as modified by regulatory statutes. More precisely, we must understand that our inheritance here is a legal discipline that develops at the pace set by commercial intercourse. So intimately related to society's economic growth, because America is among the most highly developed financial and commercial centers of the world, this supereminent principle has an importance second to none.

D. Redressing Losses Caused by Breach or Fault

If the prime contractors of the house of the law can be said to be lovers of theory, as we have seen by their construction of property, liberty and contract precepts, we can also say that they were realists. They understood that all members of society would not respect the tenets and that some provision had to be made to furnish a private remedy for those who suffered at the hands of those who breached the law. If, in the most primitive form, we took property belonging to another, the simplest remedy was a court order commanding the malfeasor to give it back. Where such a return was possible, we called it private actual redress of a breach of conduct or fault. We then encountered what can be called the law of Humpty-Dumpty:

> Humpty-Dumpy sat on a wall,
> Humpty-Dumpty had a great fall.
> All the king's horses and all the king's men,
> Could not put Humpty-Dumpty together again.

For example, the victim of a breach could not be put "together again" because the stolen horse died or was injured, or the purloined grain was consumed. Thus was created the notion of substituted redress or monetary damages as compensation for the injury.

Like every system of adjudication, our house of the law provides actual or substituted redress for the individual who has been injured by the breach of contract or duty of conduct. The law of compensation is an integral part of federal adjudication. Moreover, it is a supereminent principle that has been present in organized societies in written form at least since Biblical days. At that time, one who "hurt a field or vineyard" was required to "restore the best of whatsoever." This is classic actual tort redress. There was also substituted redress: he that kindled a fire that burned his neighbor's stacks of corn had to make good the loss. In event of "any fraud, either in ox, or in ass, or sheep, or raiment, or anything that may bring damage," it took the form of "restor[ing] double" to his neighbor.

Particularly relevant to the federal courts is the "constitutionalization" of traditional tort claims under state law, claims that allege violations of the constitution or federal statutes by federal and state officials. Since the Supreme

Court approved such actions against federal officials in *Bivens v. Six Unknown Named Agents of the Federal Bureau of Narcotics*, and—under the auspices of 42 U.S.C. § 1983—against municipal, county and state employees in *Monroe v. Pape* and its progeny, a broad range of actions have been introduced to the federal forum. Between 1961 and 1984, for example, the number of claims filed in federal district courts in a single year under civil rights statutes rose from 296 to 21,219. These claims ranged in subject matter from conversion of hobby materials to physical assaults by state officials, a public defender's performance of his counsel duties, harassment of a street vendor, failure of a social worker to foresee injuries inflicted on foster children, failure of state officials to close flood gates on a canal resulting in flood damage to property, failure of public work officials to salt roads in winter causing an auto accident and delay of public rescue services in responding to accidents.

Compensatory damages for breach of contract are familiar and are used often in the federal courts where damages relate to contract law. Here the law of damages seeks to place the aggrieved party in the economic position he or she would have been in if the contract had been performed. This involves an award, to borrow from the *Restatement of Contracts*, of both the "losses caused and gains prevented by the defendant's breach, in excess of savings made possible." Moreover, the federal courts have utilized remedies of specific redress, implicating common (if not Biblical) law, equitable concepts of replevin, specific performance and the relatively new remedy of declaratory judgment. These methods permit a federal court to order the return of an object unjustly taken, compliance with a contract or a clarification of responsibilities under an ongoing contract. These are unusual remedies, but under proper circumstances they provide the courts with a greater array of tools for doing justice between the parties when substituted redress is inadequate.

E. Punishing Those Who Wrong the Public

There is a great gap in the penal law accounts of primitive jurisprudence. All civilized systems seemed to agree in drawing a distinction between offenses against the community (state) and offenses against the individual. Generally we distinguish between crimes (*crimina*) and wrongs or torts (*delicta*). In the law of ancient communities the so-called penal law was actually a law of torts. The injured person proceeded against the wrongdoer by an ordinary civil action and, if successful, recovered compensation by money damages. As early as the Roman Twelve Tables (450 B.C.), *furtum* or theft stood at the head of civil wrongs recognized by Roman law. Other civil wrongs included assault and violent robbery, as well as trespass, libel and slander. Book IV of *The Institutes* of Justinian defines as torts: "theft, robbery with violence (*rapina*), wrongful infliction of damage or contumely." By the time of the laws of the Germanic tribes, an immense system of money compensation was in force for all actions which we now consider crimes, including homicide. As Henry Maine described:

> Under Anglo-Saxon law, a sum was placed on the life of every free man, according to his rank, and a corresponding sum on every wound that could be inflicted on his person, for nearly every injury that could be done to his civil rights, honour or peace; the sum being aggravated according to adventitious circumstances.

This is not to say, however, that in more ancient times the concept of a wrong or injury to the state or collective community did not exist. Indeed, there developed a procedure in Roman times, especially during the decline of the Republic, by which the senate delegated certain of its powers to particular *Quaestores* or commissions to investigate a particular accusation and, if it be proved, to punish the particular offender. Gradually these ad hoc commissions became permanent, and by the time of Emperor Augustus a rudimentary form of criminal jurisprudence had been established.

In the earliest civilizations, private penalties were assessed against those who wronged society in special areas that were most important to its continued existence. Thus, in addition to capital punishment for a number of offenses, including striking one's mother or father, early punishments were based on the system of "[e]ye for eye, tooth for tooth, hand for hand, foot for foot. Burning for burning, wound for wound, stripe for stripe." Other crimes involved offenses to property, agriculture and marriage. As societies became increasingly complex, the criminal law was extended to areas that had become important to them. In many instances the criminal law began to include offenses of which ancient civilizations never could have conceived, such as economic crimes with which we are evidencing increasing concern and crimes pertaining to government reporting requirements.

Federal criminal law serves a number of specific functions in our present-day federal-state system. To be sure, it performs some of the usual tasks of any law enforcement system, such as protecting the institutions and operations of the federal government against criminal activity. But notwithstanding grandstanding activity by many members of Congress, it must be emphasized that federal authorities do not have the basic responsibility of day-to-day maintenance of order in society. That responsibility is the province of local, not federal, law enforcement. Federal law enforcement is designed only to supplement local authorities in the performance of that basic responsibility. Thus, it must be understood that federal law is not limited to conduct that poses a threat to federal institutions or operations. Moreover, the same conduct, to one extent or another, is also the subject of both state and federal sanctions. Professor Louis B. Schwartz has described federal law enforcement as federal auxiliary criminal jurisdiction—auxiliary, that is, to state law enforcement.

Historically, there has been a steady growth in federal auxiliary criminal jurisdiction. Some of it has been sparked by dramatic criminal events—the Lindberg baby kidnapping and the Dillinger spree of bank robberies come to mind—but most of it has resulted from congressional activity after extensive widely-publicized hearings, especially in the era of radio and television. Facts adduced at these hearings have often demonstrated either failure or corruption in local law enforcement. The Mail Fraud Statute was first enacted in 1889, the Mann Act in 1910, the Dyer Act, which deals with interstate transportation of stolen vehicles, in 1919. Shortly thereafter came the kidnapping provision in 1932 and the federal prohibition against bank robbery of a federally-insured bank in 1934. Anti-gambling laws were enacted in 1961 and in 1964. But many prosecutions are now brought under relatively new statutes—the Controlled Substance Act of 1970, the Hobbs Act, and the Racketeer Influenced and Corrupt Organizations Act (RICO). Moreover, a favorite device of federal agents is prosecution under the Conspiracy Statute.

The number of federal prosecutions continues to rise, with the largest number of offenses being drug abuse; various types of fraud, including income tax, postal and false claims and statements; larceny of United States property; forgery; and bank robbery. Undoubtedly, in the future, the criminal law will continue to expand, coming to apply to areas of conduct that may seem surprising to us today. As society becomes more complex—economically, scientifically and industrially—the criminal law may become a necessary tool for the allocation of scarce resources.

The Supereminent Principles in History

It is possible, I am sure, to conjure up certain aspects of federal law which do not neatly fit within the specifics of the five supereminent principles that compose our house of the law. Federal taxation, for example, may come within a fuzzy area. But even here, I believe that most tax litigation centers on regulations governing income from use, sale or purchase of property, or employment contract income. Whether it can be argued that the supereminent doctrines are all-inclusive is not absolutely critical to my basic thesis. This thesis, I must emphasize, is that it is necessary to clarify and simplify the law—in both lawyers' briefs and judges' opinions—because too many current offerings describe a body of substantive law much more complicated and eccentric than it is in fact. I believe that the structure of court opinions will be more professional, briefs more clear, and the outlines of the house of the law cleaner and more distinct if wholesale dependence on citations gives way to a reference to the relevant primary discipline of the law, to a relation back to fundamentals and to the reasons these fundamentals exist in the first place.

This reference back to fundamentals brings into focus the second characteristics of the supereminent principles. Beyond their predominance in today's federal litigation, these principles boast a formidable ancestral chain and impressive relationship to legal systems of bygone eras. A brief examination of their role in those systems helps to explain *why* they loom as the dominating principles of the modern era.

These five principles have their roots in formidable legal systems of past societies. Historically, four of these—creating and protecting property rights, fulfilling promises, redressing losses caused by breach or fault and punishing those who wrong the public—can be identified in all societies possessing a social order. The fifth of the series—creating and protecting a liberty interest— has certainly been with us at least since Roman times. A quick glance at the written laws that have governed principal societies in the ancient and modern worlds is illuminating. Regardless of the variations of time and geography, vicissitudes of incidents and circumstances in particular empires, kingdoms, republics or fiefdoms, considerable resemblances are seen. The ends of law— preserving the public peace, just dispute settlements, maintaining a comfortable social and physical environment, reasonable security of expectations, tolerable adjustment of conflicting social interest and channeling of a social change—have been advanced by different means. Hence a variation of those means does exist, but the ends seem to have remained the same. Perhaps more accurately stated, fundamental legal concepts remained the same but their definitions changed as community values changed.

A. *The Institutes* of Justinian

In my view, the Anglo-American legal tradition begins with the promulgation of *The Institutes* of Emperor Justinian on November 21, 533 A.D. An attempt at a contemporary codification of Roman law as it had developed for some 1000 years, *The Institutes* range from eloquent abstractions to very precise statements of legal consequences that followed detailed sets facts. Thus, Justinian's introduction reminds us that "[j]ustice is the constant and perpetual desire to give to each man his due right," and that the precepts of the law are "to live justly, not to injure another and to render to each his own."

The Institutes were divided into four discrete books. Book I, dealing with rights of the person, described rights of freed men and slaves, outlined paternal power and family rights, and set forth the law of marriage, adoptions and guardianships. Book II, concerning the law of things, described both corporeal and incorporeal rights, including ownership and possession of real property and chattels as well as usufructs, and set forth the law of wills, gifts and transfers. Book III described intricacies of intestacy and gave us the first details of the law of obligation of contracts. Book IV described the Roman law of torts.

Henry Sumner Maine has written that "[n]either Ancient law nor any other source of evidence discloses to us society entirely destitute of The Conception of Contract," yet it is apparent that Roman law was the first jurisprudence to raise the enforcement of promises to the legal dignity it enjoys today. Originally, that with which the law armed its sanctions was not a naked promise, but a promise accompanied by solemn ceremonials. As the Roman jurisprudence of obligation developed, one or two steps in the ceremonial were dispensed with first; then others were simplified or permitted to be omitted on certain conditions; finally, a few specific contracts were separated from the rest and allowed to be entered into without ceremonial form. The selection of these types were influenced by the activity and energy of social and commercial intercourse. Slowly the agreement itself, the mental engagement, isolated itself from technicalities and became the major ingredient of legal inquiry.

Among Rome's greatest contributions to the law was its exposition of the law of obligations. Over the decades, if not centuries, it developed four types of contract—the Verbal, the Literal, the Real and the Consensual. Each class was named for certain formalities which were required over and above the mere agreement of the contracting parties. Book III of Justinian describes these "four species" of contract and treats each category separately and in great detail. It also treats quasi-contractual obligations, "obligations which, properly speaking, cannot be said to arise from contract but which, because they do not derive their existence from *delict*, are treated as arising quasi-contractually." Perhaps it is in Justinian that we see the seeds of the controversy that has plagued us down through the centuries—the confusion between implied contracts in which acts and circumstances are symbols of the same ingredients which are manifested by words in an express contract, and quasi-contracts which are not contracts at all.

Book IV contained the Roman law of torts, or *delicti*, defined as a "wrongful act, not deriving from agreement, which causes damage to another for which the latter may recover a penalty from the wrongdoer." These torts were sins of commission only, and not of omission. Named as specific torts were theft, robbery with violence and wrongful infliction of damage or "contumely." "Contumely" was defined as any deliberate affront to another, whether by conduct or by words. It served as the residual tort for wrongs against the personalty of another with almost unlimited scope, including assault and battery, defamation, imputations upon a woman's chastity and trespass on another's land.

Tort redress in Roman law was originally private revenge—actual retaliation by the victim, putting the body of the wrongdoer at the mercy of his victim. The law then developed to permit buying off vengeance by agreement of the parties in a suitable alternative (substituted) redress. Finally, the law came to require a monetary penalty as the primary remedy in all circumstances, whether the quantum was fixed absolutely or to be assessed by the judge in a legal action.

The beauty of the Justinian *Institutes* is its clarity, as well as its order. It is important today as a constant reminder that many legal concepts currently in use in federal courts also were in use in a civilized society more than 1000 years ago. *The Institutes* can be regarded as the cornerstone of our supereminent principle of liberty; thus, the opening first words of Book I: "Justice is the constant and perpetual desire to give to each man his due right." This basic notion was reflected by precepts of law: to live justly, not to injure another and to render each his own. Thus, from *The Institutes* we derive our basic definition of liberty: "Liberty, from which the expression free men is derived, is the natural ability to do anything one pleases unless it be prohibited by force or law."

B. Blackstone and the Law of England

The most popular exposition of our fundamentals took place in England in the four years between 1765 and 1769 when William Blackstone published his *Commentaries*. According to Lord Denning, Blackstone "was the greatest exponent of the common law that we have ever had." Although the Emperor Justinian announced his promulgation after ten centuries of Roman law experience, Blackstone's efforts came seven centuries after the Battle of Hastings in 1066, the date usually associated with the birth of common law. Obviously influenced by Justinian, Blackstone too utilized four books, but his compilation did not precisely track *The Institutes*. He assembled substantive qualities of rights and wrongs, private and public concerns, and persons and property to give us a symmetrical and durable statement of common law. Even the briefest summary discloses the relationship between four of our five supereminent principles, the law of contracts being essentially ignored.

Blackstone's Book I, *The Rights of Persons*, details most of the ground covered by Justinian, with one major exception—he has virtually nothing to say about slavery, a subject that occupied so much of the Roman law of persons and property. Students of contract law seem unhappy that Blackstone relegated contracts to a relatively insignificant portion of *The Rights of Persons*. They contend that Blackstone did not respect the specificity that this discipline demands, so amply covered by Justinian. Book II, *The Rights of Things*, bears a close resemblance to Justinian's Book II. It describes the law of property in thirty-two chapters, twenty-two of them dealing with real property.

Book III, *Of Private Wrongs*, summarizes the law of torts, but this book treats procedure more than it does the substantive law. In recalling the society of Blackstone's day, Professor Thomas G. Barnes, of the University of California at Berkeley, offers an explanation for this phenomenon. Professor Barnes reminds us that Georgian England was an "age of fast horses, careening carriages, drunken foul mouths, atrocious fires, a gutter-press, considerable unrest in growing towns and declining countrysides, bad food and worse drink, ... lighted squibs, of quacks, frauds, whores, and monte banks—in short an age well-supplied with tortfeasors." Blackstone's final Book IV, *Of Public Wrongs*, is a treatise on criminal law, dealing with an analysis of common law definitions.

A vital part of English law that was centuries old at the time of Blackstone was the profound commitment of the English to individual liberty. Blackstone stated:

> [T]rial by jury ever has been, and I trust every will be, looked upon as the glory of the English law.... [I]t is the most transcendent privilege which any subject can enjoy, or wish for, that he cannot be affected either in his property, his liberty, or his person, but by the unanimous consent of twelve of his neighbors and equals.

Although sometimes said to be a charter of liberties only for a small baronage, the *Magna Carta*, signed by King John at Runnymede on June 15, 1215, was subsequently so frequently reissued and confirmed that the Great Charter must be considered the source of liberties under law of all English and American freemen. Because the *Magna Carta* is more often cited than read, the magical Clause 39 deserves to be set forth:

> No Free-man's body shall be taken, nor imprisoned, nor disseised, nor outlawed, nor banished, nor in any way be damaged, nor shall the King send him to prison by force, excepting by the judgement of his Peers and by the Law of the land.

It is upon this clause that our own sense of liberty, expressed or implied in the Constitution, is anchored. It served as the philosophical base of the 1628 Petition of Right and the 1689 Bill of Rights. Moreover, contemporary due process language appeared as early as 1368, when—to prevent abuses by false accusers—Edward III decreed that: "[N]o man be drawn to answer without presentment before justices, or matter of record, or by due process and original writ, according to the ancient law of the land."

The constitutional significance of *Magna Carta* is immense. Bryce measured it in profound terms:

> The Charter of 1215 was the starting point of the constitutional history of the English race, the First link in a long chain of constitutional instruments which have moulded men's minds and held together free governments not only in England, but wherever the English race has gone and the English tongue is spoken.

Rudyard Kipling has expressed a similar feeling:

> And still, when mob or monarch lays
> Too rude a hand on English ways,
> A whisper wakes, the shudder plays
> Across the reeds at Runnymede.

C. Hebrew Law

Yet there are laws even more ancient than *Magna Carta* that contain clear resemblances to our present legal system. Ancient Jewish law, for example, is recorded in the first five books of the Bible, the *Pentateuch*. Interpretation and application of this law over early generations developed a rich oral tradition, culminating in a body of writings known as the *Talmud*. Generally, the *Talmud* is a set of books consisting of the *Mishna*, which contains originally oral law supplementing scriptural law, and the *Gemara*, a collection of commentaries on and interpretation of the *Mishna*. Notwithstanding this extensive source, we need look no further than the *Pentateuch* itself to establish the prevalent existence of the five supereminent principles.

Biblical law sought to protect the most basic liberty interests of an individual to be free from physical assault and battery. Victims of assault and battery were entitled to compensation for all harm caused, including the amount expended to be cured. The law of the Hebrews also regulated promises that established a debtor-creditor relationship. For example, the imposition of an usurious interest rate was proscribed if the debtor was poor, but the practice was expressly allowed if the borrower was not Hebrew. The law also required that a lender who took as security for a loan the borrower's raiment return this collateral by sundown so "that he may sleep in his own raiment."

Hebrew law embodied as well familiar notions regarding the redress of losses occasioned by fault. In this respect theft was viewed largely as a civil offense, with emphasis placed upon compensation of the victim. One who stole and killed an ox was required to restore to the victim five times the value of the ox. In this context, the recovery of triple damages under the Sherman Antitrust Act is not a new concept. Principles of negligence also were evident in Hebrew law. For example, if injury resulted from an animal falling into an open pit, liability attached to the person responsible for the pit.

Finally, while the focus of early Jewish law was to compensate the victim of wrongs, some wrongs were deemed such serious crimes against society as to be punishable by death. These included murder, striking one's mother or father, cursing one's mother or father and kidnapping.

D. The Visigothic Code

The law of the barbarians, the dark era of the law, shared many characteristics of modem law and is easily classifiable within our five categories. By "barbarians" I mean the loosely organized Indo-germanic tribes which inhabited northern Europe after the decline of the Roman Empire, consisting of the Ostrogoths, Visigoths, Lombards, Burgundians, Thuringians, Bavarians and other lesser groups. The Visigothic Code, written in approximately 650 A.D., represents the most sophisticated of these legal systems.

As did all the older systems, the Visigothic Code had a well developed set of inheritance and intestacy laws. Because of the German "spirit of equality," the laws were generally not very intricate. The Visigothic Code did not specifically enumerate liberty interests. However, the Code's "aim," according to Samuel Scott, was "to provide the highest degree of safety for both prince and people." All were subject to the laws, even the King. The Code also provided a primitive framework of due process requirements, such as access to a court before a duly appointed judge and the power to appoint an attorney. The Code also contained extensive provisions concerning the enforcement of business promises, particularly those involving the transfer of land. Its law of sales contained a fairly well-developed requirement of formality, requiring a written agreement to be drawn up by a notary and witnessed by as many as twelve witnesses, depending on the value of the article sold. This reflects, of course, the influence of Roman law's use of ceremony as an ingredient of contract jurisprudence. Defective chattels could be returned, and a vendor of land was required to either defend a purchaser from eviction or give him lands of equal value. Once a bargain was struck and earnest money delivered, the vendor could not back out.

The Visigothic Code contained elaborate listings of substituted redress, termed "compositions," for every offense which occurred to the drafters' imaginations as possible to be committed by one man against another. In this regard, the Code drafters' objective was to eliminate the socially requisite revenge and the perpetual enmities caused thereby. If the offender had insufficient funds, recourse would be had to his personal property. Enumerated wrongs ranged from defamation, with a schedule of fines for the various subjects defamed, to violation of corpses, murder and wrongful death, with a schedule of recompense depending on the social rank of the victim. For offenses which engendered animosity, the Code prescribed payment of an additional amount called a "faida," which was analogous to punitive damages. Refusal to pay this amount entitled the person injured to kill the offender.

Notwithstanding the private redress of wrongs, offenses against the sovereign—treason, cowardice and desertion—were considered public acts and punishable by death. Some civil wrongs, such as murder, were also punished by death if the perpetrator could not pay the composition. Further, civil violations sometimes carried an additional fine, called a "fredum," to be paid to the prince or chief due to the prejudice caused by the criminal's acts to the society at large. This fine, a quasi-criminal punishment, would either be specified in the codes for the particular wrong, or would be a set proportion of the composition.

Summary

The five supereminent pillars that support the house of the law are not newly created. They all boast a rich and prodigious history. Property interests and corresponding rights, however created and protected, can be traced to every society, even the most ancient. Liberty interests have been coextensive with the aspirations of a given civilization, often depending upon citizenship, religious affinity and ancestral caste. Notwithstanding the hiatus in Medieval England, a formal obligation to fulfill promises and a procedure to enforce this obligation has been part of the law sired by ancient Rome. Even the most ancient codes allowed private redress for the breach of an agreement or to compensate for an injury caused by the fault of another. As societies became more sophisticated, punishment by the sovereign was provided for those who wronged the public weal, with penalties taking the form of corporal punishment, banishment or death in place of earlier provisions that called for private redress in kind or in money.

Whatever the level of civilized society, it was, and is, most important that members of the community understand both the nature of the law and the penalties for its breach. The lesson that we derive from all legal societies is that the clearer the exposition of the law, the more it is capable of community comprehension. The more extensive this comprehension, the more adherence to the law can be expected. The more complete this quality of adherence, the more we approach the ideal balance of order and liberty.

Chapter Two

The Role of the Courts in Contemporary Society

Author's Note: *This is a paper that first appeared in 1976 at the bicentennial observance of the American Bar Association, whose general theme was* Common Faith and Common Law: A Declaration of Kinship of the English and American Legal Professions. *In the Foreword of a collection of papers delivered to an attendance of English and American representation, the ABA president, Lawrence E. Walsh, diplomatically observed:*

> *The Bicentennial does not celebrate the naked act of separation. That act simply started the running of the 200 years. But what we celebrate is the fusion of a nation — a powerful nation — and its emergence as one of the leaders of the world. We celebrate the survival of a nation — dedicated to the proposition that all are entitled to liberty, and the pursuit of happiness.*

Professor Harry W. Jones, Cardozo Professor of Jurisprudence at Columbia University, was in charge of later editing the papers presented for discussion. Describing the opening topic, The Role of the Courts in Contemporary Society, *he would write:*

> *In his moving remarks at the opening of the first session of the* Common Faith and Common Law *program, the master of the Rolls, Lord Denning, said that the logic of history in the common law countries has entrusted to the courts, as the highest of their duties, with responsibility to maintain and nurture the Rule of Law. Our tendency in the United States is to identify the "rule" or "supremacy" of law with the judicial enforcement of constitutional limitations. In the United Kingdom, as will be seen in the papers of this book, judicial action to maintain the supremacy of law takes other forms, less direct but, it would seem, equally effective. Thus, for example, government officers and authorities are held in England to full compliance with the "standing laws." And Acts of Parliament*

are interpreted strictly, sometimes super strictly, when they seem to come into collision with traditional liberties. Perhaps the English and American version of the Rule of Law are not so dissimilar in practice as they seem in theory. The first of the two essays in this chapter is by one of England's most esteemed judges, Mr. Justice Templeton of the High Court of Justice, Chancery Division. The second, "An American View of the Judicial Function," is by Judge Ruggero J. Aldisert of the United States Court of Appeals for the Third Circuit. Since Holmes, judges have become among the most influential of American jurisprudential writers. One thinks of Cardozo, Frank and Hand and, more recently, of Traynor, Schaefer and Friendly. Scholarly author of The Judicial Process: Readings, Cases and Materials *(1976), Judge Aldisert is a worthy addition to the goodly company of American judge-jurisprudents.*

My paper was later published under the title The Role of the Courts in Contemporary Society *in 38 U. Pitt. L. Rev. 437 (1977). Excerpts follow.*

To describe the role of the courts in contemporary American society is a Janus-faced assignment. It can be a description of what we are, or an expression what we should be. To propose what we should be requires that we know what we are; to know what we are, we must first know what we were; and to appreciate what we were requires an overview of two centuries of American judicial experience.

To be sure, our judicial systems were English in origin and in practice. Colonial courts had functioned from the beginning as integral parts of the British judicial system. When the colonies changed to statehood and separate courts were established within the state and federal sovereignties, an English model was adopted in each of the several jurisdictions. Aside from cutting the umbilical cord from the Privy Council, substantive laws and procedural rules of the original states did not undergo major revolutionary changes. By nationality we were Americans; by legal tradition we were still English. Often, the continuity of legal tradition was made explicit by reception statutes that enacted into law for the new states the pre-existing English common law and, in some instances, Acts of Parliament. By these statutes, a developed and flowering body of law was rooted instantly into the new American legal soil. As time went on, however, the transplant began to take on characteristics indigenous to its new environment.

American judges in the early nineteenth century took a traditional view of their function. The English common law judge sat as a settler of disputes between private parties, deciding questions of "lawyer's law" and pronouncing what Roscoe Pound would later call "rules in the narrower sense," precepts attaching a definite legal consequence to a definite, detailed state of facts. But the American environment was different from the English, and soon began to make special demands on the courts. In America, unlike Great Britain, a system of dual sovereignties existed. And, in America, a written constitution had been adopted—a primal document tracing its origins in part to the Magna Carta and the Petition of Right and in part to the peculiar exigencies of the new "united states" where sovereign power was to be divided between the state governments and the national government.

Within fourteen years of the Constitution's adoption, however, a new dimension was added to the judiciary's traditional role of dispute settler. Resolving a conflict between a private citizen, one William Marbury, and a public official, James Madison, the Secretary of State, the Supreme Court set a precedential stage for a new judicial function—that of interpreter of a written constitution. Thus the Court allocated to itself a role that would still serve as a source of criticism of the American judicial function on the decision's 200th birthday: it declared an act of a correlative branch of government unconstitutional, *i.e.*, null and void. Moreover, the Court deigned to command the executive what it could and could not do under the Constitution. Appropriately, perhaps, for present purposes, the Supreme Court did not "settle" the dispute between Marbury and Madison in the sense of resolving the conflict between the two litigants. It dismissed Mr. Marbury's petition for lack of jurisdiction. Rather, *Marbury v. Madison* marked a departure from the traditional dispute-settling role of the courts, and an arrival of a new function, that of interpreting a written constitution. Said Chief Justice Marshall: "It is emphatically the province and duty of the judicial department, to say what the law is. Those who apply the rule to particular cases, must of necessity expound and interpret that rule." Whether or not it was so intended, the judicial branch early established itself as protector of the Constitution and, thereby, as overseer of the constitutionality of the actions of the executive and legislative branches of the federal government.

Thirteen years later, the Supreme Court added further dimension to the function of interpreting the federal constitution. Proceeding from the federal level to the state level, the Court, in *Martin v. Hunter's Lessee*, pronounced unconstitutional a decision of the highest court of the state of Virginia. The legal umbilical cord to mother England, severed in 1776, had been replaced by another, linking the formally sovereign state courts with the Supreme Court of the United States, a court of strictly "limited" jurisdiction sitting at the apex of the national legal system. The Constitution defined the rights and obligations of the parties, state and federal, to the system of dual sovereignties, but one of the parties, the federal government, speaking through its Supreme Court, had the final authority to interpret the document.

Marbury v. Madison and *Martin v. Hunter's Lessee* early established the role of the Supreme Court as an interpreter of the Constitution—a significant expansion of the judicial role from the traditional dispute-settler mold. As we have seen the Supreme Court, and other courts, develop the interpretive function over the years since those formative decisions, we have surely understood the wisdom of words spoken, long before the days of Justices Marshall and Story, by Bishop Hoadly: "Whoever hath an absolute authority to interpret any written or spoken laws, it is he who is truly the lawgiver, to all intents and purposes, and not the person who first wrote or spoke them."

Still another connection to the federal courts was consummated at the turn of the century in *Ex Parte Young*. This time the link was forged in a conflict involving a Minnesota railroad tariff. In a delightful bit of political science fiction, the Court held that Minnesota's Attorney General was a state officer for fourteenth amendment purposes to confer jurisdiction, but that he was a private citizen for eleventh amendment considerations of state immunities. However exotic and metaphysical may have been the rationale, the decision took hold and acquired formidable jurisprudential dignity in the decades that followed. Without the legal road-bed that this case laid down, the procedural vehicle for federal civil rights actions could not have rolled as easily against state officials in the fourteenth amendment revival exercises of the stupendous sixties.

Having brought the coordinate branches of the federal government, and the state governments, within its "limited" jurisdiction, the Supreme Court began in the early decades of this century to interpret the substantive content of some of the more ambiguous phrases in the Constitution. But this was not ordinary interpretation, this was interpretation with a vengeance—what Dean Griswold has referred to as "decisional leapfrogging": "[T]he first decision is distilled from the language of the Constitution, but the next expansion begins from the reasoning of the last decision, and so on down the line until we reach a point where the words of the Constitution are so far in the background that they are virtually ignored." Operating in the common law tradition, reasoning from example and inbreeding newly distilled constitutional principles, the Supreme Court's interpretations authorized incursions by judges—both state and federal—into realms of policy traditionally entrusted to other public decision makers.

The march of federal judges into new decision-making fields continued through the era of substantive due process. Although Lochnerism suffered a setback, replete with breast-beating apologies in which the Court publicly disavowed substantive due process as a method of substituting the Court's views of proper legislation for those of state legislatures, it has returned recently under a new rubric and raiment: today American courts announce new vigors of the Equal Protection Clause, or delight in the surrealistic "penumbras" to the Bill of Rights, or discover new rights of privacy extending from "the Fourteenth Amendment's concept of personal liberty" and "the Ninth Amendment's reservation of rights to the people."

American courts reached the zenith of jurisdictional and jurisprudential expansion in 1963 when the Supreme Court cast another stout mooring line connecting the states' highest courts to the federal judicial system. Unlike that which tied the state judiciary to the apex of the federal court pyramid in 1816, this one wrapped around the very base of the federal judicial pyramid—the district courts. Under guise of inquiry into "detention simpliciter" of state prisoners in actual custody, the Supreme Court vested federal district courts—*trial* courts—with authority to review fact-finding decisions and federal constitutional law interpretations of state court systems in criminal cases, including decisions of the states' *highest* courts. These are a few distinctive landmarks on the legal journey from 1776, and recognizing them can help in arriving at an appreciation of the legal landscape of today.

As the judicial role expanded from orthodox dispute settling and spilled over into broader areas of policy making, the methodology of the decisional process underwent a change. The dawn of the Nineteenth century found American courts in the full bloom of traditional common law decision making. Making a decision involved comparing the facts at hand with the recorded cases of the past, searching for a controlling rule; that failing, the technique required going back to more general principles as starting points for legal reasoning. Facts being the key ingredients, profound respect was due the doctrine of stare decisis. Previously established rules and principles of law in large measure controlled the decisional process. The most significant feature of the common law, past and present, and the essential element in its historic growth is that it is preeminently a system built up by gradual accretion of special instances. Stability, reckonability and predictability in the law were foremost. Blackstone had expressed it:

> The doctrine of the law then is this: that precedents and rules must be followed, unless flatly absurd or unjust; for though their reason be not obvious at first view, yet we owe such a deference to former times as not to suppose that they acted wholly without consideration.

Statutes in derogation of the common law were strictly construed. Where a factual complex was not unerringly controlled by a prior decision or a statute, judges resorted to the three methods of decision making later classically categorized by Cardozo. Where precedent or statute did not provide the answer, a judge might resort to the "method of philosophy," seeking to apply logic to arrive at a unifying and rationalizing principle that would decide the case. Or he might apply the "method of history," seeking illumination from the past of a directive force that might provide the resolution of the problem. Or he might use the "method of custom," hoping to find an answer in norms of behavior.

As the century came to a close, Roscoe Pound would decry excessive rigidity in American decision-making processes. He described our system as conceptual jurisprudence, a slavish adherence to *elegantia juris*, the symmetry of law, and suggested that we resembled too much the rigid German *begriffsjurisprudenz*. In his classic, "The Causes of Popular Dissatisfaction with the Administration of Justice," Pound sounded a call for the end of mechanical jurisprudence: "[T]he most important and most constant cause of dissatisfaction with all law at all times is to be found in the necessarily mechanical operation of legal rules." Blind adherence to precedents—to the rules and principles derived therefrom—he attacked as "mechanical jurisprudence" and "slot machine justice." He advocated "pragmatism as a philosophy of law."

Pound was trumpeting a theme more softly played by Oliver Wendell Holmes a decade earlier that the social consequences of a court's decision were legitimate considerations in decision making.

If Roscoe Pound's 1908 warning against mechanical jurisprudence did not create a new American school of jurisprudence, at least it spawned widespread respectability for social utilitarianism. It added a new dimension to law's traditional objectives of consistency, certainty and predictability—namely, a concern for society's welfare. A few years after Pound's warning, Cardozo delivered his classic Storrs lectures at Yale. He stated thus his theme: "The final cause of law is the welfare of society. The rule that misses its aim cannot permanently justify its existence." A half century later, in many legal disciplines, the once desired objective of *elegantia juris* in legal precepts, institutions and procedures has become subordinated. In all but a few areas of static law, mechanical jurisprudence is more historical than operational. In 1974 Professor Harry W. Jones elegantly stated the new spirit of legal purpose: "A legal rule or a legal institution is a *good* rule or institution when—that is, to the extent that—it contributes to the establishment and preservation of a social environment in which the quality of human life can be spirited, improving and unimpaired."

Achieving law's utilitarian purpose within a framework of reasonable predictability and stability is thus the ultimate, if sometimes elusive, objective. For the sociological jurisprudent, the task is a most difficult one, for "social welfare" admits of no easy definition. Cardozo suggested that

[i]t may mean what is commonly spoken of as public policy, the good of the collective body.... It may mean on the other hand the social gain that is wrought by adherence to the standards of right conduct, which find expression in the *mores* of the community. In such cases, its demands are those of religion or of ethics or of the social sense of justice, whether formulated in creed or system, or immanent in the common mind.

Justice James D. Hopkins described public policy "as the outgrowth of the social ideals of the community, slowly changing as the needs and viewpoints of the community change."

Notwithstanding lack of precise definition, the reality is that contemporary American courts are resorting more and more to the method of sociology as a primary decisional tool. They are considering the pragmatic effects of alternative courses of decision. They are attempting to vindicate social needs of all who would be affected by their decisions, irrespective of whether those affected were the litigants before them. They are looking to the general state of contemporary legislative policy and the felt needs of the society—insofar as they can discern those needs in an increasingly pluralistic society. They are considering economic forces, scientific developments and identifiable expressions of public opinion. This decisional process has deontological as well as teleological overtones. It bears a remarkable resemblance to classical natural law.

The sociological method is now in full flower in at least two important and dynamic disciplines of law: constitutional law and tort law. Contemporary American courts—state and federal alike—are judicially formulating public policy. The articulations of these decisions—the opinions written—become primary methods of the decisional process and, as such, qualify as "performative utterances." So as not to be accused of deciding by magisterial caprice, personal bias, idiosyncrasy or unstructured opinion, and to avoid criticism of *ipse dixit* declarations of public policy, the courts have taken to setting forth "reasoned elaborations" for their interest-conflicts resolutions.

More often than not, the distillation of public policy derives from a subprocess of the judicial process now popularly known as "balancing interests." Competing interests are identified and categorized as individual, public or social interests; they are variously compared, evaluated; accepted, rejected, tailored, adjusted, and, in general, subjected to the "political contrivance" of compromise. The result is what Professor Jones has described as "a reasoned accommodation of opposed interests." With public policy playing such a prominent role in contemporary adjudication, and with a seemingly inexhaustible inventory of social interests pressing upon judges and jurists for attention,

Dean Pound's "A Survey of Social Interests" should be mandatory reading for today's law student and the subject of refresher courses for lawyers, legislators and judges.

Pound recognized that "[i]n the common law we have been wont to speak of social interests under the name of 'public policy.' " But he emphasized that the extent to which this technique may be considered valid depends, in the first instance, on whether all relevant identifiable interests are placed on the scale.

The extent to which the technique of balancing interests (first so described by Justice Hugo Black) may be considered valid, depends, in the first instance, on identifying all the interests. The expression "balancing interests" is useful, perhaps, but seriously misleading. The expression implies that the subject matter of the judicial process is somehow *quantifiable*. It is not. The best that can be hoped is that all the interests at stake in a case are *identifiable*. Having identified the interests at stake, a judge can at least consider them. I doubt that he is ever really able to "balance" them. His accommodating of the competing interests, his priorities, if you will, in resolving the interests conflicts will be durable and acceptable to the extent that a reasoned accommodation of the interests is regarded and accepted as fair. Before the accommodation takes place, however, like types of interests must be identified. As there are apples and oranges, so there are interests and interests.

Whatever the labels attached to its components, modern jurisprudence views law as a social process, the final aim of which is the society's welfare. Today law is no more (nor less) than one of many methods of ordering and channeling the energies of society; its only measure is its effect on society. Thus, the path seems clear for unabashed and open policy determination by the courts: functional and result-oriented if the impression conveyed is of a new jurisprudence, or doctrinaire and conceptual if, upon close analysis, certain elements of this new jurisprudence disclose a fealty to older, more orthodox concepts.

The expansion of the American judicial function beyond the perimeters of orthodox, private dispute settling, and the concomitant emergence of new emphases on sociological methodologies in decision making, highlight another respect in which contemporary American courts differ from those in which some of the Founding Fathers practiced: today judges make, as well as interpret, law.

This truism may seem self-evident, but public acknowledgment of this proposition required a long gestation period. Judicial ears had long been cocked to venerable principles and aphorisms that disclaimed lawmaking as a proper judicial function. Francis Bacon admonished: "Judges ought to remember that the office is 'jus dicere,' and not 'jus dare'; to interpret law, and not to make law, or give law." The Blackstonian view was that judges do not create law, they simply discover it, and even when they overrule precedent, they do not "make" law:

> For if it be found that the former decision is manifestly absurd or unjust, it is declared, not that such a sentence was *bad law*, but that it was *not law*; that is, that it is not the established custom of the realm, as has been erroneously determined.

As recently as 1918 John M. Zane declared: "The man who claims that under our system the courts make law is asserting that the courts habitually act unconstitutionally."

Modern jurisprudence, however, recognizes that the judge can, and indeed must, make law as well as apply it. Were it otherwise, there would be little room for the employment of public policy as a tool in judicial decision making. Yet there are limits. In 1917 Holmes counseled: "I recognize without hesitation that judges do and must legislate, but they can do so only interstitially; they are confined from molar to molecular motions." The natural law would not admit to such a possibility; it held that law was only discovered by the operation of the universe and could not be created by *any* human institution. Similarly, under the tenets of early positivism, with its emphasis upon the command of the legislature as the voice of the sovereign, inquiry into the judge's creative function was impermissible. Only in this century has the judge been recognized, albeit grudgingly, as a lawmaker. A more than little nudge in this direction came from John Chipman Gray: "[T]he Law is made up of the rules for decision which courts lay down; ... rules for conduct which the courts do not apply are not Law; ... that the courts apply rules is what makes them Law...."

In 1842 *Swift v. Tyson* flatly said that "it will hardly be contended that the decisions of courts constitute laws. They are, at most, only evidence of what the laws are, and are not, of themselves, laws." By 1972 *Illinois v. City of Milwaukee* would set the record straight and emphasize that in the context of state "laws," court decisions were "laws"; similarly, federal common law decisions were "laws" just as surely as those of statutory origin.

Despite the bashfulness of the judiciary to admit it, the brute fact is, as Professor Robert A. Leflar relates: "We know that courts make law, in fact, that they have made most of the law that we have. This is the way the common law has always been made." Sir Rupert Cross, quoting Mellish, L.J., suggests that it has not been otherwise in England: "The whole of the rules in equity and nine-tenths of the common law have in fact been made by judges."

Examples of recent judicial lawmaking may be found in abundance. Some are firmly grounded on considerations of public policy; others embody judicial pronouncements relying on the Cardozan method of philosophy, evolution or tradition. To identify but a few, the Supreme Court has created a wrongful death action for maritime law, and Massachusetts has announced a common law wrongful death action in tort. In 1973 Florida abolished the contributory negligence rule, and replaced it with comparative negligence; California followed suit in 1975. The "Fall of the Citadel" in products liability cases and the abrogation of hoary immunity rules are likewise the products of judicial lawmaking.

Although the precise limits of judicial lawmaking have not been staked out, the power undoubtedly is a broad one. Holmes and his followers propounded the "interstices" doctrine, but the cases illustrate that judicial lawmaking has often exceeded interstices. In practice it might appear that the only limitations are those which are "functional"—such as the inadequacy of facilities for extensive fact gathering, confinement to the facts of record, and the like. Ultimately the test of judge-made law, as with any law, is its effect on social welfare and its acceptance by society. The judge who makes law, therefore, must focus *openly* on policy considerations as he or she seeks to keep the law in tune with changing societal values.

It may be argued that this approach pays lip service only to the doctrine of separation of powers. The clear and obvious answer must be that the federal and state constitutions must be read against the backdrop of the common law tradition—which tradition has given to the courts the authority to interpret rules enacted by the legislature, and to fashion the aggregate of legal precepts that govern society. Further, if legislative authority disagrees with judicial action, it can overrule that action by statute. As the highly pragmatic legal philosopher John Chipman Gray would tell us, "The State requires that the acts of its legislative organ shall bind the courts, and so far as they go, shall be paramount to all other sources."

Still another development in the American judicial function must be examined if we are to appreciate fully the role of the courts in contemporary American society. Phenomenally and somewhat paradoxically, as the courts have enlarged their lawmaking roles, so too have the legislatures enacted laws vesting the courts with greater responsibilities. At times the growth in statutory law—individual legislative acts as well as comprehensive codes—has seemed exponential. Simultaneously the courts have been called upon to interpret volumes of exasperatingly detailed regulations promulgated by the Executive Branch. And where the legislature or the executive has not acted, prestigious private organizations— notably the American Bar Association and the American Law Institute—have suggested voluminous codes of substantive and procedural law which, while not possessing the sanctions of positive law, have exerted a potent, often persuasive, effect on the state and federal judiciaries.

A full generation ago Justice Frankfurter said that "even as late as 1875 more than 40% of the controversies before the [Supreme] Court were common-law litigation, fifty years later only 5%, while today cases not resting on statutes are reduced almost to zero." If the count has not changed since Frankfurter's day, it is only because zero is so low. Judge Charles E. Wyzanski, Jr., has suggested that "[i]n two generations the law has moved in ways unforeseeable by any nineteenth century lawyer. The center has shifted from the common law adjudged in the courts, to enacted law administered by executive agencies subject to limited judicial reviews." Similarly, Lord Patrick Devlin has lamented:

> The work done by the Judges of England is not now as glorious as it was.... I doubt if judges will now of their own motion contribute much more to the development of the law. Statute is a more powerful and flexible instrument for the alteration of the law than any that a judge can wield.

The annual grist for our separate, sovereign legislative mills must be measured in the hundreds of tons. Such legislative proliferation raises profound questions as to how our public policy is actually formulated. The reality that special legislative staffs—not elected legislators—draft many statutes draws into doubt the long-held notion that legislative enactments are the true expression of public policy, derived from the representatives elected by the people. Assuming, of course, that a statute does express some public policy—and I am convinced that many do not—the question arises whether that policy has derived from elected representatives of the people or from appointed specialists of the legislative staff.

Whatever reservations we may have about the process, the proliferation of legislation has made statutory construction of the essence in the day to day work of American judges. Judges have progressed from reliance on so-called canons of construction so deftly eviscerated by Karl Llewellyn. They have played with the Mischief Rule of *Heydon's Case*, the Golden Rule and the Literal Rule. They have dallied with what American jurisprudence has called the Plain Meaning Rule:

> It is elementary that the meaning of a statute must, in the first instance, be sought in the language in which the act is framed, and if that is plain, and if the law is within the constitutional authority of the law-making body which passed it,—the sole function of the courts is to enforce it according to its terms.... Where the language is plain and

admits of no more than one meaning the duty of interpretation does not arise and the rules which are to aid doubtful meanings need no discussion.

Impressive authorities have warned us, however, not to depend too much on the actual language of a statute. Cardozo said: "When things are called by the same name it is easy for the mind to slide into an assumption that the verbal identity is accompanied in all its sequences by identity of meaning." Holmes told us: "A word is not a crystal, transparent and unchanged, it is the skin of a living thought and may vary greatly in color and content according to the circumstances and the time in which it is used." Learned Hand said: "[I]t is one of the surest indexes of a mature and developed jurisprudence not to make a fortress out of the dictionary; but to remember that statutes always have some purpose or object to accomplish, whose sympathetic and imaginative discovery is the surest guide to their meaning."

Today current wisdom requires judges to ascertain the "legislative intent," a task somewhat akin to pinpointing the intent of a testator or of disputing parties to a contract. Proper judicial construction, in the modern view, requires recognition and implementation of the underlying legislative purpose; the judge, the theory holds, must accommodate the societal claims and demands reflected in that purpose. To do this, as Justice Roger J. Traynor puts it, we need "literate, not literal" judges, lest a court make a construction within the statute's letter, but beyond its intent.

Recourse to legislative history, the debates and committee reports, is a favorite pastime of federal courts. This is so because the Supreme Court justices have found it to be a useful technique, and also because the Congressional Record and committee reports are usually available. The practice is open to criticism. With typical incisiveness, Professor Leflar has observed: "I think that it was Chief Justice Hingham, I'm not sure, who said that the devil himself 'knoweth not the mind of man.' It is difficult to discover intent; and when you cannot discover with any authority the state of mind of one man, the process of discovering the states of mind, the intents of 535 men, who make up the Federal Congress, becomes an extremely difficult matter."

The proliferation of state and federal statues has not lessened the burdens of the judiciary. Constitutional law, of course, is virtually entirely judge-made. As Professor Jones has noted:

> The text of the Constitution covers about eight and one-half pages, fifteen pages with its twenty-six amendments. The most widely used law school course book on constitutional law runs to 1,462 pages, consisting almost entirely of closely edited Supreme Court decisions and

the writer's scholarly comments on those decisions.... James Madison and his colleagues ... would have to read a constitutional law *casebook* before they could even begin to follow the course of an argument in a present-day constitutional case.

The proliferation of state and federal statutes, therefore, has not lessened the burdens on the judiciary. Not all statutes contain the specificity of an Internal Revenue Code. Indeed, many partake of an indefiniteness that is in part traceable to the nature of the statutory beast, but which, more recently, seems a function of legislative inability to reach meaningful compromises on detailed subject matters. Often the result of this statutory explosion is that the legislature simply turns over the matter of making law to the courts.

The law flowing from the Sherman Antitrust Act is essentially judge-made law, emanating from a skimpy statutory text. The Taft-Hartley Act gave the federal courts virtually carte blanche authority under section 301 to promulgate a federal common law for labor relations. But the Sherman and Taft-Hartley Acts at least articulate national policies for trade regulations and labor; these policies furnish polestars for the guidance of the courts. Other statutes are not this specific; some merely create procedural devices for the resolution and clarification of important issues and delegate to administrative agencies and the courts the actual resolution of these problems. Frequently, the problem is legislative ambiguity. As former Attorney General Levi reminds us:

Our political institutions have often placed a premium on ambiguity in policy formulation, an ambiguity which is itself a cause of our present dissatisfaction. The responsibility thereby placed on the courts—to discover and implement social policy—is certainly difficult if not intolerable. There is an exigent need for our other institutions—and not only governmental—to clarify paramount issues and to develop remedies which work with least social cost.

Still another type of statute, of which the Civil Rights Act of 1964 is an example, demonstrates the failure of the legislative bodies to arrive at a consensus. In many instances in recent years our legislature has functioned more efficiently as a forum for discussion of issues than as a legislative organ expressing a consensus about how to treat the problems it considers. Legislative histories are contradictory; statutory texts contain waffle words. Here, too, ultimate statements of public policy by necessity have had to emerge from the courts. With the exception of those courts having certiorari jurisdiction—the Supreme Court and its analogue in some states—most courts are in the unfortunate position of *having* to decide. They do not have the luxury possessed by the legislature of avoiding decision in sensitive cases.

Whether the judge be a lawmaker, a precedent setter, a rule definer, or a garden-variety interpreter of statutes, he or she is nevertheless performing an important judicial function. As Judge Friendly asks:

> Who would want to contradict Judge Learned Hand? "When a judge tries to find out what the government would have intended which it did not say, he puts into its mouth things which he thinks it ought to have said, and that is very close to substituting what he himself thinks right.... Nobody does this exactly right; great judges do it better than the rest of us. It is necessary that someone shall do it, if we are to realize the hope that we can collectively rule ourselves."

Let us pause to take stock. We have seen that, as early as 1803, the judicial function in the United States moved from the relatively simple resolution of "lawyer's law" disputes to the delicate review of actions of coequal branches of government. We have seen that the sociological method of decision making supplanted conceptual jurisprudence as a dominant organon of the judicial process. We have witnessed public acceptance of the judge as a lawmaker and a simultaneous burgeoning of judicial statutory construction in an era of proliferating codes and statutes.

I believe that these factors have combined to strengthen the American court system as the dominant institution in contemporary American society. But all is not well. During the last decade, public confidence in key governmental and private institutions in general has waned. As we enter our third century as a nation of free men and women, created equal, therefore, we do well to ponder certain important questions which present themselves: is the current malaise symptomatic of a short-term institutional illness, or of a long-term societal condition or disease? If the former, are major measures necessary to effect a cure, or does the passage of time hold the answer? If the latter—if we are facing a long-term institutional disease—we must attack its root causes. What, then, are those causes and how do we go about remedying the problems' in the most expeditious and least disruptive manner? These are the topics that weigh heavily these days with me and my judicial brethren.

And yet, if I could make bold one observation on the role of American courts in contemporary society, ever mindful of the risks that inhere in overstatement and oversimplification, it would be this: too large a segment of the public currently depends too much upon court systems to vindicate private and public rights. If this condition persists, I see a real danger of judges, especially appellate judges, becoming "Platonic Guardians" or philosopher kings if not in ivory towers, certainly in lonely, monastic chambers. Removed from the pushes and pulls of societal clashes, appellate judges are deciding all pervasive societal issues on the basis of cold records and partisan advocacy; they do not cast eyes on the litigants themselves. Nor do they view the trauma, sense the emotions or hear the strident voices.

I have elsewhere noted a tendency among elected local, county and state officials to avoid unpopular decisions that would vindicate constitutional rights—a tendency to toss these "hot potatoes" to the courts for resolution. State and federal judges are not the only government officials who have taken oaths to uphold the laws and defend the Constitution. Is it too much to ask—nay, demand—that these other officials fulfill the obligations embodied in those oaths or yield their official posts in favor of those who will? Simply stated, the courts must not become the only government house in which justice is administered.

As it is important that all government officials—local, state and federal—be vigilant in protecting rights guaranteed by the Constitution, by statute or by regulation, it is even more important that the public—the American people themselves—begin to understand that there are limits to the capacities of the judicial system. The public must understand that the system, like any other mechanism, will break down if overtaxed; and it must understand that in several areas, the system is dangerously close to overload. If recourse to the courts continues unabated, it may well become impossible for them to continue traditional, dispute-settling functions. Moreover, because respect for the courts is predicated on the effectiveness and enforceability of its decrees and orders, it is critical that courts not be requested to grant relief that cannot be enforced. Thus, a judicial order purporting to solve a complex social, political or economic problem runs the risk of being ignored or becoming unenforceable, with a concomitant loss of respect for the judiciary as an institution.

The solution and the ultimate responsibility, then, rests with the public—with the American people themselves. It is they, the people, who must decide who the decision makers should be today and in the decades to follow. Shall difficult decisions be made by the local school boards elected by neighbors, or by an unknown federal judge sitting 100 miles distant? Shall decisional responsibility lie with state representatives elected from local districts, or with a panel of United States Circuit Judges sitting 300 miles away and, conceivably, composed entirely of non-resident judges? Shall the elected governor and the executive branch administer state mental hospitals and prisons? Shall trustees run the university? Or shall judges be our administrators and supervisors?

I submit that the public must insist that *all* public officials "protect and defend the Constitution of the United States." The public must recognize the truth in Chief Justice Stone's remark: "Courts are not the only agency of government that must be assumed to have capacity to govern." More important, they must become aware, with Professor Charles L. Black, Jr., "that the judicial power is approaching the limits of its utility for major strategic innovation." The change must come from the people, for it is they who began the process of judicialization. They must insist that the proper role for the American court is to settle specific, molecular disputes, not to solve molar social problems. These limits on judicial power are essential to a responsible political democracy; they presuppose three coequal branches of government, and an assumption of full responsibility by each branch. Upon entering our third century, we can demand no less than that each branch assume its full constitutional duty.

We should heed the great Judge Learned Hand, who in 1942 cautioned: "[T]his much I think I do know—that a society so riven that the spirit of moderation is gone, no court can save; that a society where the spirit flourishes, no court need save; that in a society which evades its responsibility by thrusting upon the courts the nurture of that spirit, that spirit in the end will perish."

Chapter Three

Precedent:
What It Is and What It Isn't; When Do We Kiss It and When Do We Kill It?

Author's Note: This chapter contains substantial excerpts from an article bearing the same title that appeared in 17 Pepp. L. Rev. 605 (1990). The article expands remarks delivered at the Mid-Winter Meeting of the Conference of State Chief Justices, Orlando, Florida, January 25, 1989.

The title of this offering is inspired by Holmes' sparkling apothegm:

> When you get the dragon out of his cave on to the plain and in the daylight, you can count his teeth and claws, and see just what is his strength. But to get him out is only the first step. The next is either to kill him, or to tame him and make him a useful animal.

The doctrine of precedent is everyone's dragon. If facts in the putative precedent are identical with or reasonably similar to those in the compared case, the precedent is recognized as legitimate, and it is applied. In such cases, all of us—student and professor, lawyer and judge, commentator and philosopher—consider it merely, as the Italians say, *un dragonetto* (a small dragon). But if the material facts in the compared case do not run on all fours with the putative precedent, the doctrine becomes *un dragone* or, to give equal time, *una dragonessa* (a full grown, ferocious dragon). Wrestling with such a dragon can be the most difficult and controversial job in the judging business.

I realize that literature on how to deal with this dragon abounds. To borrow Rabelais' Judge Bridlegoose,

> The subject has been well and exactly seen, surveyed, overlooked, reviewed, recognized, read and read over again, tossed and turned about, seriously perused and [we have] examined the preparatories, pro-

ductions, evidences, proofs, allegations, depositions, cross-speeches, contradictions … and other such like confects and spiceries.

Undeterred, I make bold to mount my charger, draw my lance and gallop into the lists to volunteer some advice on how to tweak the dragon's tail. Perhaps the dragon will prove too elusive, or I too bold or too meek, but ever persistent I will press on, hoping to tame this dragon. I bring with me experience, not only as a judge, to be sure, but also as one who has explored and meandered in the judicial process thicket, seeking trails to understand what it is all about.

First I will discuss some definitions of precedent and the overarching doctrine of *stare decisis*. I then will explore what I call the four different models of precedent. From this I will move to a consideration of precedent as a method of classification containing varying degrees of abstraction. This will lead to a study of both generalization and analogy. I wrap it up with some views of precedential vitality, and close with the distinction between precedent and persuasive authority.

Let's take a moment to review some basics. Precedent is an often misunderstood concept. Some believe it is more understandable than explainable. I tried my hand at a definition in *Allegheny County General Hospital v. NLRB* in 1979:

> A judicial precedent attaches a specific legal consequence to a detailed set of facts in an adjudged case or judicial decision, which is then considered as furnishing the rule for the determination of a subsequent case involving identical or similar material facts and arising in the same court or a lower court in the judicial hierarchy.

Chief Justice Marshall expressed the reason for this definition in 1821:

> It is a maxim not to be disregarded, that general expressions, in every opinion, are to be taken in connection with the case in which those expressions are used. If they go beyond the case, they may be respected, but ought not to control the judgment in a subsequent suit when the very point is presented for decision. The reason of this maxim is obvious. The question actually before the Court is investigated with care, and considered in its full extent. Other principles which may serve to illustrate it, are considered in their relation to the case decided, but their possible bearing on all other cases is seldom completely investigated.

Stare decisis is the policy of the courts to stand by precedent. The expression *stare decisis* is but an abbreviation of *stare decisis et non quieta movere* (to stand by or adhere to decisions and not disturb that which is settled). Consider these words. First, *decisis*. This word means literally, and legally, the decision. The doctrine is not *stare dictis*. It is not "to stand by or keep to what was said." The doctrine is not *stare rationibus decidendi* or "keep to the *rationes decidendi* of past cases." Rather, a case is important only for what it decides: for "the what," not for "the why," and not for "the how." It is important only for the decision, for the detailed legal consequence following a detailed set of facts. Thus, *stare decisis* means what the court *did*, not what it *said*.

Strictly speaking, the later court is not bound by the statement of reasons, or *dictis*, set forth in the rationale. We know this because a decision may still be vital although the original reasons for supporting it may have changed drastically or been proved terribly fallacious. In a large number of cases, both ancient and modern, one or more of the reasons given for the decision can be proved to be wrong, but the cases have retained vitality.

Priestly v. Fowler, announcing the common law fellow-servant rule, is one such case. The court based the holding on the alleged consent of a servant to run the risk. Yet there was no evidence that such consent was ever requested of, or given by, fellow servants. Of this case, it has been said that Lord Abinger planted it, Baron Alderson watered it, and the devil gave it increase. The concept, however, was almost immediately adopted in the United States in *Farwell v. Boston & Worcester Railroad*. Chief Justice Shaw reasoned that an employee consented to assume the risk of negligence by a fellow servant upon accepting employment. Again, there were no facts to support the assertion that the employee actually consented to anything. This was a concept built out of thin air. Yet, the fellow-servant rule remained the law in the United States for many years.

Precedent can be discussed in the context of four common types of opinions:

1. The textbook common law model. Here the opinion discusses only the adjudicative facts. Facts are carefully and meticulously set forth so that the reader may quickly become acquainted with the material facts that form the subject of the holding. The court does not suggest how it would decide another case based on a change in the material facts. The fabric is tightly woven. There is no room, there is no give, to stretch the holding beyond the stated facts.

2. A variation of this purist model exists when, in addition to the adjudicative (or material) facts, the court also discusses narrow and specific facts not in the record and gratuitously suggests how it would decide a case based on those non-record facts. Such a discussion is easily recognized as *obiter dictum*. Consider this example: operating his car at an improperly high rate of speed, the driver-defendant attempts a turn and whips across the centerline and crashes into oncoming traffic. The court decides the case in favor of the plaintiff and says by way of *dictum*, "Of course, although the facts are not present here, if the steering wheel sud-

denly becomes defective, we would have a products liability case and the defendant would not have been liable."

3. A third model occurs when the court suggests how it would decide an entire series of cases based on a broad array of facts not in the record. So long as this discussion does not implicate the adjudicative facts at bar, it also is recognized as *obiter dictum*. Consider the same operative facts presented in our second model. This time the court says, "If the manufacturer designed a defective brake, a sticking accelerator, a poorly designed steering mechanism, the plaintiff would have a valid cause of action against the car dealer and manufacturer." This is only dictum. The facts of the case do not discuss defective steering.

4. A fourth model is an opinion in which the court's statement of its conclusion is broad enough to cover not only record facts but also additional facts not in the record. Here, the court's decision is not *obiter dictum*. It is truly the decision of the case, arrived at in the common law tradition, but couched in a holding that is beyond a rule of law in the narrow sense. The decision takes the form of a general principle instead of a narrow rule of law.

Each of the foregoing variations announce decisions of the court and can be components of the doctrine of *stare decisis*. As precedents, however, they are not currency of equal value. Clearly, the first one, the classic common law model, possesses the strongest bite of precedent. As we go down the list of examples, numbers two and three are not precedent, and yet they are authority that can be considered by a court in a subsequent decision. The fourth variation meets the definition's technical niceties, but does not possess maximum strength, and therefore, does not achieve the reliability of a decision limited to the record material facts. An able advocate may convince a subsequent court that its original holding, although technically precedent, was only "a little bit precedent."

This fourth model causes the courts more trouble than any aspect of adjudication. It occurs when a court does not announce a narrow rule based solely on record facts, but embarks on an intellectual frolic of its own. Two examples of the fourth variation, decided in the same year, are illustrative.

In *Webb v. Zern*, Charles Webb purchased a keg of beer from a distributor, John Zern. Webb's son, Nelson, was injured when the keg exploded. The Pennsylvania Supreme Court held that section 402A of the *Restatement (Second) of Torts* was controlling and then stated: "We hereby adopt the foregoing language as the law of Pennsylvania." The court should have held: Nelson, the son, could recover in tort from the brewer, beer distributor and keg manufacturer on the theory of strict products liability, for the reasons set forth in the *Restatement (Second) of Torts*, section 402A. This holding would have met the strictures of the pure common law model. In holding as they did, the judges galloped out of the courtroom, up the hill to the legislature, and proceeded to legislate. The decision was not limited to the material facts, but rather announced a broad principle of law that could be applied to cases with materially different facts.

Another example of this type of judicial legislation can be seen in *Miranda v. Arizona*. *Miranda* was decided in 1966 and promulgated a broad legal principle, the so-called "*Miranda* Rule." For the past twenty years, courts and police departments across the country have been forced to decide what does and what does not implicate *Miranda*. The common law tradition requires starting with a narrow holding and, then depending upon the collective experience of the judiciary, either applying it or not applying it to subsequent facts. The Court did the opposite in *Miranda*.

Because the usual model was inverted in this case, the Court has spent the last twenty years chipping away at its holding. *Miranda* says that a prisoner must be advised that he or she has a right to remain silent, a right to have an attorney present during questioning and a right to the appointment of an attorney if the prisoner cannot afford one. In 1971, the Court said that *Miranda's* proscription did not apply if the statement was used only to impeach a witness. The Court subsequently held that although it was necessary to cut off questioning in a robbery case when the defendant invoked his right to remain silent, it was permissible to question about an unrelated murder if fresh warnings were given "after the passage of a significant period of time." In *Beckwith v. United States*, the Court held that the questioning of a person suspected of criminal tax fraud by Internal Revenue agents did not give rise to *Miranda*. Later the Court held that *Miranda* was not violated when a defendant who initially invoked *Miranda* waived his rights before seeing an attorney, even though his attorney attempted to see her client but was assured that he would not be questioned until the following day. In *Duckworth v. Eagan*, the Court held that informing a suspect that an attorney would be appointed for him "if and when you go to court" complied with the requirements of *Miranda*.

The end result is that the broad legal principle announced in *Miranda v. Arizona* has been consistently chipped away in the 23 years since the decision was filed. Perhaps the same results would have been forthcoming if the traditional application of precedent had been followed. For our purposes, the important point is that *Miranda* was a drastic departure from the common law tradition of incremental and gradual accretion of an original narrow rule. It was the exact opposite. We saw a broad structure erected in one case that has been subsequently subject to do-it-yourself remodeling.

Precedent then, is a doctrine with two jurisprudential concepts in tension:

- The notion that the reasoning supporting the past decision may be wrong, but the decision itself, may be right. We have mentioned this concept before. The logic of the argument, the analysis of the historical background and legislative history may all be demonstrably incorrect.
- The countervailing notion is that expressed by Karl Llewellyn: "Where stops the reason, there stops the rule."

All of us will continue to struggle with these countervailing considerations. I suggest, however, that these problems which I freely admit do exist do not go to the precedent's definition; rather, they go to the precedent's vitality. I express these tensions now solely to emphasize that for definitional purposes, *stare decisis* means no more and no less than that precedent is simply a fact-specific concept, pure and simple. The doctrine refers only to a detailed legal consequence that follows a detailed statement of material facts.

Yet another view of precedent is the perception of the doctrine as a method of classification. In this view, precedent covers the fact situation of the instant case and at least one other. It decides one case and classifies another.

Any classification is an abstraction. The art of legal advocacy is to expand or contract an abstraction to the extent it is either desirable or undesirable. If contracted, the original case retains only the highly constrictive confines of a legal rule. If expanded, the precept develops from a narrow rule of law into a full-fledged legal principle. The precepts may form the basis of what Herman Oliphant once called "a mounting and widening structure, each proposition including all that has gone before and becoming more general by embracing new states of fact."

When we expand, we indulge in the process of classification. We have two fact situations. The first has a definite legal result. We see one or two elements common to the two fact situations. We then put the two fact situations in one class, and, using the combined elements as one enlarged antecedent fact situation, we apply the legal consequence of the first case. Such a class may include multitudes of fact situations so long as a single common attribute exists.

These classes of fact situations give us a parallel series of corresponding propositions of law, each more and more generalized as we recede further and further from the original state of facts and include more and more fact situations in the successive classes. It becomes a mounting and widening structure, each proposition including all that has gone before and becoming more general by embracing new states of facts.

For example:

1. "An employee in an Executive agency [of the federal government] or an individual employed by the government of the District of Columbia may

not ... take an active part in political management or in political campaigns." 5 U.S.C. §7324(a)(2) (1982).

2. Any employee of any agency, office or department of the federal government may not take an active part in political management or political campaigns.
3. The spouse of a federal government employee may not take an active part in political management or political campaigns.
4. The parents and children of a federal government employee may not take an active part in political management or political campaigns.
5. Acquaintances, friends or business associates of federal government employees may not take an active part in political management or political campaigns.
6. No one may take an active part in political management or political campaigns.

Clearly, gradation six is far removed from the basic case and it is illegitimate as classic *reductio ad absurdum*. Yet the tendency to build a gradation of generalization upon the basic case is the centerpiece of the art of advocacy; it is external as seen in the arguments of counsel, and internal, insofar as the value judgments of individual judges are concerned.

Another example is a presently-developing concept of tort law—the tort of negligent infliction of emotional distress. At common law, there was no recovery for the negligent infliction of emotional distress. Consider this developing law in the context of a gradation of widening propositions:

1. A mother may recover for the negligent infliction of emotional distress if she watches her child suffer harm, provided the mother, herself, is in the zone-of-danger, the area of possible physical peril.
2. A child who watches his step-grandmother run down and killed may recover for the negligent infliction of emotional distress, even though he was not within the zone-of-danger.
3. A friend may recover for emotional harm if he or she witnesses another friend being harmed.
4. Bystanders may recover for emotional harm whenever they witness an accident.

Examine another example that is more typical in the judicial process. It is taken from *Donoghue v. Stevenson*, the House of Lords case that is similar to our *MacPherson v. Buick Motor Co.*: a Scottish widow bought a bottle of beer containing a snail. The court held:

> The presence of a dead snail in an opaque bottle of beverage caused by the negligence of the defendant who is a manufacturer whose goods are distributed to a wide and dispersed public by retailers that caused physical injury to a Scots woman will render the defendant liable.

This can be stated more generally:

> Whether the manufacturer of an article of drink sold by it in circumstances that prevent the distributor or the ultimate purchaser or consumer from discerning by inspection any defect is under a legal duty to the ultimate purchaser or consumer to take reasonable care that the article is free from defect likely to cause injury to health.

To extend a rule to cover a novel fact pattern is a technique that lies at the heart of the common law tradition. It is accomplished through the use of analogy or generalization. If it suits the purpose of an advocate to limit application of the precept to the original facts, the argument will be designed accordingly, and the opponent will take the contrary view.

The question for the judge is critical. Where on that gradation of propositions do we take our stand and say: "This proposition is the decision of this case within the meaning of the doctrine of *stare decisis* and we go no further?" To hold tight or to expand is a question of line-drawing. Classification, then, is simply line-drawing.

Our problem as judges is obvious: as the French General Robert Nivelle told the Germans under General de Castelnau in World War I, "*Ils ne passeront pas!*" When do we say, "You go this far and no farther"?

Professor Oliphant suggested another view of classification. Imagine standing in the middle of the field in a stadium and looking at the seats. If you focus on one seat on the lower level, the angle between you and the seat is rather slight; if you look at a seat in the upper level, it's a larger angle. The smaller the angle, the closer the classified case to the original precedent.

Karl Llewellyn put it another way. He said that precedent can be viewed as having a minimum or maximum effect. The minimum would be a strict view or small angle; the maximum, a loose view, or large angle. The problem facing judges is how to treat the precedent. Strict or loose. Lower seat or higher seat. Minimum or maximum. We must remember that this is a value judgment, depending upon the individual judge's notion of correct public policy. If we want to expand the holding, we will do so. If we want to hold tight, we will. As Llewellyn suggests, you can find that the putative precedent "holds only of redheaded Walpoles in pale magenta Buick cars." Is the process of classification strictly subjective? Is it simply a roll of the dice? I do not think so. There are certain guidelines to help us. And it is to that subject that I now turn.

How do we determine where to draw the line? Is there some guidance to know when the precedential force of one case must stop? Or is it purely personal intuition? At what level in the model classification do we say that the rule must stop? Cardozo raised the same sort of question 75 years ago:

> What is it that I do when I decide a case? To what sources of information do I appeal for guidance? In what proportions do I permit them to contribute to the result? In what proportions ought they to contribute? If a precedent is applicable, when do I refuse to follow it? If no precedent is applicable, how do I reach the rule that will make a precedent for the future?

We judges seek answers to these questions throughout our judicial careers. I do not purport to give you answers; however, I make bold to suggest a *method* to find those answers. I emphasize that I will be talking about methods, not answers. The methods are found in the canons of logic. And here I draw freely upon passages of my book, *Logic for Lawyers: A Guide to Clear Legal Thinking.*

Whether to extend or restrict precedent is inextricably wrapped up in the concept of inductive reasoning. This means reasoning from a particular to another particular, or from an assembly of particulars to an inductive generalization. Let us start with generalizations. In generalization by enumeration, we can say that the larger the number of specific instances, the more certain the resulting generalization. This simply bodes fealty to the concept of probability. It is the common law tradition of creating a principle by connecting the dots. The process of *analogy* is a little different. *Analogy* does not seek proof of an identity of one thing with another, but only a comparison of resemblances. Unlike the technique of enumeration, analogy does not depend upon the *quantity* of instances, but upon the *quality* of resemblances between things. J.S. Mill reduced it to a formula: "Two things resemble each other in one or more respects; a certain proposition is true of one; therefore, it is true of the other." In legal analogies, we may have two cases which resemble each other in a great many properties, and we infer that some additional property in one will be found in the other. The process of analogy is used on a case-by-case basis. It is used to compare the resemblance of prior cases to the case at bar. Reaching a conclusion by enumeration has the benefit of experience. Reaching a conclusion by analogy has the benefit of the high degree of similarity of the compared data.

The degree of similarity is always the crucial inquiry in analogies. Clearly, you cannot conclude that a partial resemblance between two entities is equal to an entire and exact correspondence. Here the skill of the advocate will often be the determining factor. Plaintiff's lawyer may argue that the historical event or entity in the putative precedent, Alpha, bears many resemblances to the case at bar, Bravo. The opponent will argue that although the facts in Alpha and Bravo are similar in some respects, this does not mean that those similarities are material and, therefore, relevant, or that the cases are similar in other respects; he or she will argue that a false analogy is present.

What is one man's meat is another man's poison. What is one attorney's material and relevant fact in analogical comparisons is the other attorney's immaterial and irrelevant fact. Often the art of advocacy resolves itself into convincing the court which facts in previous cases are indeed positive analogies and which are not. The judge is required to draw this distinction. The successful lawyer is one who is able to convince the judge to draw the distinction in the manner most favorable to his or her client.

Points of unlikeness are as important as likeness. Comparison without contrast is not an ideal to be followed. In examining the cases, as a scientist in a laboratory, the judge should not look for the rigid fixity of facts. Seldom are there perfectly identical experiences in human affairs.

What is "reasonable" in determining analogies may permit endless differences of opinion. And this is how it should be. The existence of varying views in multi-judge courts is one of the most vitalizing traditions animating the growth of the common law. Determining what is "reasonable," however, is closely related to the overarching process we call "reasoning," or solving a problem by pondering a given set of facts to perceive their relationship and then reach a logical conclusion. The application of "reasonableness" to "reason" is an ever-recurring scenario. If Delta has been found to be liable in set of circumstances involving Alpha and Bravo and Charlie, we have to decide, often without an exact precedent to guide us, whether Delta is also liable if only facts Alpha and Bravo are present. To do this we must determine which facts are material. Given the situation that Delta is liable if set of circumstances Alpha and Bravo and Charlie applies, we must decide if minus circumstance Charlie is material or immaterial.

Two famous cases dramatically illustrate this. In *Rylands v. Fletcher*, the defendant employed an independent contractor to make a reservoir on his land. Because of the contractor's negligence in not filling some unused mine shafts, water escaped and flooded the plaintiff's mine. The case could have been decided solely on the theory of the contractor's negligence, but the court chose to decide it on the theory of strict liability by determining that the negligence of the contractor was immaterial. Compare the actual facts of the case with the facts deemed material by the court:

Actual facts
D had a reservoir built on his land.
Through the negligence of the contractor (our circumstances C)
Water escaped and injured P.
Conclusion: D is liable to P.

Material facts as seen by the court
D had a reservoir built on his land.
Water escaped and injured P.
Conclusion: D is liable to P.

Thus by determining that circumstance C was immaterial, the doctrine of absolute liability was established in 1868 and is still alive and kicking today.

Another example is seen in the Court's treatment of segregation. In *Brown v. Board of Education*, the Court addressed circumstance B, segregation, in circumstance C, schools. It decided that under the doctrine of "separate but equal," no segregated school could be considered "equal." In *Mayor of Baltimore v. Dawson*, the Court was again presented with a segregation issue—this time minus circumstance C (*i.e.*, not in the context of schools). The Court affirmed the Fourth Circuit's ruling that the *Brown* decision applied to end segregation in public beaches and bathhouses. Segregation minus circumstance C led to the same result in *Holmes v. Atlanta* (municipal golf course) and *Gayle v. Browder* (buses). When *Browder* was decided, it was obvious that, as a matter of law, the entire doctrine of "separate but equal" was overruled and was not only limited to the facts in *Brown*—the special and particular problems of segregated education. Changing social and judicial perspectives had rendered that circumstance immaterial.

From this, we can learn something about the process of analogy, a process which lies at the heart of the system of precedents. In analogy, it is mandatory to determine which facts in the previous case are to be deemed material. The decision in a subsequent case depends as much on the exclusion of "immaterial" facts as it does on the inclusion of "material" ones.

The analytical process thus comes down to several steps: first, establish the holding of the case to learn the legal consequences attached to a specific state of facts. Then exclude any *dictum*. The next step is to determine whether that holding is a binding precedent for a succeeding case containing prima facie similar facts. This involves a double analysis: first state the material facts in the putative precedent and then attempt to find those which are material in the compared case. If these are identical, then the first case is binding precedent for the second, and the court should reach the same conclusions as it did in the first. If the first case lacks any fact deemed material in the second case, or contains any material fact not found in the second, then it is not a direct precedent.

Ultimately, law is reduced, in the case of the judge, to the art of drawing distinctions, and in the case of the lawyer, to the art of anticipating the distinctions the judge is likely to draw. To be sure, in the words of Dennis Lloyd, "[i]n a system bound by precedent such distinctions may often be in the nature of hair-splitting, this being the only instrument on hand for avoiding the consequences of an earlier decision which the court considers unreasonable, or as laying down a principle which is 'not to be extended.'" As an art, both the study and practice of law consist of problem solving. Because of the doctrine of *stare decisis*, however, problem solving must not be performed on an *ad hoc* basis. We must respect the overarching consideration that like cases be decided alike. The real question, however, is deciding what is a like case.

Our use of logical processes in the law is neither perfect nor does it claim to be. Inductive reasoning does not purport to reach truths; its aim is to produce a result that is more probably true than not. Rules of deductive reasoning go further. Properly applied, these rules command that if the premises are true, the conclusion must be true. But the genius of the common law is that these premises are not fixed in cement. In the popular idiom, they are always "up for grabs" to meet changes in our social, political, philosophical and economic climates. When invention is active, when industry, commerce and transportation bring about new forms of human relations, and when community relations change because of the extension of ethical and moral ideas, the law is dynamically able to keep pace with the variety and subtlety of social change.

The questions that face the judges of the highest courts go much further than a mere determination of when to apply a putative precedent to the case at hand. We also must decide whether to *overrule* the holding of the case. Do we bite the bullet and say so? Or do we make meaningless distinctions and, in Karl Llewellyn's expression, decide if it were a loose or strict precedent? It is essential to study the anatomy of a precedent—what it is, how it is created, how long it should endure, and whether it should be left to wither or should be nourished and strengthened.

We have repeatedly recognized that the principle of *stare decisis* should not be a "confining phenomenon." We are mindful of the observation of Justice Schaefer of the Supreme Court of Illinois: "Precedent speaks for the past; policy for the present and the future. The goal which we seek is a blend which takes into account in due proportion the wisdom of the past and the needs of the present." The doctrine of *stare decisis* is not a vehicle for perpetuating error, but rather a legal concept which responds to the demands of justice and, thus, permits the orderly growth processes of the law to flourish.

As said before, *stare decisis*, or, in its complete form, *stare decisis et non quieta movere*, is usually translated "[t]o adhere to precedents, and not to unsettle things which are established." The classic English statement is attributed to Coke: "[T]hose things which have been so often adjudged, ought to rest in peace." Blackstone's statement was more detailed:

> For it is an established rule to abide by former precedents, where the same points come again in litigation: as well to keep the scale of justice even and steady, and not liable to waver with every new judge's opinion; as also because the law in that case being solemnly declared and determined, what before was uncertain, and perhaps indifferent, is now become a permanent rule which it is not in the breast of any subsequent judge to alter or vary from according to his private sentiments.

My dear friend and colleague of happy memory, Roger Traynor, noted:

> *Stare decisis*, to stand by decided cases, conjures up another phrase dear to Latin lovers — *stare super antiquas vias*, to stand on the old paths. One might feel easier about that word *stare* if itself it stood by one fixed star of meaning. In modern Italian *stare* means to stay, to stand, to lie, or to sit, to remain, to keep, to stop, or to wait. With delightful flexibility it also means to depend, to fit or to suit, to live and, of course, to be.

In 1970, Justice Harlan set forth important values in *Moragne v. States Marine Lines, Inc.*:

> Very weighty considerations underlie the principle that courts should not lightly overrule past decisions. Among these are the desirability that the law furnish a clear guide for the conduct of individuals, to enable them to plan their affairs with assurance against untoward surprise; the importance of furthering fair and expeditious adjudication by eliminating the need to relitigate every relevant proposition in every case; and the necessity of maintaining public faith in the judiciary as a source of impersonal and reasoned judgments. The reasons for rejecting any established rule must always be weighed against these factors.

When do we overrule? We start with Roscoe Pound's warning that the law must be stable, yet it cannot stand still. No black letter guidelines determine when to follow precedent. Yet, Roger J. Traynor reminds us, "a bad precedent is easier said than undone." Thus, the decision whether to stand still often requires a balancing of hardships. We should not fall into the trap confronted by Gulliver in his Travels:

> It is a maxim among these men, that whatever has been done before may legally be done again; and therefore they take special care to record all the decisions formerly made, even those which have through ignorance or corruption contradicted the rule of common justice and the general reason of mankind. These under the name of precedents, they produce as authorities and thereby endeavor to justify the most iniquitous opinions....

The court may be inclined to overrule, according to Traynor, "if the hardships it would impose upon those who have relied upon the precedent appear not so great as the hardships that would inure to those who would remain saddled with a bad precedent." Again, Roger Traynor stated:

> Legal minds at work on this word might well conjecture that to *stare* or not to *stare* depends on whether *decisis* is dead or alive. We might inquire into the life of what we are asked to stand by. In the language of *stare decisers*: *primo*, should it ever have been born? *Secondo*, is it still alive? *Tertia*, does it now deserve to live?

The Supreme Court is fond of saying that it is difficult to overrule statutory interpretations because theoretically Congress will correct the ruling if dissatisfied. But with the Court it is sometimes a case of "do as I say, not as I do." The deed occasionally speaks louder than the word. Many statutory precedents have been explicitly overruled in the past two decades. Yet the Court seems to justify its action by suggesting categories that inform its occasional inclination to overrule. Because most state and federal cases involve statutory construction, it may be useful to summarize the reasons the Court gives for departing from its stated "general rule" that disfavors overruling statutory precedents:

- Intervening development of the law, either through the growth of judicial doctrine or further action taken by Congress.
- A precedent may be a positive detriment to coherence and consistency on the law, either because of inherent confusion created by an unworkable decision, or because the decision poses a direct obstacle to the realization of important objectives embodied in other laws.

- A precedent becomes more vulnerable as it becomes outdated and after being, in Cardozo's words, "tested by experience, has been found to be inconsistent with the sense of justice or with the social welfare."

It must be remembered that a judicial precedent may reflect as little as 51 percent of the opinion writer's point of view at the time of authorship. Depending upon the interest in the case by the non-writing judges at the time of the decision, their conviction certainly cannot be guaranteed to be any higher. Too many appellate lawyers operate on the assumption that the opinion of a unanimous court reflects 100 percent conviction and endorsement by all members of the court. Often, the minimum of effective persuasion could effectively move a court to a position desired by an advocate if it is realized that, at best, the case holding is but a narrow rule limited to a particular set of facts, and that the slightest change of facts could possibly bring about a different result.

Another factor that must be reckoned with is that we judges do change our minds. What do we say when we do this? I admire what Justice Potter Stewart said, concurring in *Boys Markets, Inc. v. Retail Clerks Union, Local 770*, where the Court reversed itself in a prior decision rendered only eight years before:

> When *Sinclair Refining Co. v. Atkinson* ... was decided in 1962, I subscribed to the opinion of the Court. Before six years had passed I had reached the conclusion that the *Sinclair* holding should be reconsidered, and said so.... Today I join the Court in concluding "that *Sinclair* was erroneously decided and that subsequent events have undermined its continuing validity ..."
>
> In these circumstances the temptation is strong to embark upon a lengthy personal *apologia*. But since Mr. Justice Brennan has so clearly stated my present views in his opinion for the Court today, I simply join in that opinion and in the Court's judgment. An aphorism of Mr. Justice Frankfurter provides me refuge: "Wisdom too often never comes, and so one ought not to reject it merely because it comes late."

I also admire the opinion of Justice Jackson, concurring in *McGrath v. Kristensen*:

> And Mr. Justice Story, accounting for his contradiction of his own former opinion, quite properly put the matter: "My own error, however, can furnish no ground for its being adopted by this Court...." [A]n escape ... was taken by Lord Westbury, who, it is said, rebuffed a barrister's reliance upon an earlier opinion of his Lordship: "I can only say that I am amazed that a man of my intelligence should have been guilty of giving such an opinion." If there are other ways of gracefully

and good-naturedly surrendering former views to a better considered position, I invoke them all.

Or Baron Bramwell's simple statement, in *Andrews v. Styrap*: "The matter does not appear to me now as it appears to have appeared to me then."

Too many advocates and commentators assume that all precedents are equivalent, that all are precedents *fortissimo*. As Judge Walter V. Schaefer has cogently observed, "To the working profession there is no such thing as an opinion which is just 'a little bit' precedent or a precedent *pianissimo*. All of them carry the same weight." This, however, is simply not so. There are precedents, and there are precedents. All are not currency of equal value.

As explained, all precedents do not have the same bite. Some are less powerful than others. Notable commentators have addressed certain aspects of this phenomenon. For example, Henry Campbell Black observed:

> A decision is not authority as to any questions of law which were not raised or presented to the court, and were not considered and decided by it, even though they were originally present in the case and might have been argued, and even though such questions, if considered by the court, would have caused a different judgment to be given.

Black has highlighted the importance of examining carefully the opinion, if not the briefs, in the prior case. Were the issues presented, considered and decided? If not, even though they could have been, the prior decision should not be considered a binding precedent on unaddressed points. If so, the prior decision is to be considered binding precedent.

Is the principle or precept deduced from the prior case contained in a thorough, well-reasoned opinion which was, itself, based upon clear and binding precedents? Is the prior case one that is seriously weakened by a trenchant dissent, or by a concurring opinion which casts doubt upon the wisdom of the majority's reasoning? Is the applicable precept found in a single case, or has it been restated and applied in several cases which have reaffirmed its value and social desirability? Clearly, the currency value of precedents varies widely. At one extreme are those that are rock-bound, the precedents *fortissimo*; at the other extreme are those that must be subject to question.

Absent formal overruling, judges must follow a precedent whether they approve of it or not. It binds them and excludes judicial discretion for the future. On the other hand, judges are under no obligation to follow persuasive authority that lacks the force of a true precedent. They will consider it, but will attach to it only the weight such authority seems to deserve. Persuasive authority can be considered merely historical comment. It depends for its influence upon its own merits, not upon any legal claim which it has to recognition, as opposed to precedent, which is considered a legal source of law. For example, these types of cases are more properly classified as persuasive authority than as binding precedent:

- Dictum.
- Decisions of courts of other jurisdictions.
- Plurality, concurring and dissenting opinions.
- The summary affirmance by the U.S. Supreme Court: a hybrid type that both is and is not precedent.
- The denial of a writ of certiorari.

A decision of a superior court is an authoritative precedent for all inferior courts in the same judicial hierarchy. There is a bit of provincialism or parochialism here. A decision of the New York Court of Appeals is authoritative precedent for all New York trial courts, but it is only a persuasive authority for courts in Pennsylvania because those courts are in another judicial hierarchy.

In the American tradition, a full-fledged precedent must be pronounced by a majority of the court. An opinion emanating from a court that reflects only a plurality view does not have the power of a majority opinion. Reasons given by the plurality are only persuasive authority. Here we must be careful to distinguish between the specific holding of a case and the reasons that support it. When concurrences are added to a plurality opinion, a true holding of the court has been established: a detailed legal consequence has accompanied a detailed set of facts. But, because the holding is not supported by a majority reasoning, the power and vitality of the holding is diluted.

Because a plurality opinion is not an opinion of the court, all appellate courts should adopt the United States Supreme Court's practice of labeling a plurality opinion as an "Opinion Announcing the Judgment of the Court," rather than simply "Opinion" or "Opinion of the Court." A few years ago we asked West Publishing Company to note this in its headnotes when only a plurality opinion is forthcoming. In such cases West usually now states in the headnotes, for example, "Opinion by Heffernan, C.J., with two others concurring." This is most helpful in determining the precedential value of a case.

I do not know whether I have helped or made a confusing subject even more so. I have tried to suggest guidelines to help you decide whether to kiss or kill the precedential dragon. In either event you must go back to its very definition. In so doing, you recognize that a case holding in the common law tradition is fact specific. When you compare a putative precedent with the case at bar, you compare facts and not the reasons stated. Yet, I freely admit that my emphasis on facts for definitional purposes is not shared by those who seem to say that the reasons given in the holding are also the precedent.

I have tried to show that reasons go only to support a decision, and when original reasons are later proved to be faulty, or when social, economic, or political conditions have changed, it is legitimate not to follow the holding because the reasoning is no longer valid. This is the theory that "where stops the reason, there stops the rule." But all is not that quick and easy. There are times when the rule must be held valid for reasons other than those stated in the original opinion.

Judges will continue to struggle with what is and is not precedent. The source of the struggle may be an uneasiness with what are and are not material facts in the compared cases, or it may be a struggle on where to hold the line in the expansion of facts from the specific to the abstract. There are guidelines, to be sure, but often it is a question of a value judgment, what Max Weber described as " 'practical' evaluations of a phenomenon which is capable of being … worthy of either condemnation or approval." He distinguished between "logically demonstrable or empirically observable facts" and "the value judgments which are derived from practical standards, ethical standards or world views." Then too, as Justice Walter V. Schaefer explained, the personality of a given judge may be the decisive factor:

> If I were to attempt to generalize, as indeed I should not, I should say that most depends upon the judge's unspoken notion as to the function of his court. If he views the role of the court as a passive one, he will be willing to delegate the responsibility for change, and he will not greatly care whether the delegated authority is exercised or not. If he views the court as an instrument of society designed to reflect in its decisions the morality of the community, he will be more likely to look precedent in the teeth and to measure it against the ideals and the aspirations of his time.

Tail-tweaking of dragons is not a task for the faint-hearted. But, you know that. You can still hear echoes of law school's first year when professors warned about and demonstrated the very difficult problems in the practice of law. I can only suggest you learn from the experience of dragon-slayers:

> "Kiss me!" cried the dragon, which had already devoured many gallant knights for declining to kiss it. "Give you a kiss," murmured the prince; "Oh, certainly, if that's all! Anything for a quiet life."
> So saying, he kissed the dragon, which instantly became a most beautiful princess; for she had lain enchanted as a dragon by a wicked magician, till somebody should be bold enough to kiss her.

"WITH GOOD LOGIC YOU MAY STILL LOSE
— BUT WITHOUT IT, YOU'LL **NEVER** WIN."

PART B

LOGIC AND LAW

The importance of logic in the law may not be de-emphasized. A person familiar with the basics of logical thinking is more likely to argue effectively than one who is not. Those who master the logical tenets laid out in the following pages will be better lawyers. Logic is the necessary supporting structure of the legal rule that emanates from the judicial opinion. This part addresses logic in three separate chapters. Chapter 4, "Elements of Legal Thinking," provides an overview of the importance and terminology of logic. Chapter 5, "Logic for Law Students: How to Think Like a Lawyer," examines in greater depth the role of logic in the law. Chapter 6, "Formal and Informal Fallacies," walks the reader through many fallacies which may render an argument unsound.

As a lawyer, you may find the discipline of parsing legalese into logical forms to be time-consuming and arduous at first, but as you become more comfortable with logic's framework, you will find that the exercise helps you more efficiently peel a case back to its essence. By familiarizing yourself with the fundamentals of logic, you can both fortify your legal position and undermine that of your opponent. Logic will not magically hand you victory at every turn, but armed with an understanding of its precepts, you will be a worthy adversary.

Chapter Four

Elements of Legal Thinking

Author's Note: *The following is excerpted from my book* Logic for Lawyers: A Guide to Clear Legal Thinking 23–29, 237–238 (3d ed. 1997).

Reflective Thinking

To study logic is to study methods and principles that distinguish correct reasoning from incorrect reasoning. The case method study of law is the study of the logical methods and principles used to make decisions. This case method is all-important because a law school education is designed to teach you how to solve complex problems. Even if you never practice law a day in your life, upon graduation you will be equipped for a galaxy of positions in both the private and public sectors for here there is a constant demand for skilled problem solvers. The case method of study is designed to develop and hone skills of analysis. An intense exposure, it is the premier educational method to learn principles of clear reflective thinking.

This does not mean that you can reason correctly only if you have studied logic. That an all-pro wide receiver may be highly gifted does not mean that he has studied the physics of a football's travel through the air or the physiology involved in running, jumping, leaping and catching. He just does it. He does it because he is possessed of what is called natural ability. Similarly, many individuals have natural logical instincts or have been sufficiently exposed to logical precepts, formally or informally, at home or in school. Taught today by the Socratic method, the study of logic in the law is similar to the study, concentration and drills that are required to develop coordination in an athletic team. But there is a difference. The study of logic is an individual endeavor.

The thesis can be stated simply: the person who studies logic—law student, lawyer or judge—and who has become familiar with the principles of logical thinking, is more likely to reason correctly than one who has not thought about the general concepts of reasoning. Logical thought in the law does not embrace all types of thinking. It does not include everything that passes through our heads. As Copi explains, "[a]ll reasoning is thinking, but not all thinking is reasoning." When you say, "I think I'll go swimming," you are engaging in a mental process, but it is not a process of reasoning. When you say, "I think that the Steelers will win today," your thinking may be based on reasoning if you first studied the teams' records, checked the disability list, or heard the weather report, but it can also mean, "I have a hunch the Steelers will win. I feel it in my bones."

Judge Joseph C. Hutcheson Jr., of the Fifth Circuit, was the judiciary's expert on "hunching":

> I knew, of course, that some judges did follow "hunches," — "guesses" I indignantly called them.... [I]n my youthful, scornful way, I recognized four kinds of judgments; first the cogitative, of and by reflection and logomachy; second, aleatory, of and by the dice; third, intuitive, of and by feeling or "hunching;" and fourth, asinine, of and by an ass; and in the same youthful, scornful way I regarded the last three as only variants of each other, the results of processes all alien to good judges. ... I, after canvassing all the available material at my command, and duly cogitating upon it, give my imagination play, and brooding over the cause, wait for the feeling, the hunch — that intuitive flash of understanding which makes the jump-spark connection between question and decision, and at the point where the path is darkest for the judicial feet, sheds its light along the way.

Logical thought is a progression of thought based on the logical relation between truths. It is unlike daydreaming, which is the development of a chain of images from a train of thought, commonly derived from what we call idle reverie, wool gathering or free association. The professor drones on in a dull lecture. You see that he wears a red tie. This reminds you of the red dress worn by Sally Mae, a friend, who recalls to mind, Jim, her brother, who works in security and uses a paper shredder, which in turn makes you think of spaghetti. Then suddenly, the professor calls upon you and you immediately think: "Where am I?"

Logical thought is reflective thinking. It consists of solving a problem by pondering a given set of facts in order to perceive their connection. For the purposes of our inquiry, reflective thinking may be understood, in the words of John Dewey, as an "operation in which present facts suggest other facts (or truths) in such a way as to induce belief in what is suggested on the ground of real relation in the things themselves, a relation between what suggests and what is suggested." What we call clear legal thinking is the application of reflective thinking to problem solving in the law. We must not establish our conclusions by intense personal desire, keenly felt emotional belief, folklore, superstition or dogmatic unquestioning acceptance. Rather, we must state grounds for our conclusion. A conclusion cannot stand on its own direct account, but only on account of something else which stands as "witness, evidence, voucher or warrant." We have to see an objective connection leading from that which we know to that which we don't know. We have to see, as Dewey describes, a "link in actual things, that makes one thing the ground, warrant, evidence, for believing in something else." Reflective thinking, therefore, is moving from the known to the unknown by an objective logical connection. The ability to think reflectively depends upon the power of seeing those logical connections. The ability to study law depends upon the power of seeing logical connections in the cases, of recognizing similarities and dissimilarities.

Simple formulas are always treacherous, but our common law tradition comes down to a recognition of a simple basic concept: if p then q; here is p; therefore, here is q. Thus, the perennial question: are the facts p or not p? There is much more to it than this, to be sure, and we will learn it, but this simplistic formula is offered now only to indicate that reflective thinking goes to the heart of logic in the law and that this mode of thinking concentrates on determining connections between statements.

Logical reasoning may be tested by objective criteria. We will set forth these standards so that you may test your own reasoning. Moreover, these criteria help you evaluate the reasoning of others. It is the purpose of logic to discover and make available those criteria that can be used to test arguments for correctness.

The logician is concerned primarily with the correctness of the complicated process of reasoning. The logician asks: "Does the problem get solved? Does the conclusion reached follow from the premises used or assumed? Do the premises provide good reason for accepting the conclusion?" If the problem gets solved, if the premise provides adequate grounds for affirming the conclusion, if asserting the premises to be true warrants asserting the conclusion to be true also, then the reasoning is correct. Otherwise, it is incorrect. The law student soon learns that these are the questions presented by the Socratic method. Lawyers learn that their adversaries ask the same questions in response to a brief. Indeed lawyers ask these questions of their adversaries' briefs. Judges will ask the same questions when briefs are read and oral arguments are heard.

The Language of Logic

The study of law involves the use of technical words of art used by logicians. You must understand some basic expressions that are important in the discussions that follow. Learn them now.

• *Proposition*: A proposition is any statement or assertion which is either true or false, and can be asserted or denied. In these respects propositions differ from questions, exclamations and commands. A proposition consists of *terms*, words or a group of words, which express a concept or simple apprehension. In the law, propositions come from many sources. We may draw them from constitutional texts or statutes, or from case law. Other propositions may come from a controlling fact, a fact that is either uncontested or has been found by a fact-finder. Examples of propositions:

> All men are mortal.
> All oral contracts for the sale of real estate are invalid.

• *Term*: A term is the simplest unit into which a proposition, and later a syllogism, can be logically resolved. When we discuss the elements of a syllogism, you will be introduced to *middle term*, *major term* and *minor term*. Examples of terms:

> All men: *middle term*.
> Mortal: *major term*.

Propositions are divided into two terms (often Middle-Major, Minor-Middle and Minor-Major) and a copula or a connecting link between the terms.

• *Inference*: An inference is a process in which one proposition (a conclusion) is arrived at and affirmed on the basis of one or more other propositions, which were accepted as the starting point of the process. Stebbing observes that inference "may be defined as a mental process in which a thinker passes from the apprehension of something given, the datum, to something, the conclusion, related in a certain way to the datum, and accepted only because the datum has been accepted." It is a process where the thinker passes from one proposition to another that is connected with the former in some way. But for the passage to be valid, it must be made according to the laws of logic that permit a reasonable movement from one proposition to another. According to Joseph Brennan, inference, then, is "any passing from knowledge to new knowledge." The passage cannot be mere speculation, intuition, or guessing. The key to a logical inference is the reasonable probability that the conclusion flows from the evidentiary datum because of past experiences in human affairs. A nickel-plated revolver was used in the bank holdup by a ski-masked robber who got away with $10,000 in marked money. A nickel-plated revolver, a ski-mask and $10,000 in marked money is found in the apartment of Dirty Dan, its sole occupant. The inference is permissible that our friend Dan was the bank robber. A moment is necessary to discuss the difference between *inference* and *implication*. These terms are obverse sides of the same coin. We *infer* a conclusion from the data; the data *implies* the conclusion. Professor Cooley explains: "When a series of statements is an instance of a valid form of inference, the conclusion will be said to *follow* from the premises, and the premises to *imply* the conclusion. If a set of premises implies a conclusion, then, whenever the premises are accepted as true, the conclusion must be accepted as true also ..." As Brennan put it, "In ordinary discourse, [implication] may mean 'to give a hint,' and [inference], 'to take a hint.' Thus when my hostess yawns and looks at her watch, I *infer* from her behavior that she would like me to go home. Her yawn and look *imply* that this is her desire." Drawing a proper inference is critical in the practice of law, as this opinion from the Court of Appeals for the Third Circuit sets forth:

> The line between a reasonable inference that may permissibly be drawn by a jury from basic facts in evidence and an impermissible speculation is not drawn by judicial idiosyncracies. The line is drawn by the laws of logic. If there is an experience of logical probability that an ultimate fact will follow a stated narrative or historical fact, then the jury is given the opportunity to draw a conclusion because there is a reasonable probability that the conclusion flows from the proven facts. As the Supreme Court has stated: "The essential requirement is that mere speculation be not allowed to do duty for probative facts after making due allowance for all reasonably possible inferences favoring the party whose case is attacked."

• *Argument*: An argument is any group of propositions where one proposition is claimed to follow from the others, and where the others are treated as furnishing grounds or support for the truth of the one. An argument is not a mere collection of propositions, but a group with a particular, rather formal, structure.

• *Conclusion*: The conclusion of an argument is the *one* proposition that is arrived at and affirmed on the basis of the *other* propositions of the argument.

• *Premise*: The premises of an argument are the *other* propositions which are assumed or otherwise accepted as providing support or justification for accepting the *one* proposition which is the conclusion. Thus, in the three propositions that follow, the first two are *premises* and the third, the *conclusion*:

> All men are mortal.
> <u>Socrates is a man.</u>
> Socrates is mortal.

• *Premise and conclusion are relative terms*: Because many arguments contain more than one syllogism (*polysyllogisms*) any premise can serve as a premise in one argument after having been the conclusion of a previous argument. Premises and conclusions require each other. A proposition standing alone is neither premise nor conclusion. Only when it occurs as an assumption in an argument is a proposition a premise; it is a conclusion only when it is the proposition that is arrived at and claimed to follow other premises in the argument.

• *Deductive and inductive reasoning distinguished*: For purposes of legal reasoning, we suggest that whether an inference is deductive or inductive depends upon the nature of the relationship between the given proposition and the inferred proposition. What is recommended here is a simplified, convenient formula for use by the legal profession, a clean cut approach that should satisfy all our needs, even though certain distinguished logicians, who teach to a broader census, may quarrel with the neatness, or over-simplification of our formula. Here's how we approach the dichotomy at this time: when conclusions are reached from the general to the particular we call it deductive reasoning; conclusions reached by reasoning from a number of particulars to the general or from a particular to another particular, we call induction. The two types of reasoning will be treated in depth in subsequent chapters.

The value of this inferential reasoning has been described by John Stuart Mill:

> To draw inferences has been said to be the great business of life. Every one has daily, hourly, and momentary need of ascertaining facts which he has not directly observed; not from any general purpose of adding to his stock of knowledge, but because the facts themselves are of importance to his interests or to his occupations. The business of the magistrate, [of the lawyer,] of the military commander, of the navigator, of the physician, of the agriculturist, is merely to judge of evidence and to act accordingly.... [A]s they do this well or ill, so they discharge well or ill the duties of their several callings. It is the only occupation in which the mind never ceases to be engaged.

How Logic Will Help You

This thesis has been straightforward. I do not say that knowledge of these materials is absolutely essential to studying or practicing law. A person may reason correctly without knowing a single rule of the syllogism; conversely, a person may know all the details of logic and not be able to discover truths that are necessary in the law. A guide to logical reasoning, or logic in the law, is tautologically speaking, simply a guide.

But what I do suggest is that an understanding of what I have said here should assist you:

- To develop clarity and consistency in your approach to law.
- To avoid error in analyzing reported judicial opinions.
- To avoid error in preparing and presenting a written or oral argument.
- To detect error in the reasoning process mounted by your adversary.
- To think and reason about difficult matters.
- To avoid the pitfalls of both formal and informal fallacies.
- And most important, to develop and improve the specific mental discipline which the study and practice of law demands and requires.

The importance of this mental discipline, commonly called "learning to think like a lawyer," was well summarized by Nicholas F. Lucas, who as a law student many years ago, observed:

> It is by this mental training rather than by the explicit, positive knowledge of its technical rules, that logic gives us the power and habit of thinking clearly. Probably more than any other science, a careful study trains and develops the reasoning powers, not merely the power of thinking consistently, but the power of discovering truth.

A final word. Logical reasoning and avoidance of fallacies does not always guarantee a solution. There is still the dilemma and counter-dilemma, one of which, "Litigiosus," kept ancient Greek logicians busy for many years:

> Protagoras, the Sophist, is said to have agreed to train Euathlus in the art of pleading. Half of the fee was to be paid when the course was completed; the remaining half when Euathlus should win his first case in court. Euathlus delayed undertaking any suit, and Protagoras eventually sued his pupil for the other half of the agreed fee, urging the following dilemma:

> If this case is decided in my favor, Euathlus must pay me by judgment of the court; and if it is decided in his favor, he must pay me by the terms of our contract.
> But it must be decided either in my favor or in his.
> Therefore, he is in any case obligated to pay.

Euathlus urged the following rebuttal:

> If this case is decided in his favor, I am free by the terms of our contract; and if it is decided in my favor, I am free by the judgment of the court.

But it must be decided in his favor or in mine.
Therefore, I am in any case freed of the obligation.

Take your time to work this out. (A couple of years will do.)

CHAPTER FIVE

LOGIC FOR LAW STUDENTS:
How to Think Like a Lawyer

Author's Note: *This article is based on my book,* Logic for Lawyers: A Guide to Clear Legal Thinking (3d ed. 1997). *This chapter excerpts from an article published in* 69 U. Pitt. L. Rev. 1 (2007), *co-authored by me and my then law clerks Stephen Clowney and Jeremy D. Peterson. Although the article is addressed to law students, the content is equally relevant to lawyers, as noted throughout the article.*

Logic is the lifeblood of American law. In case after case, prosecutors, defense counsel, civil attorneys and judges call upon the rules of logic to structure their arguments. Law professors, for their part, demand that students defend their comments with coherent, identifiable logic. By now we are all familiar with the great line spoken by Professor Kingsfield in *The Paper Chase*: "You come in here with a head full of mush and you leave thinking like a lawyer." What is thinking like a lawyer? It means employing logic to construct arguments.

Notwithstanding the emphasis on logical reasoning in the legal profession, our law schools do not give students an orientation in the principles of logic. Professor Jack L. Landau complained that "the idea of teaching traditional logic to law students does not seem to be very popular." Indeed, Professor Landau found that "[n]ot one current casebook on legal method, legal process, or the like contains a chapter on logic." In our view, this is tragic. The failure to ground legal education in principles of logic does violence to the essence of the law. Leaving students to distill the principles of logic on their own is like asking them to design a rocket without teaching them the rules of physics. Frustration reigns, and the resulting argument seems more mush-like than lawyerly. In these pages we make a small attempt to right the ship by offering a primer on the fundamentals of logical thinking.

Our goals are modest. At the risk of disappointing philosophers and mathematicians, we will not probe the depths of formal logic. Neither will we undertake to develop an abstract theory of legal thinking. This Article, rather, attempts something new: we endeavor to explain, in broad strokes, the core principles of logic and how they apply in the law school classroom. Our modest claim is that a person familiar with the basics of logical thinking is more likely to argue effectively than one who is not. We believe that students who master the logical tenets laid out in the following pages will be better lawyers and will feel more comfortable when they find themselves caught in the spotlight of a law professor on a Socratic binge.

Sifting through the dense jargon of logicians, we have identified a handful of ideas that are particularly relevant to the world of legal thinking. First, all prospective lawyers should make themselves intimately familiar with the fundamentals of deductive reasoning. Deductive reasoning, as Aristotle taught long ago, is based on the act of proving a conclusion by means of two other propositions. Perhaps 90 percent of legal issues can be resolved by deduction, so the importance of understanding this type of reasoning cannot be overstated. Second, students should acquaint themselves with the principles of inductive generalization. Inductive generalizations, used correctly, can help students resuscitate causes that seem hopeless. Third, reasoning by analogy—another form of inductive reasoning—is a powerful tool in a lawyer's arsenal. Analogies help lawyers and judges solve legal problems not controlled by precedent and help law students deflect the nasty hypotheticals that are the darlings of professors. Finally, we comment briefly on the limitations of logic.

It's Elementary: Deductive Reasoning and the Law

A. The Syllogism

Logic anchors the law. The law's insistence on sound, explicit reasoning keeps lawyers and judges from making arguments based on untethered, unprincipled and undisciplined hunches. Traditionally, logicians separate the wider universe of logical reasoning into two general categories: inductive and deductive. As we will see, both branches of logic play important roles in our legal system. We begin with deductive reasoning because it is the driving force behind most judicial opinions. Defined broadly, deduction is reasoning in which a conclusion is *compelled* by known facts. For example, if we know that Earth is bigger than Mars, and that Jupiter is bigger than Earth, then we also know that Jupiter *must* be bigger than Mars. Or, imagine that you know your dog becomes deathly ill every time he eats chocolate. Using deduction we know that if Spike wolfs down a Snickers bar, a trip to the vet will be necessary. From these examples, we can get an idea of the basic structure of deductive arguments: if A and B are true, then C also must be true.

The specific form of deductive reasoning that you will find lurking below the surface of most judicial opinions and briefs is the "syllogism"—a label logicians attach to any argument in which a conclusion is inferred from two premises. For example:

> All men are mortal.
> Socrates is a man.
> Therefore, Socrates is mortal.

According to the traditional jargon, the syllogism's three parts are called the major premise, the minor premise and the conclusion. The major premise states a broad and generally applicable truth: "All men are mortal." The minor premise states a specific and usually more narrowly applicable fact: "Socrates is a man." The conclusion then draws upon these premises and offers a new insight that is known to be true based on the premises: "Socrates is a mortal."

Gottfried Leibnitz expressed the significance of the syllogism three hundred years ago, calling its invention "one of the most beautiful, and also one of the most important, made by the human mind." For all its power, the basic principle of the syllogism is surprisingly straightforward: what is true of the universal is true of the particular. If we know that *all* cars have wheels, and that a Toyota is a car, then a Toyota must have wheels. The axiom may be stated this way: if we know that every member of a class has a certain characteristic, and that certain individuals are members of that class, then those individuals must have that characteristic.

It is no exaggeration to say that the syllogism lies at the heart of legal writing. Consider these examples taken from watershed Supreme Court opinions:

Marbury v. Madison
The Judicial Department's province and duty is to say what the law
    is.
The Supreme Court is the Judicial Department.
Therefore, the province and duty of the Supreme Court is to say what
    the law is.

Youngstown Sheet & Tube Co. v. Sawyer
The President's power to issue an order must stem from an act of Congress or the Constitution.
Neither an act of Congress nor the Constitution gives the President
    the power to issue the order.
Therefore, the President does not have the power to issue the order.

Brown v. Board of Education
Unequal educational facilities are not permitted under the Constitution.
A separate educational facility for black children is inherently unequal.
Therefore, a separate educational facility for black children is not permitted under the Constitution.

Griswold v. Connecticut
A law is unconstitutional if it impacts the zone of privacy created by the Bill of Rights.
The law banning contraceptives impacts the zone of privacy created by the Bill of Rights.
Therefore, the law banning contraceptives is unconstitutional.

We urge all law students to get in the habit of thinking in syllogisms. When briefing a case as you prepare a class assignment, the skeleton of the deductive syllogism should always poke through in your description of the case's rationale. Young attorneys should probably tattoo this on the back of their hands—or at least post it above their keyboards: whenever possible, make the arguments in your briefs and memos in the form of syllogisms. A clear, well-constructed syllogism ensures each conclusion is well-supported with evidence and gives a judge recognizable guideposts to follow as he sherpas the law along his desired footpath.

But how, you might ask, does a new lawyer learn to construct valid syllogisms? Some people come to this ability instinctively. Just as some musicians naturally possess perfect pitch, some thinkers have logical instincts. Luckily for the rest of us, the skill can be learned through patience and practice. We start with the basics. To shape a legal issue in the form of a syllogism, begin by stating the general rule of law or widely-known legal rule that governs your case as your major premise. Then, in your next statement, the minor premise, describe the key facts of the legal problem at hand. Finally, draw your conclusion by examining how the major premise about the law applies to the minor premise about the facts. Like this:

Major Premise: Cruel and unusual punishment by a state violates the Eighth Amendment.
Minor Premise: Executing a minor is cruel and unusual punishment by a state.
Conclusion: Executing a minor is forbidden by the Eighth Amendment.

Although this might look simple, constructing logically-sound syllogisms requires a lot of grunt work. You must thoroughly research the law's nooks and crannies before you can confidently state your major premise. And you must become sufficiently knowledgeable about your case to reduce key facts to a brief yet accurate synopsis.

If you find yourself having trouble organizing a brief or memo, try shoehorning your argument into this generic model, which is based on the argument made by prosecutors in nearly every criminal case:

Major premise: [Doing something] [violates the law.]
Minor premise: [The defendant] [did something.]
Conclusion: [The defendant] [violated the law.]

The prosecutor's model can serve as a useful template for most legal problems. Using it will help you reduce your arguments to their most essential parts.

In addition to providing a useful template, the above example reflects the fact that the three parts of a syllogism—the two premises and the conclusion—are themselves built from three terms. Two terms appear in each statement: the "major term" in the major premise and conclusion, the "minor term" in the minor premise and conclusion, and the "middle term" in the major and minor premises but not in the conclusion. Notice that the middle term covers a broad range of facts, and that if the conclusion is to be valid, the minor term must be a fact that is included within the middle term. Although the jargon can get confusing, the basic idea isn't hard to grasp: each statement in a syllogism must relate to the other two.

To be sure, there are other forms of deductive syllogism, but we have deliberately confined our discussion to the "All men are mortal" type—the Categorical Deductive Syllogism. Thus, we do not address the Hypothetical Syllogism (that includes an if-then statement), or the Disjunctive Syllogism (a syllogism in which one premise takes the form of a disjunctive proposition (either-or), and the other premise and conclusion are categorical propositions that either deny or affirm part of the disjunctive proposition). See *Logic for Lawyers*, at 158–68, for help with these sorts of syllogisms.

B. Finding Syllogisms in Legal Writing

But wait!—you might be thinking—this syllogism business is too simple; opinions and memos are never so straightforward. Well, yes and no. The syllogism is simple, and indeed it does undergird most legal arguments, but sometimes you have to dig a bit below the surface to excavate syllogisms. The fact that syllogisms aren't immediately evident doesn't mean that the writing is sloppy, or that it doesn't use syllogisms. But it does mean that you'll have to work a bit harder as a reader. Logician S. Morris Engel notes that "an argument's basic structure … may be obscured by an excess of verbiage…, but an argument's structure may also be obscured for us … because it is too sparse and has missing components. Such arguments may appear sounder than they are because we are unaware of important assumptions made by them.…"

Consider this one-sentence argument penned by Justice Blackmun in his *Roe v. Wade* opinion:

> This right of privacy, whether it be founded in the Fourteenth Amendment's concept of personal liberty and restrictions upon state action, as we feel it is, or, as the District Court determined, in the Ninth Amendment's reservation of rights to the people, is broad enough to encompass a woman's decision whether or not to terminate her pregnancy.

Implicit within Justice Blackmun's statement is the following syllogism:

Major Premise:	The right of privacy is guaranteed by the Fourteenth or Ninth Amendment.
Minor Premise:	A woman's decision to terminate her pregnancy is protected by the right of privacy.
Conclusion:	Therefore, a woman's decision whether to terminate her pregnancy is protected by the Fourteenth or Ninth Amendment.

The ideas are floating around in Judge Blackmun's sentence, but it requires some work on the reader's part to parse them into two premises and a conclusion.

Sometimes it's more than a matter of rearranging sentences and rephrasing statements to match up with the syllogistic form. Sometimes a legal writer doesn't mention all parts of the syllogism, leaving you to read between the lines. Logicians are certainly aware that an argument can be founded on a syllogism although not all parts of the syllogism are expressed. They even have a name for such an argument: an enthymeme. Often, enthymemes are used for efficiency's sake. If a premise or conclusion is obvious, then the writer can save her precious words to make less obvious points. Even a kindergarten teacher might find the full expression of a syllogism to be unnecessary. The teacher could say, "Good girls get stars on their foreheads; Lisa is a good girl; Lisa gets a star on her forehead." But she's more likely to say, "Lisa gets a star on her forehead because she is a good girl." In logic-speak, the teacher would be omitting the major premise because it is generally understood that good girls get stars on their foreheads. Judges and lawyers write for more educated audiences—or so we hope—and so as a law student you had better be ready for hosts of enthymemes.

In addition to handing the reader syllogisms on a platter, legal writers also have the tendency to pile one syllogism on top of another. Not surprisingly, logicians have a term for this too, but for once it is a term that makes sense and is easy to remember. A series of syllogisms in which the conclusion of one syllogism supplies a premise of the next syllogism is known as a polysyllogism. Typically, polysyllogisms are used because more than one logical step is needed to reach the desired conclusion. Be on the lookout for something like this as you pick apart a complex legal opinion:

All men are mortal.
Socrates is a man.
Therefore Socrates is mortal.

All mortals can die.
Socrates is mortal.
Therefore Socrates can die.

People who can die are not gods.
Socrates can die.
Therefore Socrates is not a god.

You have been warned. Watch for enthymemes and polysyllogisms in every opinion or legal memo or brief that you read, and be aware of them in your own writing. Your arguments will be improved.

C. Watch Out!: Flawed Syllogisms

A syllogism is a powerful tool because of its rigid inflexibility. If the premises of a syllogism are properly constructed, the conclusion *must* follow. But beware of bogus arguments masquerading as syllogisms. For example, consider the following:

Some men are tall.
Socrates is a man.
Therefore Socrates is tall.

It looks something like a syllogism, but you have no doubt spotted the flaw: knowing that *some* men are tall isn't enough for you to conclude that a particular man is tall. He might fall into the group of other men about whom we know nothing, and who might be tall, but who also might be short. This type of non-syllogism got past the U.S. Supreme Court in the *Dred Scott* case, in which the Court held that people of African descent, whether or not they were slaves, could never be citizens of the United States. One dissenting opinion noted that the Court's ruling relied on a bad syllogism, simplified here:

Major Premise: At the time of the adoption of the Constitution, *some* states considered members of the black race to be inferior and incapable of citizenship and of suing in federal court.

Minor Premise: Dred Scott's ancestors at the time of the Constitution were members of the black race.

Conclusion: Therefore, Dred Scott's ancestors were considered to be inferior and incapable of citizenship and of suing in federal court.

Mistakes of this sort remain extremely common in legal writing. Certain buzzwords, however, can help distinguish valid syllogisms from fallacious ones. *Alarm bells should sound immediately if you spot terms in the major premise like "some," "certain," "a," "one," "this," "that," "sometimes," "many," "occasionally," "once," or "somewhere."* To be legitimate the major premise must bespeak *"all"* or *"no."* Remember at all costs that the principle behind the syllogism is that what's true of the universal is true of the specific. In deductive reasoning, you reason from the general to the particular. Accordingly, if you're unsure about the nature of the general, you can't draw proper conclusions about the particular.

Remember this: just because two things share a common property does not mean they also share a second property. Some other examples of this fallacy may help. Business executives read the Wall Street Journal, and Ludwig is a Journal reader, therefore Ludwig is a business executive—WRONG! All law students are smart, and John is smart, therefore John is a law student—WRONG AGAIN! You get the idea.

So far, we've considered only two logical fallacies. Logicians have many more. Although we cannot provide an exhaustive list of fallacies, here is a quick check you can run that often will uncover flaws in a deductive syllogism. Logicians have come up with a series of letters to identify different types of propositions. The letters "A" and "E" describe universal propositions, "A" being affirmative and "E" negative. Meanwhile, "I" and "O" describe particular propositions, "I" being affirmative and "O" negative. The letters come from two Latin words: *Affirmo* (I affirm) and *Nego* (I deny). Logicians would describe the three propositions in our friendly "All men are mortal" syllogism as AII. Now for the check: for the major premise to be valid, it must be either "A" or "E." You can't make a major premise out of an "I" or an "O." The IAA form, for example, is not a valid syllogism. And your minor premise and conclusion must be either an "I" or an "O." If your tentative syllogism doesn't meet these requirements, you'll know something is wrong.

Certain logical errors crop up again and again, and so you should take particular care to avoid them. Don't cite inappropriate secondary authorities or cases from outside jurisdictions; logicians consider that an appeal to inappropriate authority. Don't rely on attacks on your opponent's character. Don't rely on appeals to emotion. Don't rely on fast talking or personal charm to carry the day. A cool head coupled with rigorous legal research, rather than rhetorical tricks, will turn a case in your favor.

It is critical to read every legal document you come across with care. Bad reasoning can seem persuasive at first glance. Logical fallacies are especially hard to spot in briefs, memos and court opinions because of the dense writing and complex fact patterns. Yet the effort is worthwhile. The ability to detect and avoid logical missteps will improve your writing immensely and develop your ability to "think like a lawyer"—the skill that professors and partners so admire.

Inductive Reasoning: Generalizations

Deductive reasoning and its adherence to the "Socrates is Mortal" type of syllogism is the spine that holds our legal system together. Justice Cardozo estimated that at least nine-tenths of appellate cases "could not, with the semblance of reason, be decided in any way but one" because "the law and its application alike are plain," or "the rule of law is certain, and the application alone doubtful." After five decades on the bench, Judge Aldisert can confirm that Justice Cardozo's statement remains true today. In the language of logic, this means that practicing lawyers spend most of their time worrying about the minor premises of syllogisms (*i.e.,* can the facts of the case be fit into the territory governed by a particular rule?).

In law school, however, you will be asked to concentrate on the ten percent (or less) of cases that can't be resolved so easily. In the classroom, knotty and unsettled questions of law predominate. Where an issue of law is unsettled, and there is no binding precedent to supply a major premise for your syllogism, deductive logic is of no use to you. By focusing on such cases, your professors will drag you kicking and screaming into the land of induction, the second category of logic.

Inductive generalization is a form of logic in which big, general principles are divined from observing the outcomes of many small events. In this form of inductive logic, you reason from multiple particulars to the general. To see how this works, suppose that you are asked to determine whether all men are mortal—the premise of the first syllogism we discussed. If nobody hands you the simple statement "All men are mortal," and you lack a way of deducing it, you have to turn to inductive reasoning. You might use what you know about particular men and their mortality as follows:

> Plato was a man, and Plato was mortal.
> Julius Caesar was a man, and Julius Caesar was mortal.
> George Washington was a man, and George Washington was mortal.
> John Marshall was a man, and John Marshall was mortal.
> Ronald Reagan was a man, and Ronald Reagan was mortal.
> Therefore, all men are mortal.

The principle underlying this way of thinking is that the world is sufficiently regular to permit the discovery of general rules. If what happened yesterday is likely to happen again today, we may use past experience to guide our future conduct. The contrast with deductive reasoning is stark. Whereas syllogisms are mechanical and exact—if the premises are true and properly assembled, the conclusion must be true—inductive logic is not so absolute. It does not produce conclusions guaranteed to be correct, no matter how many examples scholars assemble. Thousands of great men may live and die each year, but we will never know with absolute certainty whether every man is mortal. Thus, inductive reasoning is a logic of probabilities and generalities, not certainties. It yields workable rules, but not proven truths.

The absence of complete certainty, however, does not dilute the importance of induction in the law. As we stated at the outset, we look to inductive reasoning when our legal research fails to turn up a hefty, hearty precedent that controls the case. When there is no clear statute—no governing authority—to provide the major premise necessary for a syllogism, the law student must build the major premise himself. To use Lord Diplock's phrase, this requires him to draw upon "the cumulative experience of the judiciary"—the specific holdings of other cases. Once he has assembled enough case law, he tries to fashion a general rule that supports his position.

You might wonder how this works in the real world. Let's start with something mundane. Suppose a professor asks you to determine what happens to the contents of a jointly-leased safe deposit box if one of the lessees dies unexpectedly. Do all of the contents pass to the survivor, or does the dead man's estate claim his possessions? The Oklahoma Supreme Court faced this question in *Estate of Stinchcomb*. Finding that the state had no binding case law on point, the court turned to inductive reasoning. Its research demonstrated that judges in Illinois, Nevada and Maryland had all ruled in favor of the dead man's estate. From these individual examples, the Oklahoma Supreme Court inferred the general rule that "a joint lease in and of itself alone, does not create a joint tenancy in the contents of the box."

Inductive generalizations, then, are easy enough to understand. You can get in trouble using them, however. Most importantly, you must be careful to assemble a sufficient number of examples before shaping a far-reaching rule, or you will be guilty of the fallacy of "hasty generalization." In logic-speak, this fallacy occurs when you construct a general rule from an inadequate number of particulars. It is the bugaboo of inductive reasoning and often surfaces in casebooks and classroom discussions, as well as on TV talk-shows and in newspaper editorials. Think about your overeager classmates who rely on nothing more than their personal life experiences to justify outlandish policy proposals. They're often guilty of creating bogus general rules from exceptional circumstances. Judges, lawyers and law students all must be careful not to anoint isolated instances with the chrism of generality.

The difficulty comes in knowing how many instances are sufficient to make a generalization. Three? Ten? Forty thousand? This is where the art comes in. As a rule of thumb, the more examples you find, the stronger your argument becomes. In *O'Conner v. Commonwealth Edison Co.*, a federal judge in Illinois lambasted an expert witness for attempting to formulate a universal medical rule based on his observation of only five patients:

> Based on the five patients [Dr. Scheribel] has observed with cataracts induced by radiation therapy, he developed his "binding universal rule" that he applied to O'Conner, thus committing the logical fallacy known as Converse Accident (hasty generalization).... It occurs when a person erroneously creates a general rule from observing too few cases. Dr. Scheribel has illogically created a "binding universal rule" based upon insufficient data.
>
> For example, observing the value of opiates when administered by a physician to alleviate the pains of those who are seriously ill, one may be led to propose that narcotics be made available to everyone. Or considering the effect of alcohol only on those who indulge in it to excess, one may conclude that all liquor is harmful and urge that its sale and use should be forbidden by law. Such reasoning is erroneous....

Don't let yourself make the same mistake.

Raw numbers are not enough to give you a reliable generalization, however. Consider this classic blunder: in 1936, *Literary Digest* magazine conducted a massive polling effort to predict the outcome of the Presidential election between Alf Landon and Franklin Roosevelt. The Digest polled well over two million people, and the vast majority indicated they would vote for Landon (keep in mind that modern news organizations base their polls on the responses of 1,000 people). In the actual election, however, Roosevelt won 523 electoral votes and Landon received only eight. How did *Literary Digest* get it so wrong when it had crafted its rule from a massive number of particular examples? It seems the *Digest* focused its polling efforts on car owners—an unrepresentative group of the American public in 1936. From this example, it should become clear that the strength of an inductive argument rests not only on the number of examples you turn up to support your generalization, but also on the representativeness of the sample size. Keep this in mind when your opponent makes an argument based solely on the use of statistics, as is the case in many antitrust, securities and discrimination claims.

You will never completely escape the risks posed by the fallacy of hasty generalization. We can never know with certainty that an inductive generalization is true. The best that can be hoped for is that expert research and keen attention to statistics will divine workable rules that are grounded in the wisdom of human experience. If your professor demands absolute certainty of you, you'll have to explain to him that it cannot be achieved, at least not with an inductive generalization. Notwithstanding its shortcomings, inductive generalization remains a vital tool, because the ability to shape persuasive legal arguments when no clear precedent exists is often what separates a star attorney from your run-of-the-mill ambulance chaser.

Analogy

Anyone who has struggled through a first-year torts course knows that hypothetical questions play a central role in the law school classroom. Professors invent elaborate factual scenarios and ask students to distill the correct result from a handful of cases read the night before. Then they change the situation slightly; does the answer change? Now alter a different parameter; same result, or a different one? The imaginative fact patterns do not end with law school; judges, too, rely on outlandish hypotheticals to test the validity of a lawyer's argument. Yet, notwithstanding the importance of hypothetical questions in legal thinking, the ability to manage them remains poorly taught and rarely practiced. We believe that the careful use of analogy—a form of inductive reasoning—can get you past a nasty hypothetical. Analogy can help a budding lawyer advance untested legal arguments in the classroom and the courtroom. We stress that mastering the principles of analogy is not just another garden-variety lawyer's skill. Rather, it is one of the most crucial aspects of the study and practice of law.

Unlike most concepts employed by logicians, the use of "analogy" is not confined to the realms of higher mathematics and philosophy. Most law students, and even most laypersons, are familiar with formal analogies of the "Sun is to Day as Moon is to _____?" variety. The use of informal, off-the-cuff analogies guides most of our own everyday decision-making. I own a Honda Civic that doesn't overheat, so I conclude that my friend's Honda Civic will never overheat. My eyes don't water when I cut an onion; I conclude that my brother's eyes won't water either. This type of reasoning has a simple structure: (1) A has characteristic Y; (2) B has characteristic Y; (3) A also has characteristic Z; (4) Because A and B both have Y, we conclude that B also shares characteristic Z. At base, analogy is a process of drawing similarities between things that appear different.

In the world of the law, analogies serve a very specific purpose. Attorneys use them to compare new legal issues to firmly established precedents. Typically, this means that a current case is compared to an older one, and the outcome of the new case is predicted on the basis of the other's outcome. Professor Edward Levi, a top American authority on the role of analogy in the law, described analogical reasoning as a three step process: (1) establish similarities between two cases, (2) announce the rule of law embedded in the first case, and (3) apply the rule of law to the second case. This form of reasoning is different from deductive logic or inductive generalization. Recall that deduction requires us to reason from universal principles to smaller, specific truths. The process of generalization asks us to craft larger rules from a number of specific examples. Analogy, in contrast, makes one-to-one comparisons that require no generalizations or reliance on universal rules. In the language of logicians, analogy is a process of reasoning from the particular to the particular.

An example might help to clarify the distinction. Imagine you are asked to defend a client who received a citation for driving a scooter without a helmet. After scouring Westlaw, you find there's no controlling statute. There are, however, two precedents that could influence the result. One opinion holds that motorcyclists must wear helmets; the other case says that a helmet is not required to operate a bicycle. Does either control the issue in your case? Without a clear universal rule or past cases on point, deductive logic and inductive generalizations are of little help. Instead, you must rely on the power of analogy to convince a judge that helmet laws don't apply. To defend your client, you must suggest that driving a scooter is similar to riding a "fast bicycle." You might argue that small scooters can't go faster than well-oiled road bikes. Thus, a scooter presents no more danger to its operator or other drivers than a bicycle. You could also argue that scooters, like bikes, can't be driven on highways. The process of drawing these comparisons and explaining why they are important is the heart of reasoning by analogy. The idea is to find enough similarities between the new case and old precedent to convince a judge that the outcomes must be the same.

A proper analogy should identify the respects in which the compared cases, or fact scenarios, resemble one another and the respects in which they differ. What matters is relevancy—whether the compared traits resemble, or differ from, one another in relevant respects. A single apt comparison can be worth more than a host of not-quite-right comparisons. You might be wondering how to tell whether a comparison is a fruitful one or whether it's not quite right. Well, that is where art once again enters the picture. As John Stuart Mill remarked:

> Why is a single instance, in some cases, sufficient for a complete induction, while in others myriads of concurring instances ... go such a very little way towards establishing an universal proposition? Whoever can answer this question knows more of the philosophy of logic than the wisest of the ancients, and has solved the problem of Induction.

Notwithstanding the best efforts of logicians, no one has devised a mathematical equation for determining whether an analogy is strong or weak. In the words of Copi and Burgess-Jackson, "It is a matter of judgment, not mechanical application of a rule." Thinking back to our scooter example, your opponent will argue vigorously that a scooter resembles a motorcycle because both have quick-starting, gas-powered engines that are beyond human control. This comparison may strike the judge as more powerful than yours, convincing him to rule against your client.

The Court of Appeals for the Third Circuit discussed all of these principles in detail in an important class action antitrust case, *In Re: Linerboard*, where the principal issue on appeal was whether the holding in *Newton v. Merrill Lynch* applied to the case at bar:

> For Appellants' argument to prevail, therefore, they must demonstrate that the facts in *Newton* are substantially similar to the facts in the case at bar, what logicians call inductive reasoning by analogy, or reasoning from one particular case to another. To draw an analogy

between two entities is to indicate one or more respects in which they are similar and thus argue that the legal consequence attached to one set of particular facts may apply to a different set of particular facts because of the similarities in the two sets. Because a successful analogy is drawn by demonstrating the resemblances or similarities in the facts, the degree of similarity is always the crucial element. You may not conclude that only a partial resemblance between two entities is equal to a substantial or exact correspondence.

Logicians teach that one must always appraise an analogical argument very carefully. Several criteria may be used: (1) the acceptability of the analogy will vary proportionally with the number of circumstances that have been analyzed; (2) the acceptability will depend upon the number of positive resemblances (similarities) and negative resemblances (dissimilarities); or (3) the acceptability will be influenced by the relevance of the purported analogies. [Citing logicians.]

For Appellants to draw a proper analogy, they had the burden in the district court, as they do here, of showing that the similarities in the facts of the two cases outweigh the differences. They cannot do so, for two significant reasons. First, in *Newton* it was clear that not all members of the putative class sustained injuries; here, all members sustained injuries because of the artificially increased prices. Secondly, in *Newton* there were hundreds of millions of stock transactions involved, thus making the putative class extremely unmanageable; here, an astronomical number of transactions is not present. [Thus, their argument fails.]

Let's turn to other examples of the process of analogy. Imagine you discover that Able Automobile Company is liable for violating the antitrust laws by requiring a tie-in purchase of a refrigerator manufactured by Mrs. Able with the purchase of any Able car. It is not difficult to see by analogy that liability also would follow from these facts: Baker Automobile Company requires a tie-in purchase of a refrigerator manufactured by Mrs. Baker if you want to buy a Baker Mustang.

But consider the following: State College had a championship basketball team last year. Team members came from high schools *A*, *B*, *C* and *D*. State College has recruited new players from high schools *A*, *B*, *C* and *D* for this year's team. Therefore, State College will have a championship basketball team this year. Is the resemblance relevant? We must ask if the resemblance—players from the same high schools—is meaningful. Does it help us get to the conclusion we seek to draw? If one good player came from a particular school, does that mean that another player is likely to be similarly good? Probably not, unless the high school is extremely unusual and accepts as students only good basketball players. More likely, what we have here is an analogy based on irrelevant similarities, and such an analogy is of no use at all.

As mentioned earlier, law professors love to test your ability to work with analogies by inventing grueling hypotheticals. They do this for a few reasons. First, as we've already discussed, the imagined fact patterns force you to grapple with questions of law that aren't amenable to syllogisms. Second, a professor can easily and repeatedly change the facts of a hypo, allowing him to ask questions of many students and to probe the boundaries of a particular legal issue. Finally, the fear of getting trapped in the tangle of a knotty question encourages students to study the law with care and to absorb its details. If you do find yourself in the Socratic spotlight, remember the basic principles of analogy; they can be your lifeline. Begin by discussing the facts of a similar case that you are familiar with, and then lay out particulars of the hypothetical the professor has asked. Draw as many comparisons between the two cases as you can. If the relevant similarities outweigh the relevant differences, the outcomes of the cases should be the same. The more practice you get working with analogies, and the more adept you become at articulating why certain similarities or differences are relevant, the better you will fare when it's your turn to face the music.

Logical Limits:
When There Is More to the Story

We hope we have convinced you that logic is the lifeblood of the law, and that understanding basic logical forms will assist you both in law school and in your practice as a lawyer. We would be remiss, however, if we were to send you out into the world without acknowledging that there is more to the law than assembling logical expressions. Consider the following:

> All federal judges are body builders.
> Judge Aldisert is a federal judge.
> Therefore, Judge Aldisert is a body builder.

What's wrong with this statement? It's a rock-solid syllogism, adhering to the blueprint of logical validity expressed by the "Socrates" syllogism. Just the same, Judge Aldisert does not spend much time pumping iron. You see the problem, of course: the major premise is false. Not all federal judges are body builders. In fact, we doubt any of them are. The point is an obvious but important one: make sure your premises are true. If you use an untrue premise as a lawyer, it's an invitation to the other side to pillory you. If you do so as a judge, you may fashion a dangerous precedent.

Separately, logic is not the whole game. Even if your premises are true and your logical statements constructed properly, it is crucial to recognize that judges are motivated by more than the mandates of logic. Judges have notions of how things should be—of what is wrong and what is right—and often strive to do justice as much as to fulfill the mandates of precedent. They have biases, too. In reading cases, writing briefs, and arguing before a court, you will be more effective if you flesh out the logical bones of your arguments and attempt to appeal to the judge in other ways as well.

But always bear in mind: *an argument that is correctly reasoned may be wrong, but an argument that is incorrectly reasoned can never be right.* You may find the discipline of parsing legalese into logical forms to be time-consuming and arduous at first, but as you become more comfortable with logic's framework, you will find that the exercise helps you more efficiently peel a case back to its essence. A solid footing in logic will help you feel more secure when you find yourself in a complex doctrinal thicket. And while the fundamentals of logic laid out in this article will not give you a magic carpet on which you can float above the legal briar patch, we believe they will give you a machete that will help you start hacking your way through the tangle.

CHAPTER SIX

FORMAL AND INFORMAL FALLACIES

Author's Note: *The following is excerpted from my books* Winning on Appeal: Better Briefs and Oral Argument 273–279 (2d ed. 2003), *and* Logic for Lawyers: A Guide to Clear Legal Thinking 139–141, 165 (3d ed. 1997). *This chapter aims to introduce the reader to various fallacies by providing an overview. For a more in-depth treatment, see* Logic for Lawyers.

In ordinary speech, the word fallacy is used in many ways. A perfectly proper use of the word is to designate any mistaken idea or false belief: "Any team that Mike Ditka coaches will be a winning team." "All lawyers are thieves, all doctors, quacks."

In ordinary usage then, fallacy can be used to describe a false or erroneous idea. In the law, the term becomes a term of art; it refers to the logical form or content of a syllogism. Nevertheless, the terms "fallacy" or "fallacious" are often used to describe a premise in a syllogism as false or untrue. Thus, you will find judges and lawyers sometimes using the expressions in the lay sense to describe something that is not supported by the facts.

Notwithstanding its popular or lay use, logicians and the legal profession generally use the term "fallacy" in a narrower sense to describe a type of incorrect argument, rather than a description of falsity or error in a statement. Several types of fallacies rear their ugly and unwelcome heads in the law. One type of fallacy occurs when we neglect the rules of logic and fall into erroneous reasoning. Other fallacies, generally called informal or material fallacies, meticulously follow logical form but suffer from improper content or emphasis. A fallacy, then, is not merely an error but a way of falling into an error.

The name comes from the Latin, *fallax,* which suggests a deliberate deception, but most fallacies are not intentional. Fallacies are dangerous because they are false conclusions or interpretations resulting from processes of thinking that claim or appear to be valid but fail to conform to the requirements of logic. A fallacy can be defined, in Ralph Eaton's words, as "any argument that seems conclusive to the normal mind but that proves, upon examination, not to establish the alleged conclusion," or more succinctly, a form of argument that has intuitive appeal but does not withstand rational scrutiny. They have been identified as such ever since Aristotle described these arguments: "That some [lines of] reasoning are genuine, while others seem to be so but are not, is evident. This happens with arguments, as also elsewhere, through a certain likeness between the genuine and the sham." Common fallacies abound in all writings—speeches, commentaries, legislative debates, political oratory, TV editorials, columns, articles, household and family discussions, and personal conversations. For our purposes, the most useful classification appears to be two categories—formal and informal fallacies.

Formal Fallacies

Formal fallacies arise when there is an error in the logic, or formal structure, of the argument quite apart from the content of the premises. They can be discovered without any knowledge of the subject matter with which the argument is concerned. Our inquiry into formal fallacies begins with the categorical syllogism. The rules of the categorical syllogism form guidelines upon which a deductive or inductive argument in proper logical form may be based. Conversely stated, to depart from any of these rules is to commit a logical fallacy of form; it is to commit what is known as a formal fallacy.

I furnish now only a catalog or listing or tally of formal fallacies without describing or defining them. Here again for further study I refer you to *Logic for Lawyers*.

A. Fallacies in Categorical Syllogisms

Categorical syllogisms contain three terms, two premises and one conclusion. These, then, are the rules that you must follow to avoid formal fallacies:

Rule 1: A valid categorical syllogism must contain exactly three terms, each of which is used in the same sense throughout the argument.

Rule 2: In a valid categorical syllogism, the middle term must occur in at least one premise.

Rule 3: In a valid categorical syllogism, no term can occur in the conclusion which does not occur in a premise.

Rule 4: No categorical syllogism is valid if it has two negative premises.

Rule 5: If either premise of a valid categorical syllogism is negative, the conclusion must be negative.

Rule 6: No valid categorical syllogism with a particular conclusion can have two universal premises.

Violation of any of these rules is a formal fallacy and renders the argument invalid.

B.   Fallacies in Hypothetical Syllogisms

In law we often encounter a compound proposition called a hypothetical or conditional proposition. Hypothetical or conditional propositions are the darlings of law professors and of appellate judges asking questions at oral argument: "If we follow that rule, what will be the result in a case where ..." This type of compound proposition is not categorical, for it does not directly assert the existence of a fact. Instead it contains a condition — "if," "unless," "granted," "supposing," and it is divided into two parts: the *antecedent* and the *consequent*.

- If the offer is accepted before the offeror revokes, the revocation is invalid.
- *Antecedent*: the offer is accepted before the offeror revokes.
- *Consequent*: the revocation is invalid.

The conditional proposition can be combined with other propositions to form a hypothetical argument.

- If the defendant was denied due process, the conviction is invalid.
- The defendant was denied due process.
- Therefore, the conviction is invalid.

Valid hypothetical arguments cannot be constructed by making either of the following moves, which constitute the two fallacies in this area:

1. Denying the antecedent
2. Affirming the consequent

C.   Fallacies in Disjunctive Syllogisms

Disjunctive propositions present their conditions as alternatives. A disjunctive proposition expresses an "either-or," or an "if, then-not" relation between at least two component propositions. A disjunctive syllogism may consist, for example, of a disjunctive proposition as the major premise, a minor prem-ise categorically affirming or denying one of the alternative propositions, and a conclusion that categorically affirms or denies the other alternative. Such ar-guments are subject to the fallacy of the imperfect disjunctive.

1. *Fallacy of Missing Disjuncts*: This goes to the incompleteness of a dis-junction and is committed whenever a disjunctive proposition asserts the truth of at least one of a pair or set of disjuncts when in fact there are other possible or alternative disjuncts not enumerated.
2. *Fallacy of Nonexclusivity*: This fallacy occurs whenever one assumes that affirming one disjunct shows the other to be false when in fact it is pos-sible for both to be true.

Informal (Material) Fallacies

An informal fallacy is one that cannot be detected merely by examining the form of the argument but must be detected in some other way. It is any other argument that does not properly establish the supported conclusion. An ar-gument contains an informal fallacy when at least one of its premises is not true, or when the rules of inference are not properly respected.

Material, or factual, fallacies do not result from violations of formal logic rules. They are called "material" because they exist not in the form of an ar-gument, but in its factual content or matter. For this reason, they cannot be set right without some knowledge of the subject. It is difficult to condense into a single definition everything encompassed by material fallacies, yet two basic tenets of logic provide keys to their understanding:

- Logical reasoning presupposes that the terms shall be unambiguously defined and used in a uniform manner throughout.
- The discipline of logic demands that the conclusion be derived from the premises rather than assumed.

Material fallacies can sneak up on us as readily as do fallacies of form. Lo-gicians, scientists and other careful scholars are especially adept at detecting and avoiding them. Professors William and Mabel Sahakian describe them as "nu-merous, deceptive and elusive—so elusive that a person untrained in detect-ing them can easily be misled into accepting them as valid." Logicians differ as to the precise categorization of material fallacies, because some resemble or relate to a type of argument rather than a type of logic, but for my purposes, I will follow in major part the classification set forth by the Sahakians.

A. Fallacies of Irrelevant Evidence

Fallacies of irrelevant evidence are arguments that miss the central point at issue and rely instead upon emotions, ignorance and other irrelevant matters.

1. *Fallacy of irrelevance* (or irrelevant conclusions, *ignoratio elenchi*).
2. *Fallacies of distraction*
   a. *Argumentum ad misericordiam*, or the appeal to pity.
   b. *Argumentum ad verecundiam*, or the appeal to prestige.
   c. *Argumentum ad hominem*, or the appeal to personal ridicule.
   d. *Argumentum ad populum*, or the appeal to popular opinion.
   e. *Argumentum ad antiquitam*, or the appeal to tradition.
   f. *Argumentum ad terrorem*, or the appeal to fearsome consequences.

B. Miscellaneous Material Fallacies

1. *Fallacy of accident* (or *dicto simpliciter*): applying the general rule to exceptional circumstances.
2. *Converse fallacy of accident* (or the fallacy of selective instances or hasty generalizations): deriving a general rule from an inadequate sample of instances.
3. *False cause* (or *post hoc ergo propter hoc*): concluding from the conjunction of two events that one caused the other.
4. *Conclusion that does not follow* (or *non sequitur*): employing premises that do not support the conclusion reached.
5. *Compound question* (or poisoning the well): phrasing the question so as to prefigure the answer.
6. *Begging the question* (or *petitio principii*, arguing in a circular): assuming as true what is to be proved.
7. *You yourself do it* (or *tu quoque*): meeting criticism with the argument that the other person engages in the very conduct she is criticizing.

C. Linguistic Fallacies

1. *Fallacy of equivocation*: using terms that are vague or signify a variety of ideas.
2. *Fallacy of amphibology*: using statements whose meaning is unclear because of the syntax.
3. *Fallacy of composition*: concluding that a property possessed by one member of a group is also possessed by all members of the group.

4. *Fallacy of division*: concluding that a property possessed by the whole is also possessed by each of the parts individually.
5. *Fallacy of vicious abstraction*: taking a statement out of context.
6. *Argumentum ad nauseam*: sustaining one's position by repetition or other needlessly lengthy argument.

Fallacies: A Final Word

Our understanding of fallacies can be sharpened in the course of daily life. Read editorials and opinion pieces, and put the reasoning to the tests. Are the authors guilty of erecting strawpersons and knocking them down, thus committing the fallacy of irrelevant conclusions? Do they beat their breasts over an answer expressed in a news conference by the president or governor or mayor when the question was loaded with three or four compound parts? Does the content of the piece truly follow logical form? Does it appear as a categorical, hypothetical or disjunctive syllogism? Do you see *ad hominems* or other fallacies?

Pay attention to TV correspondents in their 60-second sound bites following news accounts. Are they guilty of the fallacy of hasty generalization by prophesizing broad consequences from one single event in a fast-breaking story? Do you detect any fallacies of distraction? Appeals to pity or to the masses? Are they guilty of *dicto simpliciter*, attempting to project a general rule from that which obviously is an exception to the rule? For the apogee of political science fiction, analyze carefully the comments of senators and congresspersons who blithely offer comments on sudden events without a whit of understanding of the underlying factual premises.

Or at the friendly corner tavern, listen to the loud defense of conclusions on church, school, family, religion and politics. Without entering the discussion yourself (do not ever try to use reflective reasoning in a bar), attempt to identify the premises employed by the discussants. Are there any premises? Listen to conclusions that they draw from current facts. Are these permissible inferences, that is, inferences that would reasonably follow in logical sequence based on past human experience, or are they sheer speculation? How about: "I know the game was fixed! How could a team lose three in a row to the Mets when they beat them six times straight."

In the tavern or the cocktail lounge, take an end seat and drink deeply of *non sequiturs* and *post hocs*.

But do not get smug. All of us commit fallacies every day in reaching judgments—all of us, and that includes judges, lawyers, professors, preachers and authors of books. We do this because our thinking is not always reflective. We are "thinking" every waking moment of the day. At any time, there is always a penny for our thoughts. We have daydreams and reveries. We build castles in the air. We conjure up mental pictures and random recollections. We sometimes "think" and "conclude" because we want a certain conclusion. We think that wishing will make it so.

Sometimes, we unwittingly insert a note of invention and add it to a faithful record of observation. We simply want to believe something. We are certain our kids do not do the bad things that others do. We are totally convinced that our best friends did not say what others reported that they said. We are constantly influenced by emotions, beliefs and social wants and demands. We are human; we are not computers.

So sometimes we do draw conclusions by a process that lies somewhere between a flight of fancy and a dispassionate weighing of the relevant considerations that should be employed to reach a reasoned conclusion. We must all confess to this. But by now you have learned that what is derived is reflective thinking and that this involves more than a sequence of ideas. To do our jobs as members of the legal profession, and of community and family units, and to earn the respect of those who know us, and the accolade that we are clear thinkers, we have an obligation. That obligation is to employ reflective thinking when called upon to solve a problem, any problem whether at home, school, church, office, business or in our social relations. We must respect the canons of reflective thinking, what John Dewey called "a *con*-sequence—a consecutive ordering in such a way that each determines the next as its proper outcome, while each outcome in turn leans back on or refers to, its predecessors."

What John Dewey said over three-quarters of a century ago is important and should be our watchword:

> The successive portions of a reflective thought grow out of one another and support one another; they do not come and go in a medley. Each phase is a step from something to something.... The stream or flow becomes a train or chain. There are in any reflective thought definite units that are linked together to a common end.

If we follow these watchwords, we will go a long way in avoiding the pitfalls of fallacy.

WORKIN' ON THE CONVEYOR BELT
AT APPELLATE COURTS U.S.A.!

PART C

AVOIDING ASSEMBLY LINE JUSTICE

The chapters in Part C discuss the situation of the appellate courts, examining both the relative competencies of the state and federal systems, and the consequences of a crushing caseload for the appellate judicial system. As I set forth, lawyers should not reflexively consider federal courts to be superior, but instead should reflect critically on the claims leveled at the differences between state and federal venues. Once in the federal system, too many trial lawyers appear before appellate courts without recognizing that the environment on appeal is a galaxy away from that of the trial courtroom. They must understand the burden of current caseloads and the resulting importance such caseloads lend to good writing. I set forth this severe institutional problem with actual statistics, and highlight that your appeal faces extreme competition with other appeals in the assembly line.

Also offered is a "Seniors' Solution" to the problem of mushrooming caseloads: seven senior circuit judges—five of whom (including myself) are former Chief Judges of judicial circuits—have tackled the alarming trend of ever-increasing caseloads by proposing a fundamental change to considering appeals.

Lawyers must understand the state of the appellate courts. Gone are the antediluvian days of the federal courts of appeals. By highlighting this problem, providing statistics, sharing recurring criticisms, offering suggestions along the way, and proposing a structural solution, the hope is to help the lawyer both better understand this institutional crisis and become a better advocate before an appellate court.

CHAPTER SEVEN

STATE COURTS AND FEDERALISM

Author's Note: *In the summer of 1981, The National Center for State Courts and the Marshall-Wythe School of Law of the College of William and Mary in Virginia sponsored a symposium on "State Courts and Federalism in the 1980s." Four distinguished law professors delivered papers:*

> Paul M. Bator The State Courts and Federal Constitution
> Robert M. Cover The Limits of Jurisdiction Redundancy Interest,
> Ideology, and Innovation
> Martha A. Field The Uncertain Nature of Federal Jurisdiction
> Burt Neuborne Toward Procedural Parity in Constitutional Litigation

A state judge and I, as a federal judge, were asked to deliver commentary on the scholarly papers under the rubric: "Response of the Judiciary." My colleague was a judge on the Arizona Court of Appeals. Her name: Sandra Day O'Connor. Later that year she would begin her distinguished career on the U.S. Supreme Court. A portion of my 1981 Comments, which were published in 22 Wm. & Mary L. Rev. 821 (1981), *are reproduced here.*

Although this article was published 30 years ago, my observations and sentiments have not changed. Indeed, if anything, the cases reaching the U.S. Courts of Appeals have reached new lows of drudgery, with the continued "federal courtization" of society. Before choosing between federal and state venues, or before appearing in federal courts, lawyers should be aware of the state of the federal docket. They should also critically reflect on the all-too-common refrain of federal court superiority and federal judge competency. This article provides my views on why lawyers should not reflexively consider federal courts to be superior.

———

Each of the four highly analytical, uniformly thoughtful and stimulating papers that are the subject of these comments deserves an exhaustive commentary. My role is not to respond in kind by setting forth an essay of my own, but to react informally to the intellectual feast so temptingly displayed in the

preceding pages. My reaction is, of necessity, personal and unabashedly influenced by my experience, and, therefore, these contentions are intuitive rather
than conclusive. Moreover, my reaction is probably atypical because it is colored (or shall I say jaundiced?) by twenty years in the state and federal judiciary and about a dozen years of intimate involvement in continuing education
programs for state and federal appellate judges.

My experience prevents me from looking upon state and federal courts as
inanimate institutions, or state and federal judges as faceless dancers in a blood-
less ballet. I came to know most of the federal appellate judges through the
Federal Judicial Center educational programs, which I chaired from 1974 to 1979.
Moreover, about half of the present judges of the highest courts of the states
and the Canadian provinces, a number of United States circuit judges and one
Supreme Court Justice have been my students at the Senior Appellate Judges
Seminar sponsored by the Institute of Judicial Administration at New York
University School of Law. I have heard the discussions of these state and federal judges around the seminar table, and I have read their opinions in the law
reports. More importantly, I have learned to know them as men and women
who are more than cardboard figures in black robes, and more than statistics
on a chart. My perspective, then, on the judges of the state and federal courts
probably differs both from that of the authors whose papers are my topic and
from most of my audience.

In this response to the papers, I will focus on what I consider to be a dis-
turbing bias toward litigating federal issues in federal court instead of state
court. In my view, the preeminence of this preference in academia, in Congress,
and among some judges and members of the bar has extracted from our society a heavy toll. Several aspects of that price deserve critical attention. First,
the assumptions of those who prefer federal courts have caused a completely
unwarranted perception that state courts lack competence to deal with federal
issues. There simply is no evidence that the state courts today are incapable of
dealing with most of these disputes; to the contrary, there is considerable reason to believe that the state judiciary is as qualified as the federal courts. A second item of that price is the serious dilution of federal appellate court resources
caused by Congress' indiscriminate dumping of relatively trivial matters on
the courts of appeals' dockets. The deluge of petitions seeking judicial review
of routine administrative action is but a single example of how our attention
has been drained from the truly significant cases. Federal appellate courts have
been inundated with litigation redundant to full and fair state court proceedings, a practice contrary to accepted principles of the finality of judgments.
Yet another cost of excessive federal court litigation is the very real and immediate financial burden of the litigation itself, brought about chiefly by the

liberal, perhaps better described as indulgent, policy of notice pleading. Notice pleading, when combined with abuse of discovery, has become a new weapon of economic coercion to force the surrender of those with truly meritorious claims or defenses.[1] These comments, therefore, are chiefly a response to the papers in particular and to a certain "party line" in general.

My first observation is that if one views judges, in Professor Cover's formulation, as primarily enforcers of and apologists for a social order, then the social order is in good hands whether one looks to the state or federal courts. My own evaluation of both state supreme court and federal circuit judges is that most meet Professor Bator's test of "[c]onscientiousness, dedication, idealism, openness, enthusiasm, [and] willingness to listen and to learn—all the mysterious components of the subtle art of judging well."

I am not blind to the differences between United States circuit judges and state supreme court justices. Perhaps some of the former are more eloquent stylists in speech and print, with credentials from more prestigious law schools, and with more combined experience in what I call ABA-type law firms. I am not yet convinced, however, that the Ivy League-Chicago-Stanford axis has a monopoly on acceptable jurisprudential temperament.

Nor do I believe that political experience, perhaps collectively greater among state judges, handicaps judging even federal constitutional issues. Indeed, when a judge is confronted with complex constitutional disputes about what, where and by whom a societal decision should be made, questions that underlie a host of fourteenth Amendment suits brought under 42 U.S.C. § 1983, a firsthand knowledge of the intimacies, superstitions and realities of political life may stand the judge in better stead than exclusive reliance on scholarly, but often naïve, treatises.

Professor Neuborne and I agree that if most plaintiff's lawyers, especially civil rights advocates, had their "druthers," the needle in the forum compass con-

---

1. It is with much pleasure that I note the Supreme Court has now discovered the error of the ways of pure notice pleadings. After shouting for years my disenchantment with the inefficacy of notice pleading, in 2007 I was delighted with the Supreme Court's first steps to require pleading a modicum of facts in *Bell Atlantic Corp. v. Twombly*, 550 U.S. 544 (2007), and later *Ashcroft v. Iqbal*, 129 S. Ct. 1937 (2009). The Court now holds that the requirement that pleadings contain a short and plain statement of the claim showing that the pleader is entitled to relief demands more than an unadorned "the defendant harmed me" accusation. The Court does not require detailed factual allegations (which I prefer), but the complaint must contain sufficient factual matter, accepted as true, to state a claim to relief that is plausible on its face; a claim has "facial plausibility" when the plaintiff pleads factual content that allows the court to draw a reasonable inference that the defendant is liable for the misconduct alleged.

stantly would be "jammed in the 'federal' position." Professor Bator has assigned the general reasons for this phenomenon:

> The federal courts are to be preferred because ... federal judges are more competent and expert in adjudicating issues of federal law; are more independent in resisting popular and political pressure; and are likely, through institutional perspective, to be more sensitive to claims of federal right and more zealous and even conscientious in upholding them against assertions of state power, than are state judges.

Professor Bator then summarizes the bases of these assumptions, such as how better pay, higher prestige and the security of life tenure attract better lawyers to the federal bench. The federal courts' insulation from majoritarian pressures and their distance from the "grind of legal administration," as compared to the position of the state courts, are of especial importance to his thesis. Without necessarily endorsing the concept, he notes the assumption that federal judges have a built-in institutional bias in favor of federal rights while state judges are more likely to be grudging in their protection of federal claims when those claims conflict with local authority. Those embracing this view believe that federal courts have more experience and, therefore, are more skilled in deciding federal questions. Professor Bator emphasizes that these contentions are intuitive, "rest[ing] on human insight rather than on expressed evidence or scientific measurement."

My own intuition, seasoned by first-hand experience, suggests that federal judges should be more competent, but they are not necessarily so; they should have more experience and expertise in federal constitutional questions than their state court counterparts, but they do not always; they should have institutional preferences, but these are not apparent.

Turning first to experience in federal constitutional issues, the favorite apologia for committing section 1983 cases, including state prisoner actions, to the federal courts, I defend the thesis that when it comes to the high profile issues of due process and equal protection, the state courts' experience outstrips that of the federal courts by a wide, wide margin. Virtually every criminal case today implicates fourth, fifth, or sixth amendment claims applied to the states through the fourteenth amendment, or the fourteenth amendment itself: *Miranda* warnings, search and seizure, speedy trial, severance, competency of counsel and due process, to name only a few recurring issues. Consider, for example, the number of cases raising constitutional issues articulated by the Supreme Court in recent years that are processed each day in the criminal courts of any large city. Consider also the direct and collateral appeals on these same issues before the state appellate courts. In 1980, Pennsylvania judges alone processed 61,681 indictable offenses, while the entire federal judiciary processed only 27,968. By sheer number of criminal cases, the state trial and appellate judges have experience that greatly overwhelms that of the federal judiciary.

In addition to volume of cases, general state court jurisdiction, as compared to limited federal jurisdiction, gives state judges the opportunity to pass on federal constitutional claims in traditional state court litigation that rarely occur in proceedings initiated in federal court: municipal zoning, family law and child custody suits, pendent constitutional issues accompanying substantive appeals in civil service disputes, workmen's and unemployment compensation proceedings and tax assessment matters. In addition, a growing number of civil rights cases are being brought initially in state courts under section 1983.

Aside from racial discrimination, school prayer and a very few other cases, most law suits implicating "unpopular constitutionals principles" originate and remain in the state courts. Obscenity and defamation cases come immediately to mind. Such locally unpopular causes arise, for instance, when local police attempt to close a pornography shop, when a state tort defamation complaint implicates a first amendment issue, or when a state judge clears a courtroom because the testimony is not for tender ears. Because the federal issues arise as defenses to an ongoing proceeding and not as elements of the claim, state courts are virtually always the only available forum.

Next, I turn to the familiar buzz-word "expertise," and for a moment limit consideration to federal non-constitutional issues. The familiar line goes like this: let FJ stand for federal judge, FI stand for federal statutory issue, and E for expertise. $FJ + FI$ always result in E. I agree completely, but that is as far as the formula goes. The professional literature is sterile when it comes to evaluating the E in this formula. A brief review of the Third Circuit's caseload, which I take to be reasonably typical of the other U.S. Courts of Appeals, will assist in understanding my perspective. The Third Circuit, like the other U.S. Courts of Appeals, is required to consider all appeals from final judgments of district courts, final decisions of the Tax Court and final orders of administrative agencies. In addition, the U.S. Courts of Appeals are the enforcement courts for orders of the National Labor Relations Board and a number of other agencies.

This jurisprudential menu reminds me of Army Tropical Ration B, which the U.S. Marine Corps forced on us in the Pacific Islands during World War II. The menu ran for ten days and then repeated itself, and of the thirty meals, the main ingredient in twenty of them was Spam. We had it fried for breakfast, baked at noon and served cold in the evening. We had it boiled, broiled and breaded. We had it with canned pineapple, and sometimes with raisins (when my men were not fermenting the raisins for Dugan's Dew, a kind of Central Pacific Jack Daniels), but there it was, the same old Spam. We island hoppers became experts on it. We United States circuit judges are also experts on the jurisprudential Spam of federal non-constitutional issues force-fed our way.

Seven or eight of the thirty cases a panel must decide each sitting turn solely on whether there is substantial evidence in the record as a whole or an abuse of discretion by an agency charged with administering the Social Security Act, the Occupational Safety and Health Act, the Immigration and Naturalization Act, the Longshoremen and Harbor Workers' Compensation Act, or the National Labor Relations Act. The cases certainly give the federal appellate court experience, and federal judges, before long, develop expertise in deciding them. The difference between the expertise required for judicial proceedings under the federal Administrative Procedure Act and that required of our state court brothers and sisters in the twenty-eight states using the Model State Administrative Procedure Act, however, is almost imperceptible: the reviewing court should hold unlawful and set aside agency actions, findings and conclusions found to be "arbitrary, capricious, an abuse of discretion, or otherwise not in accordance with law" or "unsupported by substantial evidence."

Another four or five cases in our regular allotment are criminal cases from the limited spectrum of federal prosecutions: narcotics, bank robberies, white collar crime (RICO) and state official corruption. The mine-run of these cases presents a familiar list of contentions: insufficiency of evidence, failure to sever counts, improper admission of evidence and the improper application of the coconspirator exception to the hearsay rule. Again, one hardly can argue that these cases lend themselves to development of unique federal court expertise.

Then come the Title VII employment discrimination cases. Almost without exception, each sitting's list now has at least one appeal by someone who has lost before the EEOC, lost in a district court, and now has conjured up myriad notions of why he or she was fired or not promoted. Additionally, there are two or three pro se civil appeals by litigants who either could not get even a community services lawyer to handle their frivolous complaints in the district court, or having lost with a lawyer want to try again on their own. Finally, the list will include four or five miscellaneous appeals in which, as Cardozo would say, "The law and its application alike are plain."

The regular panel allotment leaves about nine or ten cases that present issues belonging in the United States courts of appeals: cases in which the rule of law is certain, and the application alone doubtful, or cases in which the rule itself is uncertain—that much-welcomed case where, in Cardozo's words, "a decision one way or the other, will count for the future, will advance or retard, sometimes much, sometimes little, the development of the law." It is out of these rare cases, then, that federal courts must judges the credentials to justify the arguments in favor of federal court expertise on federal issues.

Although not all federal circuit judges share my views, I suggest that most will agree with my characterization of the dreariness presented by the courts of appeals' docket. Some federal judges are leaving their posts because of disenchantment with salaries, but my good friend Griffin Bell, one of the truly great judges and lawyers of our time, left the Court of Appeals for the Fifth Circuit because he simply became fed up with the mundane quality of most of the matters presented to United States circuit judges. The idiom "make a federal case of it" is now passé because it no longer can be said that "a federal case" describes litigation involving substantial sums or complicated legal issues. In my view the federal court has become a "nickel and dime" court. The average civil case that I processed as a judge on the Allegheny County Court of Common Pleas from 1961 to 1968, a court of general jurisdiction, involved more money than the median of civil money damage cases I have reviewed during my thirteen years as a United States circuit judge.

Even though the judges on our court must now decide cases at a rate of more than one per day, most of us are able to contend with this onslaught because the number presenting genuinely arguable issues has not increased in proportion to the total number of filings. A veteran circuit judge can quickly analyze the issues in most briefs and come to a decision. Nevertheless, if the federal courts are to live up to their reputation as "the elite," someone must soon devise a garbage-detector to filter the mess that is now descending upon us.

Meanwhile, the state supreme courts, our much maligned partners in the federal-state judicial fraternity, are getting the truly significant cases—both in the common law tradition and in the context of federal and state constitutional law. As certiorari courts, they can pick and choose the arguable, vital issues largely ignored by law reviews. They can allow new approaches to problems to germinate and develop in the lower courts without being forced to pronounce their judgments on them prematurely. They are feasting on *gnocchi al pesto* and *abbacchio al forno*, while we U.S. circuit judges stick to our Spam, now and then a Big Mac, and occasionally a rare delicacy. It is that rare delicacy, in the final analysis, that makes the job worthwhile.

I am presenting a dark picture to make a deliberate point: whatever has been the theoretical basis for federal court jurisdiction, Congress has now dumped a heap of offal on those courts that increasingly drains their attention. Federal circuit court jurisdiction now includes too many cases that do not belong in the same tribunal charged with adding an important gloss to the greatest legal document in the history of the world, the U.S. Constitution, and also charged with adjudicating and defining critical rights and liberties of our people. The same judges who have the responsibility for defining the true public policy of the Civil Rights Act of 1964, our antitrust policy under the Sherman and Clayton Acts, our national labor policy under section 301 of Taft-Hartley, and the critical financial consequences of the federal securities acts, should not be troubled over a suit under the Civil Rights acts for six packs of cigarettes, or the sale of a used car brought under the Odometer Tinkering Act or the small claims brought under the Truth in Lending Act. Federal judges, again speaking theoretically, should be the experts manning the big guns in the litigation battlefield. Instead, we are wasting, if not exhausting, our energies, running around with cans of insect repellent. The reality is that United States circuit judges have become experts, but they are experts who stand alongside a conveyor belt that moves every day of the year and who examine everything that passes by, spending much valuable time deciding what conveyed material should be rejected outright without argument or opinion, what requires a moderate amount of concentrated attention, and what demands close inspection, much care and bright polish. The time is long overdue for those who sincerely believe that federal judges are in fact the elite, experts in a rare craft—and now I speak especially to the law professoriat, the ACLU, the corporations, the institutional litigants, and others who really care about such things—to do something about taking us off the assembly line and putting us back into the craftsman's shop.

Chapter Eight

Life in the Raw in Appellate Courts

Author's Note: *It is welcome news that the University of Mississippi School of Law and other institutions are now sponsoring Criminal Appeals Clinics. The program is welcomed because we face a serious problem of adequate representation of defendants in criminal appeals. The author volunteered to assist in the program. The following is a revised excerpt of the Foreword in the special edition of* 75 Miss. L.J. 645 (2006).

When I was researching for the first edition of my book, *Winning on Appeal: Better Briefs and Oral Argument* in 1991, I received views of chief justices of over 30 states and chief judges from United States courts of appeals. Coalescing with my own experience of having been a federal appellate judge since 1968, our views on the general quality of briefs were summarized:

- Too long. Too long. Too long.
- Too many issues or points.
- Rudderless; no central theme(s).
- Failure to disclose the equitable heart of the appeal and the legal problem involved.
- Lack of focus.
- Absence of organization.

Writing a convincing brief does not get you "brownie points" or a star on the forehead. The prize is that you win the case. Writing a bad brief will not send you to sit in the corner of the school room. Instead, you lose the case. It is that simple.

Eleven years later, as I prepared the second edition of *Winning on Appeal*, I solicited comments from 19 state chief justices, 9 United States circuit chief judges and more than a score of other state and federal appellate judges. They made the same dreary complaints that their predecessors expressed more than a decade before. My experience also was unchanged, notwithstanding sitting regularly with the Courts of Appeals for the Fifth, Seventh, Ninth and Tenth Circuits, in addition to sitting with my own court, the Mighty Third.

I chalk this up to one phenomenon: too many trial lawyers appear before appellate courts without recognizing that the environment on appeal is a galaxy away from that of the trial courtroom. On the trial level, the main purpose is to persuade the fact-finder to translate a congeries of testimony and exhibits into rock-bound facts. In these surroundings, the lawyers control the time. Trials are measured in days, weeks and months.

Not so in an appeal. Your principal briefs are limited to about thirty pages or 14,000 words, and ordinarily you only get fifteen minutes to argue your case. Too many lawyers do not realize that on appeal more is *not* better.

Much is written about the burdens of proof in the trial court, while little is written about the burdens on appeal. A presumption exists on the appellate level that the trial court committed no reversible error. We see this in those cases where, because of recusals, an appellate court is evenly divided. When this occurs, the judgment of the trial court or the lower appellate court is affirmed.

Using statistics of the United States Courts of Appeals that generally track any intermediate state appellate court, your chances of getting a reversal are mighty slim.

United States Courts of Appeals Percent Reversed

Percentage of Cases Reversed on Appeal (All Regional Circuits)

Nature of Proceeding	1998	2000	2002	2004	2006	2008	2010
All Appeals	10.4	9.5	9.6	8.4	8.7	9.3	8.4
Criminal	6.5	6.3	5.4	6.0	6.2	6.6	5.6
U.S. Prisoner Petitions	10.3	11.1	8.9	8.4	7.5	9.7	10.2
Other U.S. Civil	11.0	11.8	10.7	11.8	11.7	11.8	13.0
Private Prisoner Petitions	7.5	9.1	9.8	8.8	9.6	9.7	8.5
Other Private Civil	15.2	11.8	13.4	12.0	12.9	13.6	12.1
Bankruptcy	14.4	14.7	12.1	15.9	13.3	15.5	16.0
Administrative Appeals	6.6	7.0	13.1	5.4	7.9	7.6	7.1

Percentage of Cases Reversed in the Court of Appeals for the Third Circuit

Nature of Proceeding	1998	2000	2002	2004	2006	2008	2010
All Appeals	9.7	11.4	11.6	12.2	13.3	10.3	8.4
Criminal	7.8	7.2	6.8	8.3	14.6	7.8	5.3
U.S. Prisoner Petitions	11.9	15.8	9.4	7.7	5.1	11.3	3.8
Other U.S. Civil	6.9	12.6	11.4	12.3	12.6	9.9	7.3
Private Prisoner Petitions	8.0	8.7	14.6	13.5	14.1	11.2	14.2
Other Private Civil	11.3	12.1	13.8	16.1	15.5	15.5	11.9

Bankruptcy	6.7	23.1	21.2	36.7	12.7	14.6	14.3
Administrative Appeals	13.8	19.6	16.9	7.5	12.6	6.9	7.4

The appellant today fights to succeed amid a crushing caseload where nationally about 9 out of 10 cases are affirmed. And in direct criminal appeals, only about 1 case in 20 is reversed. That is the true reality show that the lay public and trial lawyers do not see.

My experience in riding the circuits has taught me that if an appeal presents an issue of institutional or precedential significance, oral argument will be granted by the court. Various courts have different procedures through which this decision is reached, but judges seem to err on the side of granting oral argument in unworthy cases, rather than denying the opportunity in deserving cases.

They did not teach you in law school or at the fancy CLE seminar that when you are writing a brief you have an extremely important hurdle to mount if your client is going to get a real bang for his buck: you must convince the court to grant you oral argument. And this no small challenge. There is a handicap sheet out there that gives the odds that the judges will grant oral argument in your case. The statistics are in full blossom for you to digest. Records of the U.S. Courts of Appeals for the last 20 years show the trend and the history of the various circuits:

Circuit	Percentage Argued in 1990	Percentage Argued in 2010
ALL CIRCUITS	44.9%	26.7%
D. C. Circuit	57.3%	48.8%
First Circuit	67.5%	28.8%
Second Circuit	75.8%	38.6%
Third Circuit	27.3%	14.7%
Fourth Circuit	37.3%	12.9%
Fifth Circuit	30.1%	24.6%
Sixth Circuit	49.7%	31.2%
Seventh Circuit	56.8%	48.7%
Eighth Circuit	42.4%	23.0%
Ninth Circuit	49.5%	30.0%
Tenth Circuit	36.9%	31.3%
Eleventh Circuit	45.0%	14.4%

The comparison of these years illustrates that in the United States courts of appeals a significant development in the judicial process has taken place during the span of about two decades. It is a nationwide decline of 18.2% of cases being argued. The decline has been across the board in every Circuit, with the

Fifth Circuit holding firm at limiting argument to about one in four. On average less than three cases out of ten are now calendared for oral argument. I am informed also by my own experience: judges will no longer vote for oral argument where the law is clear and the application of facts to the law equally plain.

This should be a signal to lawyers that today, more than ever, the appellant's brief takes on a vital and decisive role. You must not only write to persuade the court to reverse the judgment of the district court, but you must meet a threshold burden of demonstrating in your brief that, on the basis of the proper standard of review, a serious reversible error was committed in the trial court to deserve oral argument. An arguable question of law has to be presented.

Because these pages represent a perspective from the bench, I pause to reflect on the caseload for each active judge on the United States Courts of Appeals. I will speak of "then" and "now." In 1969, my first full year as a United States circuit judge, each active judge on my court was responsible for deciding 90 appeals a year. I went to Philadelphia six times a year from my home in Pittsburgh to hear oral arguments, and in each sitting we had to decide fifteen appeals during argument week. The national average was 93 appeals per judge per year. That is the "then" part. I turn to the present "now" situation: how many cases must each active U.S. Circuit judge decide each year?

Cases per Active Judge

	1992	1998	2004	2010
All Circuits	399	410	432	459
D. C. Circuit	195	173	156	173
First Circuit	323	303	262	415
Second Circuit	287	296	260	535
Third Circuit	345	337	379	428
Fourth Circuit	425	550	522	644
Fifth Circuit	643	581	727	632
Sixth Circuit	338	306	348	293
Seventh Circuit	390	312	349	319
Eighth Circuit	471	457	399	502
Ninth Circuit	381	505	490	516
Tenth Circuit	396	318	254	242
Eleventh Circuit	605	613	711	664

The national average means that each active United States circuit judge must decide 459 appeals each year. After deducting Saturdays and Sundays, each judge must decide more than one case each day. The One-a-Day brand was a great name for vitamins, but I doubt that it is equally great in describing the caseload for United States circuit judges. Whether presenting or defending an appeal, your case moves along an assembly line. Think about it. Statistically speaking, judges have less than one day to give the case full treatment: studying briefs; researching the law; perhaps hearing argument; conferencing with colleagues; making the decision; writing a precedential or not-precedential opinion; studying other writers' opinions; and deciding motions and petitions for rehearing. This does not include attending to correspondence and the telephone. That is over one case a day in the highest federal court to which a litigant has a right to take an appeal.

Thus, your appeal faces extreme competition with other appeals in the assembly line. That is "now," the modern day appellate court.

I believe that the statistics I have set forth above paint a true picture of today's environment in appellate advocacy. No advocacy program will be complete without a recognition of these stark facts of life in our appellate courts.

CHAPTER NINE

"The Seniors" Suggest
a Solution

Author's Note: *The following is an unpublished article prepared by me for my colleagues as a private memorandum of the work by "The Seniors," a group of senior U.S. Circuit Judges including five former chief judges in the mid-Nineties. I resisted several suggestions that it be published because as an unadulterated optimist, I still hoped that somehow our project could find a sponsor so that we could finish our task. But a decade and a half has now passed, and the time has come to publish the foregoing, as a tentative solution offered up by "The Seniors" those many years ago.*

In 1994 a group of seven senior circuit judges—five of us being former chief judges of judicial circuits—formed an informal think tank, calling ourselves "The Seniors." The "old" chiefs included former chief judges William J. Bauer, Seventh Circuit; John C. Godbold of both the Fifth and Eleventh Circuits; Pierce Lively, Sixth Circuit; Paul H. Roney, Eleventh Circuit; and myself, Third Circuit. Our other two members were Joseph F. Weis, Jr., Third Circuit, former chairman of the prestigious Federal Courts Study Committee, and Thomas M. Reavley, Fifth Circuit, a judicial philosopher who believes that "some fundamental adjustments in thinking are needed" in the U.S. Courts of Appeals.

We preferred not to be a committee of a formal structure like the Judicial Conference of the United States because we felt that our ideas were too revolutionary to be accepted by a body whose committees always kept an eye focused on the Congress or judicial traditionalists.

In a September 6, 1994, Overview we stated the purpose of our study:

The Seniors seek a solution to the astronomical caseload now plaguing the U.S. Courts of Appeals. We have seen the case load per active judge increase from 93 fully briefed appeals per judge in 1969 to an average of 428 in 1993, as Judge Aldisert indicated in his detailed report, circuit by circuit, to the American Law Institute in 1994. This means that every federal appeal moves along an assembly line of one case every 4.9 hours per active judge. For a first hand discussion of the crushing case load in the Fifth Circuit, see Judge Reavley's insightful review in the *Texas Tech Law Review*.

The various courts of appeals have designed various procedural mechanisms to handle the onslaught, but we have decided to go further. Much further.

It becomes necessary to make reference to Judge Reavley's review in the *Texas Tech Law Review* of Professor Thomas E. Baker's insightful book, *The Problems of the U.S. Courts of Appeal*. Judge Reavley made some startling observations of the crushing case load in his own Court of Appeals for the Fifth Circuit. He began by noting that in 1993, new appeals in his court numbered 6,695, and then observed:

> [In 1994], one judge on our court wrote 248 opinions (including the one-liners) and the average number of opinions was 216 (average termination was 698) for each active judge. Each active judge is required to produce an opinion almost every working day. In addition, he must review two other opinions of panel colleagues and deal with motions and petitions for rehearing, judicial matters that exceed 1,000 in number over the year. I understand how some of our judges despair at having become little more than case processors and editors of their clerks' opinions. Many judges join Professor Baker in lamenting the loss of appellate ideals and traditions.
>
> While I do not rule out the need for the structural reforms discussed in this book, I would offer priorities for Congress and for circuit judges.
>
> If we will only look at the dockets of these courts, we will see that most of these appeals should have never been in federal court to begin with, and, once there, they should be given no more than summary processing.

With Judge Aldisert's presentation before the ALI discussing caseloads of active judges in all circuits and Judge Reavley's discussion of the Fifth Circuit case load in his law review article, it is clear that we have our work cut out for us.

We conclude that we seek the answer to two questions:

- Does each recipient of a district court judgment have an absolute right of appeal?

· If the answer is yes, what kind of appeal?

We offer a suggestion, introduced by the following:

> This is heady stuff. We have agreed to work together and re-invent the wheel. To commence a study that will begin where the common law left off. This, to begin before any statute gave English, and then American, litigants a right to appeal from a trial court. SENIORS COMMITTEE, WORKING PAPER NO. 1 (on file with author).

Emphasizing that "[o]ur primary function is to brainstorm and formulate solutions; our secondary function is to decide to whom we make these recommendations," we announced:

> Our recommendations must be the best solution possible—academically or theoretically speaking—within the framework of the Constitution. We will not proceed on the basis of what the Judicial Conference of the United States or Congress would accept. We are a think tank, not a legislative committee. We will address the problem from the standpoint of our long experience as federal appellate judges.
>
> We understand the realities of the appellate process: error correcting and law making. We should think about what percentage of cases are error correcting only. Aldisert made an educated guess in his ALI presentation, making reference to Cardozo's stated experience in the New York Court of Appeals:
>
> What also makes the [crushing case loads in the U.S. Courts of Appeals] at least marginally functional, is that most federal appeals each year come within the two categories suggested by Cardozo, more than 70 years ago: those in which "[t]he law and its application alike are plain and those in which the rule of law is certain, and the application alone doubtful."
>
> In his GROWTH OF THE LAW 60, 164 (1924) Cardozo said that at least nine tenths of the cases coming to the New York Court of Appeals, "could not, without semblance of reason, be decided in any way but one. The law and its application alike are plain. Such cases are predestined, so to speak, to affirmance without opinion." These are the cases that form the jurisprudential cholesterol clogging the arteries at the heart of the appellate process.
>
> In 1986 Aldisert suggested that 90% of the cases coming to his court came within Cardozo's first two categories. Here he was in agreement with Henry Friendly and Professor Harry Jones. Ruggero J. Aldisert, *The House of the Law*, 19 Loy. L.A. L. Rev. 755, 763 n.28 (1986).

Background

The Seniors devoted eight months to correspondence and telephone calls as we exchanged ideas and working papers. At our own expense, we held a day-long meeting at the United States Court of Appeals for the Seventh Circuit in Chicago, with Chief Judge Bauer hosting. At that time we did not have the advantage of the Supreme Court's unanimous re-affirmances in 2000 that there is not a constitutional right to an appeal. Previously we had the teachings of *McKane v. Durston*, 153 U.S. 684, 686 (1894) ("An appeal from a judgment of conviction is not a matter of absolute right, independently of constitutional or statutory provisions allowing such appeal. A review by an appellate court of the final judgment in a criminal case, however grave the offense of which the accused is convicted, was not at common law, and is not now, a necessary element of due process of law."). We also had the teachings of *Ross v. Moffitt*, 417 U.S. 600 (1974), but we were uncertain whether modern concepts had expanded the reach of Due Process. But in *Martinez v. Court of Appeal of California*, 528 U.S. 152 (2000), speaking through Justice Stevens, the Court emphasized that

> [a]ppeals as of right in federal courts were nonexistent for the first century of our Nation, and appellate review of any sort was "rarely allowed." The States, also, did not generally recognize an appeal as of right until Washington became the first to constitutionalize the right explicitly in 1889. There was similarly no right to appeal in criminal cases at common law, and appellate review of any sort was "limited" and "rarely used."

In *Smith v. Robbins*, 528 U.S. 259, 270 n.5 (2000), speaking through Justice Thomas and citing *Ross v. Moffitt* and *McKane v. Durston*, the Court reiterated, "The Constitution does not, however, require States to create appellate review in the first place."

We examined summary calendar procedures in New Mexico in which the courts decide two-thirds of their appeals in less than 100 days by doing away with transcripts, briefs and oral arguments in favor of a summary calendar in which an appellant must file a detailed docketing statement:

> The docketing statement contains (1) a statement of the nature of the proceedings; (2) the date of the judgment or order sought to be reviewed and a statement that the appeal was timely filed; (3) a concise, accurate statement of the case summarizing all facts material to a consideration of the issues presented; (4) a statement of the issues on appeal,

including how they arose and how they were preserved in the trial court, but without unnecessary detail. The statement of issues should be short and concise and should not be repetitious. General conclusory statements such as "the judgment of the trial court is not supported by the law and the facts" will not be accepted; (5) a list of authorities believed to support the contentions of the appellant. Argument on the law shall not be included, but a short, simple statement of the proposition in which the case or text is cited shall accompany the citation.

For a complete discussion of the procedure, see Thomas A. Marvel, *Abbreviated Appellate Procedure: An Evaluation of the New Mexico Summary Calendar*, 75 Judicature 86 (1991).

We looked at jurisdictions having no absolute right to appeal, but certiorari procedures. The Virginia practice provides for only three types of appeals to the Court of Appeals, all others by discretionary appeal to the Supreme Court. New Hampshire's practice provides that "[t]he right to appeal in New Hampshire is limited to the right to obtain a discretionary determination by this court as to whether it will accept the appeal." *State v. Cooper*, 498 A.2d 1209 (N.H. 1985).

Although as judges we had no power to tramp on the toes of Congress and institute a system of discretionary review in the Courts of Appeals, we did have an obligation to recommend procedures that would meet the realities of the modern era and settled on what we called a gate-keeping mechanism for all appeals.

Briefs: Are They Necessary in Every Case?

We first attacked the notion of commencing an appeal with adversary briefs. We decided that just because courts had been doing things this way for several hundred years, it did not necessarily make it the best way to process appeals today. In the spirit that it's time to wake up and smell the roses, we decided to devise a system to obtain information that judicial decision-makers wanted to hear from the lawyers in the first go-around. We no longer wanted a procedure where the first crack out of the box was for judges to read an appellant's brief, with all its one-sided verbose accoutrements.

We started with the concept that a brief is what lawyers want judges to read. That's putting the cart before the horse, we thought. In an environment where each active U.S. circuit judge is required to decide 443 cases a year, we decided that the first offering in the appeal had to be something the *judges want to hear, not what lawyers want to say.* Our solution was to replace the appellant's brief with a "Jurisdiction and Merits Statement," which would be an electronic form. This would be a gate-keeping mechanism for all appeals, a system to provide the court with the opportunity to move cases to an "Expedited Procedure Appeal" for consideration, in the first instance, by one judge we described as the Principal Judge, who would be teamed with a secondary judge, described as the Review Judge. These gate keepers would permit the Court to decide whether the appeal merits a full briefing schedule and oral argument and consideration by *three* Article III judges.

To be sure, if the appeal involves a case where "the law is not clear," the Principal Judge will no doubt certify it for formal briefing. If the case comes within the first category suggested by Cardozo, almost a century ago, it "could not, without semblance of reason, be decided in any way but one. The law and its application alike are plain. Such cases are predestined, so to speak, to affirmance without opinion." Cardozo's second category is where "[t]he law and its application alike are plain" and those in which "the rule of law is certain, and the application alone doubtful." These two categories make up about 90 percent of the U.S. Court of Appeals caseload. Certainly, where the law and its application alike are plain, it is doubtful that the gate-keeping procedure would permit these cases to proceed to full briefing and consideration by a traditional merits panel of three judges. My educated guess is that about one half of the second category in which the rule of law is certain, and the application alone doubtful would proceed beyond the Principal and Review Judges.

On the basis of our present caseloads, therefore, a large proportion of cases would be terminated by the "Expedited Procedure Appeal," thus affording much more time to concentrate on cases described by Cardozo as "where the courts work for the future" because the law is not clear.

On the basis of the contents set forth in the suggested form, the Principal Judge would either (a) summarily affirm or dismiss, or (b) order full briefing. The appellant would have the right to file exceptions to any order of affirmance and dismissal. The exceptions would be heard by the Review Judge. If the Review Judge agreed with the Principal, a final order of affirmance or dismissal would be entered; if the Review Judge disagreed, he or she would order full briefing.

On to the details. The Jurisdiction and Merits Statement would not be a Reader's Digest version of a traditional appellant's brief. The major difference is that the form would include (a) a copy of the district court's opinion, (b) a list of authorities supporting the appellant's contentions, and (c) contrary authorities relied upon by the district court or by the appellee in the trial court. No argument would be permitted on the form, but excerpts of District Court briefs filed by the appellant and appellee addressing the issues on appeal would be attached to the form.

We did not perceive the Jurisdiction and Merits Statement as an ex parte adversarial brief, but a concise summary of the issues presented together with any supporting and contrary authority. It would not be a narrative, but a carefully drafted form in which an appellant would check boxes and tersely summarize authorities set forth to support contentions. The form follows the lead of computer drop down menus. Its purpose is to implement Ernest Hemingway's exhortation: "What this country needs is a good crap detector!"

"Jurisdiction and Merits Statement" Form

We suggested the following form, titled as the "Jurisdiction and Merits Statement."

APPELLANT'S JURISDICTION AND MERITS STATEMENT

1. Within 20 (or 30) days from the time the notice of appeal is filed, appellant shall file with the Clerk four copies of the Jurisdiction and Merits Statement, (hereinafter "Statement") with proof of service of one copy on the opposing party or parties, which shall recite:

    A. The caption with the parties' names and case number assigned by the Clerk.
    B. The court or agency from which the appeal is taken, and the name of the judge.
    C. The date of filing of the notice of appeal or the date of entry of order granting leave to appeal; and
    D. The name and address of the attorney for appellee, if known.

2. Filed with the Statement will be a legible copy of:

    A. The dated notice of appeal;
    B. The order, judgment or determination appealed from;
    C. The opinion or memorandum of the District Court, or a statement of no opinion;
    D. If there was no opinion, excerpts of the record indicating the reasons, if any, articulated by the District Court for entering the judgment; and
    E. Portions of the District Court briefs of all parties addressing the points raised on appeal, and if necessary, as augmented by subsequent authorities.

3. The Statement must give the statute or case(s) supporting the assertion that the Court has jurisdiction to entertain the appeal and to review the questions raised.
4. The merits statement must include:

    A. A point-heading identification of all issues raised and where the issue was presented in the District Court; and

B. A list of authorities, with pinpoint citations, believed to support the contentions of appellant and contrary authorities known to appellant, especially those on which the District Court relied. Argument on the law shall not be included, but a short, simple statement declaring the proposition for which the case or text is cited shall accompany the citation. Use of a parenthetical sentence for each citation is recommended.

5. The Court would determine, *sua sponte*, whether it had subject matter jurisdiction and authority to review, based on the papers submitted or such other necessary written submissions.

6. The Jurisdiction and Merits Statement must follow the precise official form of the Court. Failure to file the Statement within the time provided by the rule or to utilize the precise form described in this subparagraph will be sufficient grounds for dismissing the appeal by the Court without notice.

APPELLEE'S JURISDICTION AND MERITS STATEMENT

1. Within 20 days of service of appellant's Jurisdiction and Merits Statement, the appellee (1) shall file or cause to be filed with the Clerk an appearance of counsel and (2) within the same time frame, an original and three copies of the appellee's Jurisdiction and Merits Statement on the proper form, with proof of service on each other party, which shall recite:

A. A jurisdictional statement agreeing with or contradicting that of the appellant; and
B. A point heading response to each argument in the precise order raised by appellant. The response shall include:
   (1). A list of authorities, with pinpoint citations, believed to support the judgment of the District Court or final order of the administrative agency, and any contrary authorities not included in the appellant's statement.
   (2). Argument on the law shall not be included, but a short, simple statement declaring the proposition for which the case or text is cited shall accompany the citation. Use of a parenthetical sentence for each citation is recommended.
   (3). Any relevant excerpts of the record, or briefs filed in the District Court not included in the appellant's statement.

TWO-JUDGE EXPEDITED APPEALS DISPOSITION PANEL

Single Judge Consideration and Review

1. A two-judge Jurisdiction and Merits Statement Panel or Panels shall be rotated among the active and senior judges on the Court.

2. One judge, to be known as the Principal Judge, shall have the original responsibility for each case represented by the Jurisdiction and Merits Statement. The statements will be distributed at random to each member of the panel.

   A. If the Principal Judge decides that the case is not proper for expedited disposition, it will be returned to the Clerk for full briefing. There will be no appeal from this decision.
   B. If the Principal Judge decides the case as an affirmance or dismissal, a proposed order will be transmitted by the parties by the Clerk. The appellant will be given 10 days to file exceptions to the proposed order. If no exceptions are filed, the proposed order shall be deemed a final order and judgment and so entered.
   C. If exceptions are filed, the Clerk will transmit the exceptions to the Principal Judge. The Clerk shall also transmit them to a second member of the panel, known as the Review Judge, together with a copy of the Jurisdiction and Merits Statements of appellant and appellee.
   D. If the Review Judge agrees with the original disposition, a final order and judgment will be entered for the Court.
   E. If the Review Judge does not agree with the original disposition, the case will be returned to the Clerk for full briefing.

Review of Administrative Agency Orders

The Seniors were greatly concerned about the appeal-after-appeal procedures in many administrative agencies. Take, for example, the Social Security Administration. In this agency, a claimant for disability has the opportunity to climb six rungs in an appellate ladder, administratively and judicially. Following initial rejection of claim, the claimant has the potential to receive the following review:

1. By a supervisor
2. Hearing before an administrative law judge and decision
3. SSA Board of Review
4. U.S. District Court
5. U.S. Court of Appeals
6. U.S. Supreme Court

Our collective experience indicates that the principal, if not universal, question in judicial review of administrative agencies is whether the agency determination is supported by substantial evidence. We endorsed Recommendation 20 of the Long Range Plan for the Federal Courts, as approved by the Judicial Conference of the United States and published by it in *Review of Administrative Proceedings* (1995):

In general, the actions of administrative agencies and decisions of Article I courts should be reviewable directly in the courts of appeals. For those cases in which the initial forum for judicial review is the district court, further review in the court of appeals should be available only on a discretionary basis except with respect to constitutional matters and questions of statutory or regulatory interpretation.

Efforts to Find Funds to Hold Meetings

And so it went. The Seniors' modus operandi was to identify a specific problem and then start from scratch to find a solution. An overarching concern was the question: "How may a litigant receive proper justice in a system in which every active circuit judge must decide 443 appeals a year?"

The Seniors started at square one, and were diligent with our limited resources. There was only so much we could do by telephone, e-mail or U.S. Mail in and from our individual chambers stretched from St. Petersburg, Florida and Montgomery, Alabama, through Danville, Kentucky and Pittsburgh, Pennsylvania, down to Austin, Texas and up to Chicago and then over to Santa Barbara, California. We covered the waterfront with as many Courts of Appeals as possible. Although I am a Third Circuit judge, at that time I was sitting regularly with the Ninth and Tenth, and was totally familiar with their procedures; that meant that the Seniors had the advantage of experience in seven U.S. Courts of Appeals. We estimated that the only subsidy we needed to complete our work was travel and lodging expenses for a few more meetings and that our work could have been completed with a budget of $50,000. We made applications to several private foundations, drawing up a prospectus for a grant, but none of us could get a nibble anywhere.

In a meeting with Chief Justice William H. Rehnquist, two representatives of the Seniors explained our project. The Chief Justice was very enthusiastic about our work and said that he would like to constitute us as a special ad hoc committee with appropriate travel funding. We furnished the Chief Justice with reports of our activities, and from time to time he voiced keen interest in our work. A letter from me to the Chief Justice memorialized his enthusiastic support of the "The Seniors" solution to the crushing case load in the U.S. Court of Appeal:

April 7, 1995

Dear Mr. Chief Justice:

I have advised my colleagues ("The Seniors") of your keen interest in our project to develop solutions to the crushing caseload of active circuit judges today. As explained in our get-together at the Greenbrier, The Seniors will be meeting this June in Chicago for our first meeting and at our own expense.

Although we have exchanged several ideas by mail we will start where the common law left off and discuss the following:

- Does one have an absolute right to appellate review of every district court final judgment?
- If so, what type of appeal is one entitled to?
- Given the overwhelming caseload in the courts of appeals, what should be the prerequisites to having a fully briefed appeal considered by three Article III judges?

This is a full plate; we will merely scratch the surface in June. We will then forward a brief report to you. As discussed at the Greenbrier, you can then consider constituting us an ad hoc committee.

It was great seeing and singing with you.

Cordially,

Our research soon reached a point where we absolutely needed another face-to-face meeting to have the benefit of open discussion, but delayed scheduling one until funding, approved by the Chief Justice, came through from Washington, D.C. This never came to fruition.

Having received a cold shoulder from private foundations and the Chief Justice, our work came to an end. It was not that effervescence in ideas fizzled out, but scattered as we were from Florida to California, we could not afford to dig more into our own pockets for travel and lodging. Our spirits were willing, our confidence high, convinced as we were that we were striving to fashion a solution to the crushing caseloads that everyone agreed was an extremely serious problem, but we could not move forward without face-to-face meetings with open discussions.

But at least we had the satisfaction that we tried.

A Peroratio

When I look at our court systems today, I see clouds above and on the horizon. But these are only clouds and, with the possible exception of the overload of cases facing appellate courts where litigants have an absolute right to appeal, the shadows in the sky need not comprise a permanent weather front. The ultimate solution may mean a shift in law school direction in the classroom and in the research carrel, a shift toward solving problems of judicial administration. However it happens, and I think it will, I believe candid, open-

minded scholarship and thoughtful, open-ended dialogue must take prece-
dence. When I entered law school, during the time of my law practice, and in
my early years on the bench, judges had the time and the tradition to compose brilliant essays and commentary. Burgeoning case loads now completely
consume the time and energies of those who wear the robes. The importance
of the legal academy cannot be overstated. It is there that great instruction
abides, a grand tutelage that extends far beyond students enrolled in formal
classes and ultimately embraces lawyers and judges as well.

Meanwhile, a stalwart judicial process is at work, in part following directions
from the masters of generations past, who were thoughtful students of the judicial process that paused to analyze a complex whole and to divide it into its
constituent elements. Faced with infinitely more complicated societal and economic issues than pure "lawyer's law," those who have followed have made important and necessary adjustments to the system. The impress and imprint of
what we have inherited are still out there to behold and admire. Nevertheless,
the common law tradition today continues to reach beyond what has gone before, most often advancing cautiously, hugging shores like mariners of old,
but at times, willing to launch bold, jet-powered excursions to meet, in the
words of an old friend of happy memory, Professor Maurice Rosenberg, "the
unrestrained tendency to take to the courts the most explosive issues of society—and present them with the explosive forces of advocacy."

No one has addressed this as eloquently as former U.S. Circuit Judge Shirley
Hufstedler of California in her opening statement of the Charles Evans Hughes
address before the Bar Association of the City of New York in 1971:

> We expect courts to encompass every reach of the law, and we ex-
> pect law to circle us in our earthly sphere and to travel with us to the
> alien vastness of outer space. We want courts to sustain personal liberty,
> to end our racial tensions, to outlaw war, and to sweep the contaminants
> from the globe. We ask courts to shield us from public wrong and pri-
> vate temptation, to penalize us for our transgressions and to restrain those
> who would transgress against us, to adjust our private differences, to
> resuscitate our moribund businesses, to protect us prenatally, to marry
> us, to divorce us, and, if not to bury us, at least to see that our funeral
> expenses are paid. These services, and many more, are supposed to be
> quickly performed in temples of justice by a small priestly caste with
> the help of a few devoted retainers and an occasional vestal virgin. We
> are surprised and dismayed because the system is faltering.

"WE HEAR ARGUMENT,
BUT DECIDE FROM THE BRIEFS"

Part D

The "Write Stuff"

The three chapters in Part D, what I call "The Write Stuff," reveal my concern over the rather dismal state of legal writing, a personal interest that has prevailed over the years. Part D contains separate chapters on brief writing and opinion writing, subjects that I have discussed in detail in my books and law review articles. The success of advocacy or adjudication depends on what and how you write. Part D also contains an examination of the intersection of the American law review and opinion writing. It is the law review that constantly subjects the work of appellate courts to intense, critical scrutiny, to a jurisprudential dissection of our opinions, to a microscopic examination of the contents that compose the body of judicial published work.

Supreme Court Justice William J. Brennan, Jr., was fond of telling this story about himself:

> In his first criminal trial, the young Mr. Brennan was appointed to defend a vehicular manslaughter case. A police officer who lived near the defendant agreed to be a character witness, but the young Brennan did not know that you may—and should—prepare a witness to testify.
>
> Armed with a manual on evidence, and bereft of formal education in trial practice (Harvard Law School had not offered him any), he rose to examine: "Sir, are you acquainted with the defendant's reputation for veracity in the vicinage where he resides?"
>
> The elderly Irish cop look puzzled and then volunteered tentatively, "Well, he is a good driver, I'd say."
>
> Shaken but undeterred, Brennan repeated his question word for word. This time, the witness simply stared at him. As the future Justice began a third time, the judge interrupted.
>
> "Officer, do you know the young man over there?" pointing to the defendant.
>
> "Yes, Your Honor."
>
> "Have you ever known him to lie?"
>
> "Why, no, Your Honor."

"Well, that is what Mr. Brennan has been asking you, but he went to Harvard Law School and has forgotten how to speak English."

The compleat lawyer should not—indeed, cannot—forget how to use English. This Part will help light the way forward.

CHAPTER TEN

BRIEF WRITING

Author's Note: *Part of the following was published by NITA in my book,* Winning on Appeal: Better Briefs and Oral Argument 19–28 (2d ed. 2009). *The other part is a slightly revised excerpt from my article* Perspective from the Bench on the Value of Clinical Appellate Training of Law Students, *published in 75* Miss. L.J. 645 (2006).

The Purpose of Brief Writing

An appellate brief may be defined as a written, reasoned elaboration that justifies a conclusion. It is a demonstration of written, reflective thinking expressed in a logical argument designed to educate and to persuade. In a practical sense, it is a written statement of reasons explaining why an appellate court should reverse, vacate, or affirm the judgment or final order of the tribunal from which the appeal is taken.

Briefs are written for one audience and one audience only—judges and their law clerks. They likely have the most limited readership of any professional writing. You write to persuade a court, not to impress a client. You write to persuade a court to your point of view; at a minimum, you write to convince the court to grant oral argument in your case. The key word is "persuasion." If a brief does not persuade, it fails. Every brief writer must understand this and never forget it. As you write, prop a sign, literally or figuratively, on your desk that asks, "Will this brief persuade the reader?"

Persuasion is the only test that counts. Literary style, massive displays of scholarship, citations that thunder from the ages and catchy phrases are uniformly pointless if the writing does not persuade.

Authorities may differ as to a precise definition of "persuasion." Kenneth Andersen describes it as "a communication process in which the communicator seeks to elicit a desired response from his receiver." Erwin Bettinghaus is more specific: "As a minimal condition, to be labeled as persuasive, a communication situation must involve a conscious attempt by one individual to change the attitudes, beliefs, or behavior of another individual or group of individuals through the transmission of some message."

Although both these definitions effectively express a general concept, what Bettinghaus says has a special relevance to counsel for the appellant, who has the burden of persuading the appellate court that the trial judge committed reversible error. Although not usually stated as a traditional burden of proof, in actual practice, the presumption of correctness lies with the trial tribunal. Evidence of this presumption is the jurisprudential axiom: when an appellate court is equally divided, the judgment of the trial court must be affirmed.

The appellant is required to rebut this presumption of correctness. To do this, the appellant must challenge the attitudes or beliefs expressed by the trial court and presumably endorsed by the appellate court; the appellee's task is to reinforce these attitudes or beliefs.

When considering persuasion in the abstract, however, Professor Nicholas M. Cripe reminds us that persuasion in an appellate court "differs from the common persuasive [writing or] speaking situation such as political speeches, protest rallies, legislative debates, revival meetings, jury trials, and especially commercial advertising and selling."

Appellate advocates must tackle rhetorical problems rarely encountered by other persuasive writers or speakers. They are limited to a small number of available relevant arguments. They must carefully select and present these contentions in a setting where the atmosphere and traditions render ineffectual or inappropriate techniques commonly used in other types of persuasive writing and speaking.

The audience is a concise grouping of, in the words of Cripe, "highly trained, intelligent, frequently articulate judges who likely will react unfavorably" to anything but the formal style of authoritative persuasion. Moreover, unlike most literature of scholarly persuasion, appellate briefs are not read at a leisurely pace and their contents savored and digested in a contemplative environment. Rather, briefs must compete with other demands on an appellate judge. Astronomical caseloads require judges to read large numbers of briefs while simultaneously performing other judicial functions demanding equal priority.

Elements of the Argument

In law, as in formal logic, the word "argument" takes on a special meaning. An argument is a group of propositions of which one is claimed to follow from the others, which are regarded as support or grounds for the truth of that one.

An argument is not a loose collection of propositions; it has a formal structure that one trained in the law recognizes.

The *conclusion*, or "therefore" statement of an argument—the precise relief sought in the brief—is a proposition that is affirmed on the basis of the other propositions of the argument. Logicians call these *premises*; lawyers call them points, or issues, in the brief. These points are designed to serve one purpose and one purpose only: they supply evidence or reasons for supporting the desired conclusion.

Reasoning is the process of reaching a conclusion through a series of propositions in argument form. Reasoning is reflective thinking. In a brief, we reason from something we know—the statute, procedural rule, or case law—to something that we did not know prior to our reasoning—the conclusion. Reasons, as distinguished from reasoning, are the considerations set forth in the terms and propositions in the premises "which have weight in reaching the conclusion as to what is to be done, or which we employed to justify it when it is questioned."

The conclusion in a brief is not just the major thing; it is the only thing. Indeed, it is the only game in town. The purpose of a brief is to convince the court to accept your conclusion—to reverse, vacate, or affirm the lower court's judgment. The only purpose of the brief's contents that precede the conclusion—statements of jurisdiction, standards of review, issues, facts and the discussion of legal precepts—is to set the stage for logical premises to justify the suggested conclusion.

Unlike an opinion of the court, a law review article or a professional treatise, a brief sells only its conclusion. Remember, the brief writer is a persuader. The lawyer is selling something, and that something is the conclusion.

Your brief is nothing more nor less than an expanded categorical syllogism containing premises (propositions). The conclusion you urge in your brief can only be true when (1) the other propositions (premises) are true, and (2) these propositions imply the conclusion; in other words, the conclusion is inferred from these premises.

The argument is designed to educate the court by setting forth solid reasons which, if accepted, may be incorporated into the court's opinion. The reasons must be logical, but until they appear in a judicial opinion, they are not "performative utterances" that possess the strong bite of precedent. Reasons in a brief have no life of their own. They are tools of education and persuasion only. Their role in an appellate brief differs from a law review article or legal treatise, where the focus is information and comprehensiveness. Reasons in an appellate brief are designed to do one thing: to convince a court to accept your conclusion. The only measure of their success is the extent to which they persuade the judge to accept the brief's conclusion.

The written brief always has played an important role in the American appellate court system. By contrast, the English appellate system relies entirely on oral argument. Oral argument in an American appellate court is a fleeting moment; a written brief is a permanent formality. The court relies on the written brief prior to oral argument, in the decision-making process afterward, and in the post-argument decision-justifying process—the preparation of the opinion.

Moreover, the astronomical increase in appellate court caseloads has emphasized the importance of briefs and diminished the importance of oral arguments. Crushing caseloads have imposed severe restrictions on the time available for oral argument and the length of time allotted.

Notwithstanding many exhortations about the importance of oral argument, in today's appellate environment you must write to win. Do not depend solely on your powers of speech, regardless of how great they may be. Your hopes hang on the written argument; the oral argument is only a safety net.

Gaining and Maintaining Attention

Pioneer psychologist William James once said, "That which holds the attention determines the action." To the brief writer, this means two things: (1) you must gain the attention of the reading judge, and (2) you must maintain it. Attention is a necessary condition for persuasion.

When you start to plan your brief, place yourself in the judge's shoes. The judge will pull down from the shelf the set of briefs, typically blue for the appellant, red for the appellee, gray for the reply and green for the amicus curiae. (Mine will have been tied together with "tape, red," noted in the Judiciary Act of 1789; traditions persist long and hard in my chambers.) The judge then will open the briefs and ask, "Now, what is the excuse for this appeal?" This is not an indication that the judge is prejudging the merits; it is only the presumption of trial court correctness at work.

The appellant always must be conscious of this presumption and remember that the odds of reversal favor the appellee. Keep in mind the track records: between 1997 and 2001, the appellant's odds of prevailing were one in ten in the United States courts of appeals.

Whether appellant or appellee, you must plan your brief to gain the immediate attention of the judge. You do this by:

- Leading from strength; hitting the reader between the eyes with your strongest argument.

- Expressing a message that the reader will understand.
- Structuring a presentation within the framework of the reader's knowledge, beliefs, and attitude.

John W. Davis once wrote:

> [Judges] are anxiously waiting to be supplied with what Mr. Justice Holmes called the "implements of decision." These by your presence you profess yourself ready to furnish. If the places were reversed and you sat where they do, think what it is you would want first to know about the case. How and in what order would you want the story told? How would you want the skein unraveled? What would make easier your approach to the true solution?

To gain the attention of the judge, the writing must be simple and clear. Here you may benefit from the advice of professors of speech and debate at the undergraduate level. Robert Huber at the University of Vermont taught his debate students a simple argument pattern designed to keep the argument clear, which brief writers can adopt to gain and maintain the judges' attention. The schematic is N-E-P-C: NAME IT, EXPLAIN IT, PROVE IT, CONCLUDE IT. Although devised for oral argument, this design works equally well for written briefs. Professor Cripe says, "If outlined, NAME IT would be a Roman numeral, EXPLAIN IT the capital letters, PROVE IT the Arabic numbers and small letters under the EXPLAIN IT sections, CONCLUDE IT probably a capital *D* or *E* tying up the point."

The first principle of gaining and maintaining attention is to write for the person who will read your brief. You do not write for publication. You do not write to show your colleagues how smart you are, how well you know the subject matter, or how stupid you believe the judges to be. All this may well be true. But the name of the game is "persuade the judge." You don't score points for anything else.

The second principle is subsumed in the first. To gain the judge's attention, you must immediately establish your credibility as a brief writer. Without credibility you may possibly gain the judge's attention, but you will never maintain it. Unless you maintain it, you will never induce the judge to accept your conclusion. And unless you persuade the judge to accept your conclusion, the brief is not worth the paper it is written on. Getting the judge to accept your conclusion is to appellate advocacy what the bottom line is to business.

So much for this short exposition on brief writing theory. I now pause to survey the problems that many appellate judges see in brief writing.

Criticisms of Briefs

Before I address the criticisms of briefs that judges lodge against lawyers, certain things must be said. First, writing an appellate brief is not easy. It may be the most difficult task of advocacy. What you write, in most cases, is your client's last opportunity to claim or defend. Before I criticize, let me put certain things in perspective.

On a scale of difficulty, writing a brief is much more arduous, calls for much more research, and requires much more intellectual choice and judgment than does writing a judicial opinion. It is easier for a judge to write an opinion than for a lawyer to write a brief from scratch; the judge has the advantage of both parties' work product. The brief writer has to narrow the issues; this part of the judge's task already is performed. The brief writer has to select the precedents and supply the authorities; the judge examines them, confirms their authenticity and, via independent research, ascertains their continued vitality. In so doing, the opinion writer has a distinct advantage over the brief writer, because it can be assumed that the cited authorities already have been cross-checked by opposing counsel in answering briefs.

Second, many of the criticisms leveled against briefs also may be directed against judicial opinions. There is sufficient criticism to go around to all hands—to those on the bench as well as to those at the bar. Both have much room for improvement.

But the similarity stops there. A litigant does not lose a case because a judge's opinion fails to convince. Judges' tenures seldom are affected if their work product is sloppy, turgid, rambling, repetitious and, at times, incomprehensible. But the quality of professional legal writing directly affects the persuasive powers of briefs, and, indirectly, the reputation of the lawyer in the professional community and personal standing in the law firm.

Examine, if you will, the following criticisms and decide if you are guilty of any of the practices. Remember the bottom line. For writing a convincing brief, you do not get Brownie points or a pat on the head. You win the case. For writing a bad brief, you are not directed to sit in the corner. You probably will lose the case. It is that simple.

What then are the criticisms generally expressed by judges against lawyers' briefs today? Here are some:

- Too long. Too long. Too long.
- Too many issues or points.

- Rudderless; no central theme(s).
- Failure to disclose the equitable heart of the appeal and the legal problem involved.
- Lack of focus.
- Absence of organization.
- Cluttering the logical progression with excessive citations and verbiage.
- Uninteresting and irrelevant fact statements.
- Misrepresented facts and case holdings.
- Failure to mention or properly cite cases against you.
- Failure to state proper jurisdiction (appellate and trial court).
- Failure to set forth the proper standard of review for each point presented.
- Failure to apply the standard of review properly.
- Failure to prepare an accurate table of contents.
- Failure to prepare an accurate table of authorities with page references to the brief.
- Failure to set forth a summary of argument before proceeding into a discussion of each point.
- Unclear, incomprehensible, irrelevant statements of reasons.
- When applicable, failure to state that a point is an independent reason that may support the brief's conclusion, regardless of how the court rules on other issues.
- Misrepresenting or exaggerating the adversary's arguments.
- Inaccurate or incomplete citations.
- Citing cases that have been overruled.
- Discussing unnecessary details of precedents and compared cases.
- Failure to show similarity or dissimilarity of material facts in compared cases.
- Failure to cite to the record when necessary.
- Citing to a record not contained in the appendix or excerpts of record.
- Failure to support the brief with a sufficient appendix or excerpts of record.
- Failure to complete the brief with a terse summation demonstrating why the reader should agree with the conclusion.
- Failure to state the relief requested.
- Typos, misspellings and grammatical mistakes.
- Failure to observe the court's appellate rules.
- Failure to observe color codes on brief covers when required by court rules.

The Brief-Reading Environment

Lawyers should understand the environment in which briefs are read. The general public and the legal profession generally are familiar with the working environment of trial judges—the courtroom and the chambers. But they are typically unfamiliar with where and when appellate judges do their thing. Briefs are sometimes, but not very often, read in a cloistered setting—a quiet, library-like room where the only sound may be a softly ticking clock. Briefs usually must compete with a number of other demands on the judge's time and attention.

The telephone rings. The daily mail arrives with motions and petitions clamoring for immediate review. The chambers' e-mail account spits out an urgent message or another judge's draft opinion, the reviewing of which is given a higher priority than drafting your own opinions.

The Clerk's office sends a fax with an emergency motion. The air courier arrives with an overnight delivery. The law clerks buzz you on the intercom because they have hit a snag in a case. So the deathless prose that you have been reading in the blue or red-covered brief must await another moment. Or another hour. Or another day.

So the briefs are wrapped up and taken home, where they are to be looked at after the nightly news but before your favorite evening television show. In the meantime, your spouse wants to talk with you, or the kids clamor for attention, or friends telephone. The briefs are rewrapped and set aside for another time. Or they are read in airport waiting rooms, or aboard a plane with the person in the next seat glancing across and speculating, "Gee, I suppose you're a lawyer. Let me ask you about this lawsuit I want to bring." Or the briefs are read late at night in hotel rooms with poor lighting, thus inviting soporific consequences.

Look at the numbers. When I first became an appellate judge in 1968, each active judge on the court was required to hear ninety appeals a year, which amounted to six sittings a year and fifteen sets of briefs per sitting. Each active judge on the court now has to decide approximately 485 appeals a year, participate in standing panels for pro se cases and motions, and sit in approximately seven scheduled sittings a year. This means that each judge must read approximately 1,000 briefs a year written by lawyers, plus at least fifty briefs written by *pro se* litigants and a like number of counseled responses, and frequently many reply briefs. In many of the state intermediate courts, the caseload is even more formidable.

I have described in detail the brief-reading environment for one purpose only: to emphasize that the written brief can be an effective instrument of persuasion only if it is concise, clear, accurate and logical.

Suggestions to Improve Briefs

Let me now offer some suggestions on how to avoid some of the criticisms of briefs from the bench.

A. The First Steps in Writing a Brief

Above all, make certain you have allocated sufficient time to prepare the brief. Do not let it play second fiddle to a series of depositions or other work which may be irrelevant in summary judgment or at trial. Writing a good brief takes time—both in planning what to say as well as expressing your argument effectively.

The first step in the writing process is to make an informal list of the issues that may be included. This is just an inventory. Here, you simply want to brainstorm the issues. The first step is not to use editorial or jurisprudential judgment. You simply make a list of all possible issues about which you might write. Put down every conceivable argument. This is only the beginning. Unfortunately, too many lawyers consider it the end as well. They make that list and then indiscriminately write a brief based on it.

The second step is weeding out issues that do not have a reasonable probability of prevailing in the appellate court. This may be the most difficult decision you make in writing the brief. It is certainly the most important one. What to exclude is as important as what to include. Here is the test you will use for inclusion:

LIMIT THE SELECTION OF ISSUES TO THOSE THAT MORE PROBABLY THAN NOT WILL ATTRACT THE INTEREST OF THE APPELLATE JUDGES AND GENERATE THEIR SERIOUS CONSIDERATION.

Note: I did not say issues that *possibly* will stimulate their interest. I said *probably* and this means more likely than not.

Here you must trade places with the brief reader in black robes. You must be dispassionate, detached and imperturbable. You must also be intellectually disinterested. Put aside emotions and passions, especially when you are representing the appellant. Carefully analyze the issues to ascertain where there is an *arguable* question of law, not simply an *imaginable* one. Do not expect to win by rolling the dice or throwing a handful of issues at the wall and hoping that some will stick.

A successful trial lawyer may mix the good with the bad and still succeed. In your closing speech to a jury, you can toss in a few arguments designed for emotional or populist purposes, or even one or two that smack of prejudice and superstition. You can avoid logic and get away with it. You can use fallacies of emotion and distraction. In examining and cross-examining a witness, you can permit extraneous matters to seep in and you still might get away with it.

The game changes when you climb the appellate ladder. You cannot afford to *dilute*, or shall I say, *pollute* the good with the bad. One or two perfectly good arguments should not be polluted with superfluous contentions that not only will never get anywhere, but, by their mere presence, will also weaken your good points. This is forensic infection. Bad arguments infect the good.

B. How Many Issues?

Now I come to my personal litmus test, the number of issues in a brief in *all* civil cases and a goodly number of criminal cases:

Three:	Presumably arguable.	The lawyer is primo.
Four:	Probably arguable points.	The lawyer is primo minus.
Five:	Perhaps arguable points.	The lawyer is no longer primo.
Six:	Probably no arguable points.	The lawyer has not made a favorable initial impression.
Seven:	Presumptively no arguable points.	The lawyer is at an extreme disadvantage, with an uphill battle all the way.
Eight or more:	Strong presumption that no point is worthwhile.	The lawyer needs a miracle.

To be sure, this litmus test is arbitrary, yet veteran appellate judges are virtually unanimous in complaining about the unnecessary prolixity of issues raised in most state and federal appeals. For example, former Chief Justice Malcolm Lucas of California advised: "Spend time on issues with potential merit. Shotgun approaches that do not distinguish between important and insignificant claims weaken your presentation."

C. A Caveat in State Criminal Appeals

But I rush to a big caveat. In taking state direct criminal appeals, you must consider not only your efforts before the present court. You must keep in mind other possible proceedings—state post conviction remedies and federal habeas under 28 U.S.C. §2254. Two important considerations hang heavy in state criminal appeals not present in civil appeals. First, you must avoid being procedurally defaulted for failing to raise an issue, especially a federal constitutional issue. Second, you must be totally conversant with state law setting forth what is necessary to raise properly an issue, specifically the quantum of discussion required on each point in the brief.

Because of the necessity of protecting the record for future proceedings, some of the issues you must present may not comport with the advice regarding the limited number of issues and the extent and quality of the discussion in the make-or-break issues in the present appeal. With an eye to the possibility of raising federal constitutional issues in a later Section 2254 proceeding in a United States district court, you have a twofold responsibility to ensure that: (1) you have exhausted all federal constitutional issues in the state court system, the Open Sesame to the federal courthouse door; and (2) you were not procedurally defaulted in the state judicial system from raising them there. Every lawyer practicing in a state or federal criminal court must be well-versed in that branch of federal constitutional law governing criminal law proceedings—from the start of a police investigation to filing a brief in the appellate courts.

D. The First Impression

You have limited the arguments to the points that are generally arguable issues. Your task now is to make a good first impression. In writing a brief, you do not get a *second chance* to make a *good first* impression. Always keep in mind the monstrous load of cases facing the judge. Your brief is capable of generating different first impressions. The judge may look at it and say, "Hey, this lawyer really knows the score. This lawyer has something here." That is the effect you want to make. At the other end of the scale, the impression of the judge may be: "This is what Ernest Hemingway had in mind when he said, 'What this country needs is a good crap detector.'" In your next brief, the choice is yours.

E. Arrangement of Issues

Always lead from a position of maximum strength—your strongest and most important points. This strategy requires you to produce an intelligent answer to the following question: what argument, objectively considered, based on precedent and the court's previously-stated policy concerns, is most calculated to persuade the court to your benefit? You want the point to be objectively considered by the court. It is your baby, but do not look at the baby through rose colored glasses. Look at your baby with all its warts and blemishes.

The law does change, but it changes in increments. You are not going to get an intermediate court of appeals to overrule precedent set by the highest court in the judicial hierarchy. Listen to Myron Bright of the United States Court of Appeals for the Eighth Circuit: "If an appellant can't win on the strength of the strongest claim or claims, he stands little chance of winning a reversal on the basis of weaker claims." The court needs to know just where the heart of the appeal lies. Distracting attention from arguable issues never helps an appellant's cause.

F.   State the Issue Narrowly

State the issue as narrowly as possible. The objective of appellate advocacy is to win the particular appeal before the court. Do not ask the court to make a decision with molar consequences when all you need is a molecular effect. There is a difference between succeeding as an advocate in a particular case and mounting a white charger to expound a greater cause in which you passionately believe. The law develops incrementally. There are few sea changes. Do not expect the court to change the law drastically in a single case. Write as narrowly as possible in order to win this appeal only.

G.   The Statement of Facts

In selecting the facts, the brief writer walks a very tight rope. This job requires consummate skill because you must constantly maintain a balance between being scrupulously accurate and putting the most favorable spin on your version of what happened. Do not steal the facts. Your opponent's brief (or the judge) will expose you. The exceptional advocate weighs these conflicting duties and conveys the impression that his or her client deserves to win.

It is essential that the statement of facts demand and retain the reader's attention. Do not bore the judge. Do not make the narrative difficult to follow. Do not mimic the style of an IRS regulation. Come closer to John Grisham than Beltway bureaucrats. Catherine Drinker Bowen kept a sign posted above her desk to discipline herself as she wrote her books: "Will the Reader Turn the Page?"

Consider how judges study briefs. Very seldom does the judge read one brief all the way through and then read the other brief completely. What I usually do is first read the appellant's statement of issues to learn what the case is all about and get the flavor of the case. I want to know the perimeters of the judicial inquiry. Then I read that portion of the trial court's opinion dealing with those issues. I do not read the whole opinion, merely the facts and that portion of the opinion discussing the issues presented on appeal.

Next, I read the appellant's summary of the argument, and then that of the appellee. And I do all of that before I read the statement of facts in the appellant's brief. I have already looked at the fact finder's rendition of the facts. I know the summary of both arguments. That forms the background before I start reading the facts.

From all this comes one direction to brief writing that absolutely must be followed: *never write your statement of facts until you have written the statement of issues.* This is an absolute imperative. It is your protection against writing a long-winded, rambling account of facts that will immediately turn off the judge. Keep in mind two concepts that many law clerks call "Aldisertisms":

> *Learn the difference between that which is important and that which is merely interesting.*
> *It isn't unconstitutional to be interesting.*

H. Summary of the Argument

The summary is critical because it gives the reader a concise preview of the argument and, therefore, should be crafted to allow the judge to form a mental outline of his or her pre-argument memorandum. Preparing an effective summary may be the brief writer's most challenging and important task. Former Mississippi Supreme Court Justice James L. Robertson once commented:

> I think the most important part of the brief is the Summary of the Argument. I invariably read it first. It is almost like the opening statement in a trial. From clear and plausible argument summary, I often get an inclination to affirm or reverse that rises almost to the dignity of a (psychologically) rebuttable presumption.
>
> ....
>
> I do not mean to denigrate the importance of a fully developed and technically sound argument. But I read the subsequent argument in a "show me" frame of mind, testing whether it confirms my impression from the summary of the argument.

Professor David W. Burcham, now president of Loyola Marymount University, Los Angeles, was one of my former clerks who went on to clerk for Justice Byron White and to practice law with a large Los Angeles firm before donning academic robes. He offers this observation: a brief writer should understand that the summary of argument will likely create the first, and perhaps last, impression of the Court toward the legal merits of the client's case. It should be the structural centerpiece of the entire brief.

Finally, I turn to the heart of your brief: the discussion of the issues or points you raise under the rubric of "Statement of Issues."

I. Issue-by-Issue Discussion

You proceed to the argument in a highly compartmentalized, issue-by-issue format. This is not the time for cross-pollination. The statement of your issue should be the argument heading. Use simple declarative sentences; state what you want the court to accept. Tell us this in a simple sentence. You do not have to use a "whether" statement or an interrogatory. If you want to move and influence the court to your way of thinking, set forth the point you want the court to accept in the statement of issues as well as the topic sentence in each one of your sections. Do not be a "whether" man or woman.

First Criterion: Do not wander, ramble, digress, or become unglued.

Second Criterion: Incorporate the proper standard of review in the topic sentences introducing each point. You must set forth and remind the reader of the standard of review for each issue presented.

Third Criterion: Determine whether the issues are independent of each other. "If you find on point one, you will then reverse, and it's not necessary to decide point two." The ideal brief contains several independent issues, so that if the court does not agree with you on the first issue, it might agree with you on your second or third. The tough road to hoe is when your points are interrelated, where the conclusion of the syllogism of your first point becomes the major premise for your second point. And the conclusion of your second point becomes the major premise of the third and so on. That's the difficult brief, because if you get whacked on your first point, the court can't go to your second or third point because they are logically prohibited. For example, in a *Miranda* issue, you must prove that the defendant was in custody. Without this proof, every other argument fails. Analyze your issues. Try to avoid an interdependent format by making your issues as independent of each other as possible.

Fourth Criterion: Always consider the consequences of each point you make. In considering how the law will affect other cases, appellate courts are always anxious not only about in personam justice between the parties, but also in rem justice. Always contemplate what precedential and jurisprudential institutional results will be forthcoming if the court accepts the conclusion you urge in your brief.

Much advice abounds on how to craft the discussion in your issues. For a more comprehensive discussion, I refer you to my book, *Winning on Appeal: Better Briefs and Oral Argument*.

Conclusion

In these pages I have not attempted comprehensive suggestions, but I have presented these few suggestions as advice along the way from one who has given much thought to our problems and has had the rare opportunity to have sat regularly in so many different United States courts of appeals.

What I have set forth in the foregoing represents advice of a contemporary. As early as 1851, however, the famed constitutional scholar and prolific writer on the law, Joseph Story, Justice of the United States Supreme Court and Dane Professor of Law at Harvard, encapsulated all of this in rhyme.

You wish the court to hear, and listen too?
Then speak with point, be brief, be close, be true.
Cite well your cases; let them be in point;
Not learned rubbish, dark, and out of joint;
And be your reasoning clear, and closely made,
Free from false taste, and verbiage, and parade.
Stuff not your speech with every sort of law,
Give us the grain, and throwaway the straw.
Whoe'er in law desires to win his cause,
Must speak with point, not measure our "wise saws,"
Must make his learning apt, his reasoning clear,
Pregnant in manner, but in style severe;
But never drawl, nor spin the thread so fine,
That all becomes an evanescent line.

Chapter Eleven

Opinion Writers and Law Review Writers:

A Community and Continuity of Approach

Author's Note: *This article appeared as* Opinion Writers and Law Review Writers: A Community and Continuity of Approach, 16 Duq. L. Rev. 2 (1977–1978), *which in turn was based on remarks delivered at the Duquesne University Law School Annual Law Review Dinner, Pittsburgh, Pennsylvania, May 28, 1977.*

"We are not final because we are infallible, but we are infallible only because we are final."

Justice Robert H. Jackson is responsible for this marvelous line. And so much wisdom abides in it. Even this most perceptive and gifted Supreme Court Justice, however, failed to reckon with a formidable American institution that can seriously question the notion that appellate judges are final. We may be final as far as particular litigants are concerned, but a case can be made that the last, or final, word on the law is now a privilege entrusted to, or shall I say, acquired by, the law review writers and editors of our law schools.

It is the American law review, this serious institution of scholarly criticisms—sometimes volatile, sometimes impertinent, by nature opinionated but never villainous—it is the law review that constantly subjects the work of appellate courts to intense, critical scrutiny, to a jurisprudential dissection of our opinions, to a microscopic examination of the jural sinews and fibers that compose the body of our published work. Law reviews indeed constitute an extremely valuable, extra-judicial laboratory in which our various specimens are meticulously studied and then evaluated as healthy or pathological.

Although we judges come as unwilling patients to the scalpels and incisions of law review writers, any judge sensitive to the activity or reputation of his court should welcome the diagnosis and possible surgery; at least, I do. In a system of government where the executive and legislative branches are constantly subject to public review at the ballot box, but where appellate judges are lifetime or long-term, it is the law review that serves as an informal check and balance; informal and unstructured, to be sure, but nevertheless, a respectable and ever-present force.

Time and again I find myself discarding passages in draft opinions—enthusiastic passages that were the product of much zeal and hours, if not days, of labor. I discard them because, after reflection, I become convinced that my approach would not wash; that it would not survive calm, detached appraisal, the withering gaze of critical analysis—especially the inquisitorial scrutiny of a law review examination. And, at decision conferences, my colleagues and I, in planning the outline of a proposed decision, are not above asking one another if the design we are planning can withstand this same disciplined dissection. Thus, the role of the student law review as an unabashed and immodest critic of state and federal appellate courts is much to be desired and welcomed by the bench and bar.

In this spirit, it becomes appropriate to discuss rules and measures by which judicial opinions should be evaluated. I do not suggest anything revolutionary. Guidelines and standards for *reviewing* an opinion are the same as those utilized in *writing* an opinion. For this reason, I believe that the writer and the reviewer should approach an opinion from the same vantage point. A common approach would produce continuity, and thus yield meaningful analyses to the readerships of both opinions and law reviews.

Introduction

Although the beginning point for both writers and readers of judicial opinions may be the same, the manifested ends are sometimes dissimilar: the law contained in the opinions is the law as it is; the scholarship efforts of the law review writer culminate, more often than not, in the law as it *ought to be*. When there is a coalescing between the law that "is" and the law that "ought to be," a state of jurisprudential bliss exists between academia and the courts. More frequently, however, a chasm exists between "is" and "ought" which law reviews seek to bridge. While that effort is heartily commendable, many loose planks endanger the wayfarer on that noble crossing.

The multifaceted realms of "being" and "oughtness" have been analyzed and discussed through the ages. The tension between the opinion writer and the law review writer might well be a modern-day parallel of the clash between Roman *verum*, truth, and *certum*, certainty. But my concern here is not so much with philosophical origins of the problem as with the postulate that notwithstanding the innate tension, a meaningful, productive analysis requires a significant community and continuity of approach between the opinion writer and the reviewer.

As both a reader and writer of judicial opinions, I suggest that the desired approach includes four areas which, if given greater attention from both writers and reviewers, would greatly aid both groups in their quest to "thoughtfully and disinterestedly ... [weigh] the conflicting social interests involved in the case." First, the terminology used by judges and critics alike evidences sloppiness in identifying the legal precepts which are components of various *rationes decidendi*. Second, there is often a failure to isolate precise contours of the jurisprudential dispute before the court. Third, there is sometimes a failure to avoid, or to identify, fallacies of reasoning. Finally, there is frequent failure to recognize and to evaluate the public policy judgments that inhere in judicial lawmaking.

Identifying the Legal Precepts

The importance to both writer and reviewer of ascertaining the relative weight to be accorded various precepts is heightened by the exigencies of translating into written word the respective writer's analysis. Thus, phraseology must be precise and analytical processes must be valid, if we are to have the desired continuity of approach between writer and reviewer. Where Philip Selznick has used the word "law," I shall use Pound's formulation, "legal precept," and define rules of law as precepts attaching a definite, detailed legal consequence to a definite, detailed state of facts. Rules are to be distinguished from principles, which are authoritative starting points for legal reasoning, employed continually and legitimately where cases are either not covered at all or not fully covered by rules in the narrower sense. Unlike rules, then, which emanate from specific factual complexes, principles do not attach a definite, detailed legal result to a definite, detailed state of facts.

Ronald Dworkin makes the point that rules are applicable on an "all-or-nothing" basis: "If two rules conflict, one of them cannot be a valid rule." It is here that we usually resort to principles, because "[p]rinciples have a dimension that rules do not—the dimension of weight or importance. When principles intersect, one who must resolve the conflict has to take into account the relative weight of each."

I insist that the legal precept be properly labeled or identified—but not for the sake of *elegantia juris* or preciousness. There are much more pragmatic considerations. When a specific holding of a case is suddenly anointed with the chrism of "principle" there is a very real effect on the doctrine (yes, I think it's a doctrine, not a principle or rule) of *stare decisis*. The danger of a commentator or a writer of a subsequent opinion lifting a naked holding of a given case to the dignity of a legal "principle" may give to a single appellate decision a precedential breadth never intended. It may confuse the dispute-settling role of a court with its responsibility of institutionalizing the law. Institutionalization in the common law tradition, in Harlan Fiske Stone's felicitous expression, is "preeminently a system built up by gradual accretion of special instances." And, in my view, the accretion is not gradual if you pile on an improper dimension to a specific instance.

I candidly confess to a suspicion, and it is not more than that, that a divergence of basic philosophy may exist between the traditional common law lawyer-judge and the American legal academician. Many legal commentators, both on and off the bench, appear to have an infatuation with the Continental tradition of codification. If the law is moving, stop it; freeze it; codify it. Thus appears the penchant for Uniform and Model Codes on everything from commercial and criminal law to class action procedures, the mighty efforts of the Restatements of the Law, and the frenetic activities of the American Bar Association to procreate "standards" with undiminished vigor.

It is my thesis that every holding of every case does not deserve that same size black letter law treatment that some commentators or codists wish to give it. If American case law is to develop properly in the common law tradition, it is essential that the effect of specific instances, *i.e.*, the rules of law in the narrow, Poundian sense, be given proper weight. But only proper, honest weight. And often, describing a rule as a principle, or a doctrine, is interfering with the measure of proper weight. It's putting a jurisprudential thumb on the scale.

The ability to properly identify, and distinguish among, the various components of *rationes decidendi* is an ability which should be developed in the writer or reviewer even prior to his or her taking pen to hand. Only where both parties begin with a firm grasp of the relative dimensions of the legal precepts involved in a dispute can they be assured that they will use consistent and proper designations, and thus produce meaningful analysis. Ideally, the components will be clearly identified in the opinion, precluding any guess, or value judgment, on the reviewer's part. Thus, where a judge properly identifies the guiding principles, or controlling rule, the reviewer may merely restate the court's initial precept identification and then focus his or her analysis on the choice of those precepts. If after close examination, however, it appears that an opinion contains imprecise or improper labeling, we return to square one and the reviewer's initial job is somewhat more complex. Such ambiguity itself warrants comment by the reviewer, who must ferret out some common nomenclature on which the opinion can be reviewed.

Identifying the Precise Dispute

Professor Herbert Wechsler has aptly observed that the role of the critic "is the sustained, disinterested, merciless examination of the reasons that the courts advance, measured by standards of [reasoned principles]." Thus, effective interplay between the writer and reviewer of a judicial opinion requires that the judge elaborate and justify his or her disposition of the four basic functions, and that, likewise, the reviewer remain within these bounds in examining the opinion.

We have seen that the proper terminology involves basically an intellectual grasp of concepts on the part of the individual writer or reviewer. Identification of the precise dispute implicates both a preferred methodology of analysis and an understanding of terms. The introduction of a preferred procedure heightens the importance of the community and continuity of approach between writer and reviewer. When both exposition by the judge and examination by the critic are set within the framework of the four basic functions, determination of whether the ultimate decision in a case accords with the Jones-Pound measures of being "right as possible" or "good" will be a more effective endeavor.

For example, the writer and reviewer may differ on the preferred disposition of any of the four functions. The level at which disagreement occurs (if it occurs at all) may well dictate the entire tenor and depth of a law review article. Thus, if the reviewer's sole dispute with an opinion writer is over application of a given precept to the facts at hand, there is no point in fashioning a long legal essay on finding the facts, choosing the legal precept, or interpreting it.

In many instances, however, the reviewer will dispute not so much the application of a given legal precept, but the court's choice of that precept, *i.e.*, the court's judgment regarding the similarity of fact situations under comparison. Professor Edward H. Levi has explained that "the scope of a rule of law, and therefore its meaning, depends upon a determination of what facts will be considered similar to those present when the rule was first announced. The finding of similarity or difference is the key step in the legal process."

To understand why disagreement between writer and reviewer occurs most frequently on this level, we need only consider again one of the basic distinctions between a judicial opinion and a law review article. An opinion treats a narrow fact situation, a specific case or controversy; a law review article often treats a broader subject, using the single opinion as a springboard for discussion. The good judge will identify, isolate, discern the precise dispute and usually say no more, but the reviewer will use the identified dispute as a vehicle for extended analysis of the law involved in the decision. The specificity and discrimination of an opinion of an appellate court requires maximum judicial restraint because the writing needs the approval of at least one other member of a three-judge panel to make it an opinion of the court. The reviewer may—and should—give freer rein to certain value judgments as to what something *should* be.

Disagreement between opinion writer and reviewer over the choice of legal precepts, then, must be tempered by an understanding of these distinctions. Thus enters the importance of identifying the precise dispute: not until both writer and reviewer have clearly identified the dispute, and some common ground is found, may the reviewer's jump to the "ought" begin. The good reviewer will resist the temptation to criticize unfavorably a judge merely for his or her choice of precepts when those precepts rest on a valid identification of the precise dispute. Of course, when the reviewer can demonstrate that the writer misapprehended or misrepresented the dispute, this should be done. But such a situation is not the stuff of which scholarly contributions are made. I suggest that the most fruitful approach is for the reviewer to parallel as closely as possible the court's dispute identification, and proceed to an analysis of the precepts beyond that on which the court, in the exercise of its judicial function, may embark. Examining the life and future of those precepts, judge-made or statutory, which the court deemed relevant, as well as the court's application of the law, can be a most exciting challenge. And awareness by both writer and reviewer of the importance of proper dispute identification again moves us toward the desired community and continuity of approach—leaving, it must be noted, maximum room for the reviewer's creativity and depth of analysis.

Fallacies of Reasoning

Although reasoned exposition traditionally takes the form of a logical syllogism, there is, of course, much more to the judicial process than dryly logical progression. In exercising a choice of legal precepts, for example, the opinion writer does not necessarily appeal to any rational or objective criteria; essentially, he or she exercises a value judgment and should be recognized flatly as doing so. A frequent error of law reviews is to permit the reviewer who, at bottom, disagrees with the opinion writer's choice of major precept to embark on an attack of the court's "reasoning." In fact, notwithstanding the nature of the published opinion, law reviews conduct little analysis or criticism of reasoning *qua reasoning*. I suggest that more attention should be focused on the methods utilized by the opinion writers to justify their decisions, *i.e.*, the reasoning itself. Just as it is not too much to ask whether one disagrees with the choice of the "authoritative starting point," and if so, why, it is not too much to ask whether the reviewer's quarrel is with the formal correctness of the syllogism used and, if so, where.

There is fertile ground upon which to criticize the reasoning in opinions. The reviewer's responsibility to do so, however, must extend beyond superficial critiques of "the court's reasoning" or broad accusations of fallaciousness. Any material fallacy of logic should be identified with particularity. For instance, when there occurs a fallacy of irrelevance, often referred to as irrelevant conclusion or *ignoratio elenchi*, it should be identified as such and explored. The writer, in this instance, proves a point unrelated to the issue presented or, conversely, disproves a point similarly irrelevant. The fallacy results in spending time and effort to prove something that has not been asserted and which, most likely, bears little relevance to the cause. In another form of the same fallacy, the writer assumes that he has proven his own point by disproving those of another.

Another common fallacy is the fallacy of accident, or *dicto simpliciter*, which occurs when the writer, confronted with a special, exceptional case, attempts to apply a general rule. Thus, the case which exists as an exception is brought within a universal statement from which it previously was exempted. A converse fallacy also frequently appears: the fallacy of selected instances, or the fallacy of hasty generalization. This consists of amassing a few instances and establishing a generalization or rule based on those alone. The fallacy is in the lack of a representative number of particular instances to form a valid foundation. Dean Pound suggests, in this regard, that often commentators will hastily generalize a holding into a principle.

The fallacy of false cause, or *post hoc*, involves reasoning from mere sequence to consequence, from what merely happened in chronological order to the assumption of a causal connection. Then there is *petitio principii*, or begging the question. In order to prove that A is true, B is used as proof, but since B requires support, C is used in defense of B, but C also requires proof and is substantiated by A, the proposition which was to be proved in the first place.

These are but examples of a few ways that reasoning as expressed in judicial opinions and in law review articles can go awry. A watchful eye for these defects in reasoning is often a hallmark feature of criticism and scholarly writing, and it would suit legal writers of all stripes to pay more attention to them.

Identifying Public Policy

Just as the opinion writer will strive to recognize and accommodate the relevant interests in a case, it is the reviewer's responsibility to couch any discussion in the same light. Where the law reviewer simply indicates that he or she dislikes the particular result in the case, without more, or simply expresses a value judgment, without more, the review should be sloughed off as sophomoric. Where the law reviewer merely disagrees with the court's decision because the writer—student or professor—favors certain interests or groups over others, where it is simply a question of whose ox is being gored, then, although the reviewer's right to disagree is to be respected, it is not legitimate to camouflage this basic policy disagreement as a criticism of an opinion writer's legal ability or scholarship. If what is to be written is essentially a criticism of a judge's political or social philosophy, it may more properly belong in a political science journal than in a law review. But a continuity of approach between opinion writer and reviewer in identifying and dealing with the various interests *will* yield a very important area in which various critiques should be made: where the law reviewer can demonstrate that the court has not taken cognizance of all the interests, or that there is a better adjustment that is available, then the criticism is acceptable and, indeed, warranted.

Conclusion

There are rules and measures of a good opinion which must be followed by the opinion writer. Those who would review the opinion must use the same rules and measures. The rule or measure is a complex ideal embracing standards for assessing and criticizing decisions that purport to be legal, whether made by a legislature or by a court, whether elaborating a rule or applying it to a specific case.

Most definitions of law invoke a normative system and a master ideal. Thus, St. Thomas Aquinas reminded us that law is "an ordinance of reason for the common good, promulgated by him who has the care of the community." But positive law, whether it comes from the legislature or from the court, includes an arbitrary element. It is, in Philip Selznick's formulation, to some extent brute fact and brute command: "[T]his arbitrary element, while necessary and inevitable, is repugnant to the ideal of legality. Therefore, the proper aim of the legal order, and the special contribution of legal scholarship, *is progressively to reduce the degree of arbitrariness in the positive law.*"

The function of the modern American law review is exactly that: progressively to reduce the degree of arbitrariness in the positive law. However, as a judge must resort to reasoned elaboration instead of judicial fiat, so must criticism of a judge's work be free from law review fiat. Thus appears the critical importance of continuity between writer and reviewer in the various approaches discussed herein. In effecting a proper and consistent approach, we are able to evaluate decisions not in terms of "right" or "wrong," nor in terms of subjective agreement or disagreement with the result, but rather in terms of the thoughtful and disinterested weighing of conflicting social interests. And thus will opinion writers, reviewers, readers and, indeed, the development of the law itself, be served.

CHAPTER TWELVE

READING AND EVALUATING AN APPELLATE OPINION

Author's Note: Portions of this chapter, co-authored by me and my then law clerks Meehan Rasch and Matthew P. Bartlett, first appeared as Opinion Writers and Opinion Readers, *31 Cardozo L. Rev. 1 (2009).*

Introduction

A judge is a professional writer. Whether the judge writes well or poorly, he or she writes for publication. By force of circumstance, everything he or she does in the conduct of the judicial office must be expressed in words, preferably—but alas, not always—with a high degree of clarity and precision. Other writers may have the assistance of elegant typography and graphic illustration. The judge is armed only with the figurative pen.

Unfortunately, readers and users of judicial opinions—litigants, lawyers, other judges, clerks, researchers and law students—tend to be very busy. As a result, they have highly selective reading habits. Opinion readers, especially the vast majority who were not parties to a given case, need and expect to quickly learn what the case is about, what are the key issues and the relevant facts, what legal precedent governs the situation and how it applies, and what ultimate conclusion and resulting rule of law emanates from the case. Detective mysteries and narratives with O. Henry surprise endings have their place— in fiction. Apply these techniques to the writing of opinions and you risk losing your audience. In the words of Henry Weihofen, "[e]conomy of the reader's attention requires that we minimize friction in the process of communication between writer and reader." With the number of published opinions constantly increasing, and with the constant competition for readers' attention, it is important that opinion writers bear in mind their potential readers and strive to produce a serviceable, cogent and elegant end product.

Harried opinion readers likewise will benefit from a better understanding of opinion structure and opinion writing technique as they struggle to parse— whether as students in a first year classroom or as advocates researching a case to be argued before the highest court in the land—just exactly what these dang opinions are intended to convey and why they are even written in the first place. The emphasis of this chapter is on appellate court opinions, but much of it applies also to opinions of trial judges, administrative law judges and government agencies.

The Anatomy of an Opinion

Opinion writers—and readers—must resist the temptation to evaluate an opinion in terms of their agreement with the result, or according to how congenial with their personal philosophy it may be, or simply because they want to apply a value judgment in the choice, interpretation or application of the controlling legal precept, for this too may be a personal valuation. Rather, measure opinions against the test inspired by Roscoe Pound and the late Cardozo Professor of Jurisprudence at Columbia University, Harry Jones: (a) how thoughtfully and disinterestedly the court weighed the conflicts involved in the case and (b) how fair and durable its adjustment of the conflicts promises to be. The first factor goes to the "reasonableness" of the court's decision, the second to the logical validity of the reasoning. Opinion writers must keep these maxims in mind as they prepare, and then write, and then rewrite.

As a professional writer, a judge must possess literary skills. If such skills are not natural, they *must* be acquired or learned. The judge must accomplish this himself or herself. If a judge wants to write clearly and cogently, with words parading before the reader in logical order, the judge must first *think* clearly and cogently, with thoughts laid out in neat rows. To do so is to demonstrate respect for the elements of reflective thinking and the rules of deductive and inductive logic. Any judge who is unwilling or unable to do this will confuse readers and cannot perform his or her judicial duties properly.

As the appellate case loads have increased, so has the judges' dependence upon law clerks. Law review graduates seem to be preferred because of their editorial experience. Unfortunately, that experience too often has been gained in the production of prose that only foreshadows a transfer of literary shortcomings, whole and unaltered, to the writing of opinions. Obviously, choosing the most literate law clerk is not enough. It is the judge who makes decisions and then the judge who must explain those decisions. It is the judge who holds the commission. It is the judge whose name goes on the opinion. It is the judge who must assume 100 percent of the responsibility. The law clerk is an assistant, and only an assistant. The law clerk must help in research, in the drafting process and in expressing views of the law, but—and this is a big "but"—every sentence the law clerk writes in the opinion must be totally understood and endorsed by the opinion-writing judge. To delegate some writing responsibilities to a law clerk is more than proper; it is an absolute necessity in this litigious age. This delegation, however, is legitimate only to the extent that the judge accepts the submitted language, understands what has been written, agrees with it and is willing to stake a professional reputation on it.

A. Reader Criticisms of Opinions

Readers lodge a torrent of criticisms against opinions written today: opinions are too long and burdened with too many citations. Their discussion tends to ramble, failing to clearly define and analyze issues, and they present lengthy and largely unnecessary discussions of the cases compared. Opinion writers make unstructured references to other cases without indicating what facts in those cases are material or immaterial. They fail to set forth specific reasons for choosing one line of cases over others, saying, "We think that is the better view" and, "We prefer the majority view," without explaining why. Opinions display acute "law reviewitis," being overwritten and overfootnoted, obese and sloppy instead of clean and neat. Holdings are often expressed in terms that reflect factual scenarios not contained in the records. Writers eschew those good, plain words and sentences that communicate rather than befuddle. Finally, there are too many published opinions—far too many—with no precedential or institutional value.

Certainly, some, but not all, of these criticisms are valid. Fortunately, they do not apply to all judges or to all opinions. Nevertheless, there is enough falling from grace to justify guidance to avoid some of the most common pitfalls.

These expositions are not meant solely for opinion writers. For you, dear opinion readers, we hope you will be able to utilize this anatomical guide to further develop your understanding and reading of case law. As I have advised elsewhere, "There are rules and measures of a good opinion which must be followed by the opinion writers. Those who would review the opinion must use the same rules and measures." Law students, neophyte practitioners and law clerks, recognize the components and structure of every opinion you read, whether or not the opinion writer assists you in the task. "Always be certain that you examine the entire anatomy of the opinion, that you know the proper nomenclature for all its relevant parts." Scholars, law review writers and other critics of opinions should be advised that "if the critic casts stones at the opinion writer's reasoning, the stone thrower should recognize the distinctions among the court's reasoning process, the weight given to the arguments, and the court's exercise of value judgment." Effective opinion critics also must be able to pinpoint the exact legal dispute between the parties and fully understand the judicial decision-making process and legal reasoning structure. Recognizing the (sometimes shrouded) parts of an opinion will assist you throughout your careers in communicating effectively with your primary audience, whether that be a client, judge or other practitioners and scholars. All opinion readers, critics and users will benefit from a "behind the scenes" look at the very object they are dissecting.

B. Let the Reader Recognize an Outline

A lengthy discussion of a multifaceted single issue or of multiple issues should be segmented. Each segment should be preceded by a Roman numeral or a letter. In this way, the reader has a visual outline to aid in understanding the opinion.

No one style fits all opinion writers. I prefer the U.S. Supreme Court style of segmenting each identifiable segment of the opinion with Roman numerals. The writer proceeds with each segment as a self-contained unit. This encourages coherent, concise, issue-centered writing. It separates the issue, facts and rationale into easily identifiable segments. It eliminates the need for stodgy, artificial transitional phrases because the numeral serves to indicate the transition to a new subject. In many cases the most important reason for the use of segments indicated by Roman numerals is that it shortens and clarifies the separate opinions written by judges on the same panel. A judge wishing to join in an opinion except a portion of the discussion on damages can say: "Judge Alpha concurs in the opinion of the majority and dissents only to Part III of the opinion." The net effect of this is that the reader can quickly understand where there is unanimity in the court and, if there is disagreement, precisely where it exists.

Not all opinion writers agree. Some prefer the opinion to be uninterrupted; they like it to flow like a legal essay. Others prefer subheadings to introduce the issues, in law review style. Still others follow the styles of legal memoranda by compartmentalizing with subheads titled "Facts," "Discussion" and "Conclusion." It is a matter of personal style. There is no specific convention giving the seal of approval to one over the other. Unless the opinion is very short, however, either a Roman numeral (sometimes followed by letters) or a subheading should be used to assist the reader in segmenting discrete parts of the opinion.

Conclusion

According to Walter V. Shaefer, late Chief Justice of the Illinois Supreme Court, "[A]n opinion which does not within its own confines exhibit an awareness of relevant considerations, whose premises are concealed, or whose logic is faulty is not likely to enjoy either a long life or the capacity to generate offspring." We are fortunate to have a large number of good opinion writers in the U.S. Courts of Appeals and in the state supreme and intermediate courts. Notwithstanding the complex nature of today's litigation, these opinion writers prove that a clear and cogent statement of reasons may easily explain the decision to the beleaguered reader who may be short of time and perhaps slow of comprehension. The work product of the excellent opinion writers, unfortunately, provides a stark contrast with those of their less-skilled colleagues.

Luckily, the writing of judicial opinions, like most tasks in the law, can be improved with practice. So too can the reading of opinions. A focused opinion reader who can recognize the anatomy and objective of judicial opinions will more easily absorb points the opinion writer seeks to convey. In the interest of "minimiz[ing] friction in the process of communication between writer and reader," to borrow from Henry Weihofen, we urge opinion writers to write like readers, and opinion readers to read like writers. Opinion readers only stand to benefit from wider understanding of the judicial process and of the purpose and mechanics of opinion drafting. And opinion writers must at all times keep in mind that they write for distinct primary and secondary readership markets, and craft their opinions accordingly.

Together, a better understanding and appreciation by opinion readers and opinion writers for those on the other side of the page will facilitate judicial communication and enhance the continued development of our law.

"ANYBODY CAN DECIDE, BUT JUDGES MUST DO MORE
...THEY MUST PUBLICLY JUSTIFY THEIR DECISION."

HOW JUDGES DECIDE CASES

In the Preface of the 1976 first edition of my book, *The Judicial Process: Readings, Materials and Cases*, I wrote, "A study of the judicial process is a study of how courts decide cases. It is an analysis of decision making as it actually takes place and as it ought to take place." My experience teaches me that too many lawyers think that flashing a long list of cases and trying to show how smart they are is what we judges find persuasive. In reality, ours is a common law tradition in which the judicial process is paramount to how a judge approaches and decides a case, and justifies that decision. In this Part, the lawyer can learn how to better approach and address cases, especially those in which no precedent controls and the law is not clear. To effectively persuade a judge in these cases, the lawyer must understand the judicial process culminating in the public justification of a decision. This process ranges from examining the legal philosophy and jurisprudential temperament of a judge, to comprehending the factors affecting judicial decision making, to understanding the components animating the public justification of a decision. So informed and, consequently, so armed, the lawyer can present a case that will allow the judge to craft a durable and fully justified opinion in the lawyer's favor.

Chapter Thirteen

Philosophy, Jurisprudence and Jurisprudential Temperament of Federal Judges

Author's Note: *This chapter is excerpted from an article I wrote that appears as* Philosophy, Jurisprudence, and Jurisprudential Temperament of Federal Judges, *20 Ind. L. Rev. 453 (1987). In republishing it here I have made minor changes to compensate for the nearly 25 years that have passed since it first appeared. In this article, I critically examine the labels bandied about seeking to categorize judges. Rather than relying on sophistic classifications, the lawyer who understands the difference between the philosophy of law and a philosophy of law, the significance of jurisprudence, the effects of jurisprudential temperament and the interplay between all of these factors—highlighted here by the task of constitutional interpretation—will be better situated to understand and persuade the judge.*

Introduction to Philosophical and Jurisprudential Concepts

After 50 years as a state and federal judge, I find myself somewhat uncomfortable because I am unable to pigeonhole myself into the fashionable categories used by political scientists, respected law professors, lawyers and both the print and broadcast media to describe judges. I feel somewhat inadequate because I simply don't know if I am a "liberal," "conservative," "activist," "strict constructionist," "centrist," "moderate" or "Reagan type." Although these expressions are so commonplace that obviously many must have an idea what they mean, I'm not quite sure that these expressions are likely candidates for definitional prizes in explaining what they mean. These descriptions probably originated in the political arena as handy one-word pejoratives, but they surely have caught on and are very much with us today.

I have been a judge-watcher for a long time, and my view has been an unusual one, because it has been from the inside looking both out and up; looking out at fellow appellate judges and looking up to the Supreme Court Justices who review our work. I do this watching because my avocation, if you call it that, is studying the judicial process. By this I mean a study of methods—of how courts decide cases; an analysis of decision making as it actually takes place and as it ought to take place. As a long time student in this field who believes he still has a long way to go, I put aside, for our immediate purposes, the substantive law that is the product or result of the process. In this chapter, I will content myself only with examining the process itself.

The more I think about the judicial process and one-word labels bandied about to describe those who make the process work, the more I am convinced that this splash and dash is a very ineffective attempt to cover a very complex individual—today's federal judge. As two digits may not adequately describe a nuclear physics formula, simplistic expressions cannot begin to cover very complicated judicial personalities. I think that this is true when describing any judge, but it's even more true when you describe federal judges, especially federal judges on the appellate hierarchy's two top tiers.

A. Theories of "Liberal" and "Conservative"

If you are comfortable with the most familiar dichotomy—the division between so-called liberal and conservative judges—you have your choice of a number of abstract theories. If you so choose, you can start with the clash between two renowned works of moral and political philosophy, John Rawls' *A Theory of Justice*, and Robert Nozick's *Anarchy, State, and Utopia*. Rawls expressed his conception of justice in the statement: "All social values—liberty and opportunity, income and wealth, and the bases of self respect—are to be distributed equally unless an unequal distribution of any, or all, of these values is to everyone's advantage." Nozick defended a thesis of the "minimum state," and argued that state intervention is severely limited to the narrow function of protection against force, theft and fraud, and to the enforcement of contracts. He contended: "The minimal state is the most extensive state that can be justified. Any state more extensive violates people's rights. Yet many persons have put forth reasons purporting to justify a more extensive state." Perhaps we can say that liberal or activist judges will do what they can to enforce the egalitarian philosophy of Rawls, and that the conservatives will lay back with Nozick, content that the least government is the best government.

Or you can select another method of separating the liberal sheep from the conservative goats by hearkening to the differences between Locke and Hobbes in reconstructions of the state of nature. John Locke's *Second Treatise on Civil Government* emphasized the natural rights of individuals as to "life, liberty and estate." He built on English tradition, as illustrated by Sir John Fortesque and Coke, the entire emphasis of which had always been on rights of the individual rather than the rights of people considered en masse. Locke believed that the state of nature was an era of "peace, good will, mutual assistance, and preservation" in which the "free, sovereign" individual is already in possession of all valuable rights. Yet from defect of "executive power" the individual is not always able to make his rights good or to determine them accurately with respect to the like rights of his fellows. Hobbes painted a far different picture of man's state before any government existed. He visualized it as one of "force and fraud," in which "every man is to every man a wolf." From this we may draw the conclusion that Hobbes traced all rights to government and regarded them simply as implements of public policy. Locke, on the other hand, regarded government as creating no rights, as being strictly fiduciary in character, and as designed to make secure and more readily available rights that antedate government and that would survive it. I think traces of labels of conservative and liberal peek through here.

Yet another choice is available—the dichotomy suggested by Alexander M. Bickel in *The Morality of Consent*. He stated that the liberal and conservative traditions have competed, and still compete, for control of the democratic process and of our constitutional system, and that both have controlled the direction of our judicial policy at one time or another. Bickel, too, referred to John Locke in the context of the social contract theory. He described this tradition as contractarian, a tradition that rests on the vision of individual rights that have a clearly defined, independent existence predating society and that are derived from nature and from a natural, if imagined, contract. Society must bend to these rights.

Bickel named the other tradition the Whig tradition, one intimately associated with Edmund Burke. This model rests not on anything that existed prior to society but on flexible, slow-moving, highly political circumstances that emerge as values of society evolve. The task of government, according to this tradition, is to make a peaceable, good and improving society informed by the current state of values. In discussing Burke, Bickel stated:

> [The rights of man] do not preexist and condition civil society. They are in their totality the right to decent, wise, just, responsive, stable government in the circumstances of a given time and place. Under such a government, a partnership Burke calls it, "the restraints on men, as well as their liberties, are to be reckoned among their rights," and "all men have equal rights, but not to equal things," since a level-

ing egalitarianism, which does not reward merit and ability is harmful to all and is unjust as well.

Because all these thoughtful analyses are couched in the abstract, to predict how a judge will decide a case based on a preconceived label is at best a shaky, if not a downright imperfect, diversion. Yet the effort continues unabated, with the main journalistic effort taking the form of a track record tally. It is a quantitative analysis that proceeds by inductive reasoning from decisions made in specific cases that are then generalized into a conclusion. Don't include me as a devotee of this dichotomy. I think danger exists in calling the shot either by trying to characterize the judge as an apostle of some philosopher or by running a tab on who won what case on which the judge sat. I think it is far more productive to consider at least three basic concepts that go into the judicial process: legal philosophy, jurisprudence and jurisprudential temperament.

A full discussion of these elements is necessary if we are to find what Holmes called predictability, or what Llewellyn called reckonability, in the law. Some prophetic quality is very much desired in the law. We need predictability so that, in Roscoe Pound's words, judges will find the grounds of decision, counselors the basis of assured prediction as to the course of decision, and individuals reasonable guidance toward conducting themselves in accordance with the demands of the social order.

B. Legal Philosophy

Let's start with some definitions. Because these are my own formulations, I will emphasize, with a nod to Felix Cohen, that a definition I give here is either useful or useless: "It is not true or false, any more than a New Year's resolution or an insurance policy." I make a distinction between philosophy of law and *a* philosophy of law. When I speak of philosophy, I am addressing a very broad inquiry into what the relationship between individuals and government ought to be. In this context, the problems of legal philosophy are problems of normative political philosophy. So perceived, philosophy of law deals with the chief ideas that are common to rules and methods of law as legal precepts in the aggregate. Legal philosophy also deals with the various disciplines that bear directly on the wise solution of a galaxy of problems. It inquires into the problems of terminology, legal methods, the role of precedent, statutory interpretation, underlying rationale, the use of different types of authority, the efficacy of various controls and their operation in diverse factual scenarios, and the basic issues concerning the values that are implemented.

When I speak of *a* legal philosophy, I am addressing the specific answers to these basic inquiries forthcoming from very respectable thinkers, both in academia and on the bench. Each thinker probably articulates or at least demonstrates some particular legal philosophy. Hence, each of their individual solutions to myriad problems of judicial decision-making is what I call *a* legal philosophy.

Decision-making in the law is not a science capable of being reduced to a neat formula. It is confusing and complex. It involves concepts that general philosophers have found difficult to explain—volition, will, intention, action, choice and responsibility. Philosophy of law appears to embrace the same problems present in moral evaluation. It addresses those aspects of human nature implicated in other branches of philosophy; philosophy of mind and of action as well as philosophical psychology, all of which describe the nature and relationship of thought, feeling and action. Because there are no pat answers, it should be expected that individual thinkers would come up with divergent views. Hence, the institutional imperative for a multi-judge court.

Some philosophers, for example, have argued that governments exist only to benefit their citizens—the classic Jeremy Bentham utilitarian theory—and that any governmental action is justified only when, and to the extent that, it contributes to the general well-being. Others argue for a more limited government form. They contend that persons are endowed with rights and that government actions are limited by these rights. This theory states that no action is justifiable if it interferes with these rights, and that governments exist to see that rights are protected and to promote well-being only when doing so does not involve infringement of rights. Most of these philosophers give primacy to the individual, but there are those, especially from ancient societies, as well as Fascists and Nazis, who give primacy to the state as an end in itself. Legal philosophy concerns an inquiry into what kind of society is best; *a* legal philosophy tells us what kind that is.

It is probably safe to say that most modern legal philosophy descends from Jeremy Bentham's benefit theory or utilitarianism—the goal of morality is to maximize pleasure and minimize pain. The goal is the greatest happiness for the greatest number. Bentham's basic concepts have been challenged, to be sure. The principal anti-utilitarian arguments state that other moral goals exist besides pleasure, pain and happiness, and that, moreover, these factors cannot be quantified. Notwithstanding scholarly criticism of Benthamism, I doubt that any appellate judge ever takes a strong position without sincerely believing that his solution is predicated on some theory of benefit.

Ronald Dworkin and John Rawls emphasize that a theory of rights and liberty is more realistic and accurate than the benefits theory. Where so many facets of legal philosophy are concerned, oversimplification is a perilous exercise, but I think we can generalize to the extent that two major schools of philosophical thought are popular today. The utilitarian takes it to be a self-evident truth that governments exist to benefit their citizens. I have often quoted Harry W. Jones, late Columbia Cardozo Professor of Jurisprudence, in this respect: "A legal rule or a legal institution is a *good* rule or institution when—that is, to the extent that—it contributes to the establishment and preservation of a social environment in which the quality of human life can be spirited, improving and unimpaired." Liberty is *one* of several benefits to be conferred on persons. The rights theorists believe otherwise. They believe that governments exist to preserve the independence of individuals from unwarranted interference from other individuals and from government itself. Under this theory, at least under that espoused by Professor Ronald Dworkin, in exercising rights, liberty is a "trump" over decisions to implement other benefits through law because it can be derived from the moral presumption that each person is to be treated with equal respect and concern. Dworkin teaches that we have inherited a moral commitment to equality, to equal respect and concern for others, which must underlie any allocation of benefits.

All philosophers deal with data about what people say and think and what they do. They critically interpret this data by submitting these raw materials to tests of consistency, coherence and justifiability. They test the data by considering both the merits of a particular view of society reflected in a judicial decision (or legislative action) and the role of law that the decision exemplifies. In so doing, the philosopher examines the ethical choice that has been made. When it comes to ethics, a case can be made that legal philosophers, as well as judges, fail to distinguish between their own preferences and the preferences of those affected by the action. A society that never has experienced free speech and self government may not include aspects of liberty in its notion of welfare. Migrant farm workers, unemployed urban black teenagers and shack dwellers in Appalachia may enthusiastically prefer a meaningful wage, decent housing and regular food over an abstract guarantee of free speech, free association, free mobility and free enterprise. One can argue that these liberty values are primarily middle class values that are fundamental only to that class. As Richard Neely stated, then Chief Justice of the West Virginia Supreme Court of Appeals, "Authorities of either the right or left argue that the right to a job, security from criminal violence, and a more equal distribution of wealth are far more 'fundamental' values of the working class." There are preferences in our society, and all judges must recognize this.

For our purposes, I am limiting theories of the philosophers to the uses to which a legal institution has been or may be put and not to the type of institutions they advocate. I am, therefore, not so much interested in descriptive questions about law as I am about normative questions; about how judges assess laws and legal systems in terms of their purposes and how one can evaluate the performance of judges. The inquiry involves not only metaphysics, or the study of the nature of things, but also the philosophy of language. Additionally, this study depends on the recognition that legal philosophies develop and evolve from judicial resolution of real disputes involving concrete facts. Yet though facts be uncontroverted, as we have seen in many constitutional law cases emanating from the federal courts, idiosyncratic notions of ethics run rampant in the process. Each judge is an observer, himself a part of the cosmos he observes, and he has a particular station in it. The functions of the judge's mind and emotions create private perspectives and feelings of wonder, adventure, curiosity and, ultimately, psychic satisfaction. We all have our minimum beliefs and radical presuppositions. All these go into the selection, if not the creation, of the first principle upon which we base our result. Some judges take as first principles nothing more than their accidental prejudices. On this, in constitutional law at least, hangs the distribution of access and power among various groups and institutions. These first principles are what the law of the Constitution is about. According to Bickel, "They change over time and develop, and become entrenched as they gather common assent. Beyond them lies policy, and there lie our differences."

Starting points in legal philosophy as in general philosophy are the universals, first principles of some kind, legal or moral. Critical, however, must be the understanding that although a reasoning process is always present, indeed, highly refined, satisfaction with the result is always dependent upon congeniality with the initial proposition of the analysis. The inference proceeds from one "ought to be" to another. In this respect then, legal philosophy is identical with ethical philosophy. We cannot discover an absolute ethical truth, and probably not an absolute legal truth. The closest we can come is where a particular "settled" legal precept forms the initial proposition. Where the analysis proceeds from abstract first principles and not hefty, hearty precedent, less concordance in the result can be expected.

John Hart Ely emphasized that lawyers and judges cannot be the best persons imaginable to tell good moral philosophy from bad. Clergy, novelists, perhaps historians, to say nothing of professional moral philosophers, seem more sensible for the job. I am reminded that some decades past, it was suggested that columnist Walter Lippmann, although not a lawyer, was a fine choice for the Supreme Court. From all this, we can safely conclude that legal philosophy can be perceived as a branch of a subdivision of general philosophy. We may conclude that its study is more practical than theoretical, and that it constitutes a study of general first principles, as distinguished from specific and secondary precepts.

I have dwelt on the theory of legal philosophy at length because what I propose to discuss in the musings that follow are certain concepts that may be different, one to the other, yet they are related to legal philosophy and to each other. I will discuss federal judges not from the standpoint of a label or nickname, but, as stated above, from the standpoint of legal philosophy, jurisprudence and jurisprudential temperament.

C. Jurisprudence

I perceive jurisprudence as a concept that is separate and apart from legal philosophy. The principles of legal philosophy are the abstract moral and legal principles, or doctrines or conceptions, that I have called first or supereminent principles. Standing by themselves, first principles do not carry the horsepower of legal rules. They do not describe a detailed legal consequence of a detailed set of facts. I perceive jurisprudence as something else, best described as a body of law that has formal features. It is a system of rules, promulgated by those with power and authority, backed by sanctions, and regulating public behavior. In choosing the term "jurisprudence," I am probably influenced by the expression currently in use in France to describe case law—*la jurisprudence*. Although case law in the French civil law tradition does not have the strong bite of precedent present in the common law countries, the name given to French case law nevertheless expresses at least part of what I comprehend. My meaning goes much further. I use jurisprudence to describe a system of obligatory norms, both substantive and procedural, that shape and regulate the life of a people in a given state (and here I use the term, state, in both the international and American sense). Any valid legal rule is a norm if it is considered a command in the John Austin sense. Yet this binding quality may also spring from the "will" of parties to a transaction as well as from a legislator or it may emerge from the customs of a people or from a general belief that a norm is a rule expressing the notion that somebody ought to act in a certain way.

A given jurisprudence may be in effect for a given people at a given period. For example, when we commonly refer to ancient Roman law, German law, Italian law, British law, Pennsylvania law, or law of a federal judicial circuit or the U.S. Supreme Court or Congress, we are referring to the jurisprudence of a particular system. Moreover, this jurisprudence takes the form of a body of legal precepts more or less defined, the element to which Jeremy Bentham referred when he said that law was an aggregate of legal precepts. I suppose we may call jurisprudence the by-laws of a given society or rules that govern a given social order. It is law as it is, not as it ought to be. It is more properly a juridical science than a philosophy.

I find it necessary to distinguish between legal philosophy and jurisprudence. Although these are two important elements that go into the make-up of a judge's personality, this distinction is seldom made today by those who evaluate judges and judging. Yet there are grey areas where the line of demarcation between the two concepts is evanescent, if not nonexistent. Sometimes, when we think we are addressing substantive law, it may be more philosophy than jurisprudence, or maybe a little of both. The concepts are not mutually exclusive. Take, for example, two dimensions of law articulated by Roscoe Pound. In addition to being a legal precept in the aggregate sense, law may be considered as "a body of traditional ideas as to how legal precepts should be interpreted and applied and causes decided, and a traditional technique of developing and applying legal precepts whereby these precepts are eked out, extended, restricted, and adapted to the exigencies of administration of justice." Moreover, law may be considered as "a body of philosophical, political, and ethical ideas as to the end of law, and as to what legal precepts should be in view thereof."

If a judge is truly following "a body of traditional ideas," he is probably observing the law as it "is" and not as it "ought to be." If we talk about law as it should be, we are not dealing with juridical science, or what we have been calling jurisprudence. Instead, we have entered the world of philosophical generalities. Immanuel Kant suggested that the distinction existed in two simple Latin words. When we ask *quid jus?* we are seeking some general principle of philosophy to help us decide what the law ought to be. When we ask *quid juris?* we are seeking what already has been established as part of the jurisprudence. From this I think we can say that when we seek that which must or ought to be in the law, in contrast to that which is, we are in the realm of legal philosophy. As I said before, this can be an extremely subjective exercise with deontological overtones. I think we can safely say that when a judge resorts to legal philosophy for assistance, he or she looks at law in its logical universality, seeks its origins, notes the general characteristics of its historical development, and tests it according to very personal ideals of justice, personal ideals that must be drawn from pure reason in order to avoid idiosyncratic arbitrariness.

But unfortunately the line between what the law *is* and what it *ought to be* is not always a bright one. One legal precept, pushed to the limit of its logic, may point to one result; another precept, followed with like logic, may point with equal certainty to another result. For example, assume the presence of two contradictory legal precepts and that a choice must be made between the two. Where choice of two competing precepts is involved, and often it is, are we faced with a case of what the law *is* or what it *ought to be*? Is the answer found in the jurisprudence, or is a resort to general philosophical principles necessary? Or take the questions posed by Cardozo:

> If a precedent is applicable, when do I refuse to follow it? If no precedent is applicable, how do I reach the rule that will make a precedent for the future? If I am seeking logical consistency, the symmetry of the legal structure, how far shall I seek it? At what point shall the quest be halted by some discrepant custom, by some consideration of the social welfare, by my own or the common standards of justice and morals?

D. Jurisprudential Temperament

It is here where that quality which I call jurisprudential temperament, or the judge's intuition, comes into play. This temperament invariably influences the decision. It inclines the decision one way or another. It is a major determinant of whether the case is controlled by precedent or settled law. That is to say, this temperament determines whether the result is found in the jurisprudence, or whether the result requires a choice between two competing precepts, also in the jurisprudence, or whether the case requires movement to square one—recourse to first principles. In the federal courts, especially in constitutional law spinoffs in actions brought under 42 U.S.C. § 1983, the judge's view of the role of the court is all-important. There is probably more subjectivity brought into play in these cases, more activity on the intuition scale, than in any other aspect of the law. Much of this problem can be laid at the door of the Supreme Court because it has served up a mishmash that furnishes no identifiable criteria as to what are garden variety common law torts dressed in the tinsel and glitter of Fourteenth Amendment deprivations and what are truly important and, to use a favorite word, "fundamental" rights. To federal circuit and district judges, this may be what Winston Churchill is reported to have said of a pudding someone served him: it seems to lack a theme.

Yet I hasten to add that federal court decision-making is not subjectivity run rampant. In terms of numbers, quite the contrary is true. As I indicated before, most tasks, perhaps eighty to ninety percent, involve a kind of mechanical process: the law and its application alike are clear; or the law is clear and the sole question is its application to the facts. The results in these cases are often predetermined, some, from the instant the complaint is filed. But where the result is not predetermined and the law is not clear, the courts are faced with what Hart called the "penumbral" cases, where the language of the legislation or the Constitution is intentionally general. We must recognize that some statutory language is inevitably vague because the legislator who can anticipate and decide all the particular cases that will fall under a given statute has yet to be born.

Whether judges must, in certain cases, resort to a penumbral area of the law reflects a value judgment and is indicative of the judge's jurisprudential temperament. Some judges have lower thresholds than others, and are more inclined to find solace in shades and fringes rather than the black letter law. But when they so function, it means that they have exhausted the guidance that hefty, hearty precedents can give and they feel that they must turn to other resources. These resources are found in the body of first or supereminent principles, legal or moral, that form the body of legal philosophy. Dworkin suggested that when this occurs, the decision depends "on the judge's own preferences among a sea of respectable extralegal standards, any one in principle eligible, because if that were the case we could not say that any rules were binding." In this respect, the nature of the temperament may be reflected by the particular choice of moral values offered by diverse philosophers. Those whom we may call the naturalists will claim that law is best explained by reference to natural moral principles, principles inherent in the notion of an ideal society and the moral potentiality of persons. Yet Austinian positivists will claim that law is best understood formally as a system of orders, commands, or rules enforced by power. Moreover, although consistency is required of a legal system, that is to say, stated reasons in the cases must be consistent with legal or moral principles, the collection of private moral decisions by judges need not necessarily be consistent. The judge may pick and choose in various cases among the various philosophies expressed by our writers and judges, one time following a rights theorist, another time, a garden variety Benthamite.

But to understand jurisprudential temperament is to recognize that the judge's initial reaction as to whether a case is controlled by precedent (or by unambiguous statutory language) or comes within what Hart called the penumbral area is itself a gauge of that temperament. As I said before, we judges have different thresholds, or as Emerson said, "We boil at different degrees." What makes a case controversial or difficult at times is precisely this difference. It makes the difference whether a utilitarian weighing of material benefits is preempted by a right. Dworkin offers some advice here. A useful definition of a hard case is one in which existing case law and statutes, the presence of precedents and other immediately relevant rules of decision, tend to generate or fit a result that offends the judge's intuitions about benefit and harm. These are the intuitions that constitute his temperament. Yet these reactions should not be mechanical, as the label-tossers of "liberal" and "conservative" would have us believe. Neither, however, should they be unpredictable. Our legal system is both a system and a history of reasons; reasons that judges have given for past determinations and reasons that embody many conceptions of human nature. The judge's matured decision must be informed by this history. His own determination of benefit and harm will be informed by consulting the justifications offered by other judges in other relevant opinions. Dworkin described this task as an ideal, and stated that it demands a judicial Hercules.

But alas, we are not all Hercules. Judges are merely human beings. The inflow from the cumulative experience of the judiciary mixes with what is already in the judge's mind. What is already there is an accumulation of personal experience including tendencies, prejudices and maybe biases. I don't mean conscious biases, but the unconscious ones that any person may have and which the judge cannot eradicate because he does not know they are there. One of these may be a bias in favor of the justice or equity of the particular case and against any precedent or law that seems to deny it. This is an example of temperament. When such a feeling dominates, the judge's mental notes may emphasize those facts that he deems to be significant; the insignificant, being omitted, will disappear from his memory. The facts will be molded to fit the justice of the case, what Lord Devlin calls "the aequum et bonum," and the law will be stretched. Yet another judge may possess the same intensity of justice for the case, but will refuse to stretch the law, and instead state, "We are constrained to hold ..." In these two cases, the feelings of justice are the same. But disparate jurisprudential temperaments command different results.

Another factor of temperament to be considered is the treadmill upon which United States circuit judges run these days. The judge must possess highly refined administrative talents simply to keep current, let alone to allow time for research and reflection. (Most do have sufficient administrative talents, but some do not and indeed are constantly harried.) We exhibit a wry smile when we read such statements as one emanating from Alexander Bickel: "Judges have, or should have, the *leisure*, the training, and the insulation to follow the ways of the scholar in pursuing the ends of government."

I have emphasized the complexities that abide within concepts of legal philosophy, jurisprudence and jurisprudential temperament only to illustrate the sophistication of our subject matter. I turn now to examine the interplay of these concepts when judges interpret the Constitution.

Constitutional Law Interpretation

Concededly a primary basis of criticism of the federal courts is the use of constitutional interpretation to alter social and political, as well as juridical, customs and traditions. Our remarkable Constitution is unique. British Prime Minister William Gladstone described our Constitution as "the most wonderful work ever struck off at a given time by the brain and purpose of man." Yet the Constitution is a "most wonderful work" because it is more a moral statement than a set of positive law norms, more a declaration of rights than a set of by-laws for society. The United States Constitution sets forth a frame of government that the courts must interpret constantly to accommodate the changes in community moral standards. The Constitution descends from the Magna Carta and the English Declaration and Bill of Rights of 1688 and 1689, and contains certain fundamental principles of right and justice. These principles are entitled to prevail of their own intrinsic excellence, regardless of the interpretations of those who dominate government at any particular period and regardless of those who wield the physical resources of the community.

A. John Marshall

Interpretations by prominent legal philosophers on the bench have charted the course of this nation. Among these was John Marshall, who came to the Supreme Court not only at the right time, but whose long tenure justifies his paramount place in our history. If Marshall had proclaimed only the decision in *Marbury v. Madison* he still would be remembered. Marshall, however, wrote for the Court in *Fletcher v. Peck, Dartmouth College v. Woodward, McCulloch v. Maryland, Cohens v. Virginia, Gibbons v. Ogden* and *Osborn v. Bank of the United States.* Jethro K. Lieberman succinctly has described the leadership of Marshall in these cases: "These seven decisions made the Union that the Civil War preserved. It was a breathtaking, prodigious achievement. The majestic sweep of his opinions gave flesh and blood to the Constitutional skeleton."

B. The Warren Court

Marshall steered toward one goal—his grand vision for a unified, federalized nation. His domination of the Court was perhaps matched by only one other influence in our judicial history—the justices of the Warren Court with their grand vision for an egalitarian society. *Brown v. Board of Education* was the overture, trumpeting stirring notes of the Warren Court's theme for this country. Recognizing that the theme would first produce massive discord, and realizing that the *Brown* decision could not be immediately enforced, a year after the initial decision, the Court announced the "with all deliberate speed" formula.

Shortly, a full orchestration of our society set in: the Court outlawed bible reading and all other religious activities in public schools; ordered reapportionment of the House of Representatives, of both houses of state legislatures, and of local governments on a one-man, one-vote basis; reformed numerous aspects of state and federal criminal procedure, extensively enhancing the rights of the accused, including juvenile offenders; made wire-tapping and eavesdropping subject to the Fourth Amendment's prohibition against unreasonable searches and seizures, and held that evidence obtained in violation of that prohibition may not be admitted in state or federal trials; and laid down a comprehensive set of rules governing the admissibility of confessions and the conduct of police toward persons arrested. The Warren Court greatly expanded the concept of state action under the Fourteenth Amendment, thus enabling the federal courts and Congress to reach out and prohibit private discrimination. The Court also limited the power of state and federal governments to forbid the use of birth-control devices; to restrict travel; to expatriate naturalized or native-born citizens; to deny employment to persons whose associations were deemed subversive; and to apply the laws of defamation. Egalitarianism was the watchword and accompanying themes enlarged the dominion of law and centralized the law-giving function in national institutions, including the federal courts.

Notwithstanding the great progress made under the equal protection and due process clauses, the country paid a price. In the minds of many people, the federal courts represented the ultimate relief from every social, political or economic ill. Heightened expectations became commonplace and still are present today. These expectations are chiefly responsible for the litigation explosion in the federal courts and are the source of great disappointment to many in our society who rap at our courthouse doors and often leave in dejected spirits because they do not quite understand that many limitations on our activity exist. Three quarters of a century ago, Roscoe Pound sounded a warning:

> [W]hen men demand much of law, when they seek to devolve upon it the entire burden of social control, when they seek to make it do the work of the home and of the church, enforcement of law comes to involve many difficulties.... The purposes of the legal order are [then] not all upon the surface and it may be that many whose nature is by no means anti-social are out of accord with some or many of these purposes.... [It is then that] we begin to hear complaint that laws are not enforced and the forgotten problem of the limitations upon effective legal action once more becomes acute.

C. Universal Principles

Constitutional interpretation draws essentially on universal principles. At times there appears to be a clash between two sets of ethics denominated by Max Weber as an ethics of responsibility and an ethics of conscience. Weber stated that the ethics of responsibility require accepting unpleasant truths, the limits of knowledge and of human nature, the costs of actions and sometimes the cost of refusing to take action. The ethics of conscience require reminding humankind of its moral duty to live up to its highest potentiality and refrain from acting solely out of expedient or base motives. Clearly, those societies function best in which the practitioners of the ethics of responsibility and of conscience are at least well-matched.

At other times, the collision occurs in the disagreement over interpreting the Constitution as a moral statement. The Benthamites exalt the goal of morality by maximizing pleasure and minimizing pain, thereby conferring a benefit on society. They advocate pleasure and pain as the common denominator of all morally relevant experiences. Even the Benthamites will disagree among themselves, however, as to what constitutes pleasure and pain. Our sordid history in race relations attests to that disagreement. What is deemed a long-awaited benefit to blacks may come with great pain to the multitude of red-necks.

Beyond intramural skirmishes among the utilitarians is the rights theorists' approach to the moral values contained in the Constitution. The rights theorists argue that life is more than pleasure, happiness and the avoidance of pain. The right to liberty, for example, is paramount. According to this view, the benefit of liberty has priority over all material benefits. The ever-present dilemma is to determine what things are benefits and how much divergence exists after we identify these things. When it comes to public affairs, Rawls argued that considerations of liberty must be "prior in lexical ordering" to conditions of social welfare. I think this means that no matter how abundant and equitable the distribution of material comforts may be, the most extensive liberty that is possible for all members of society cannot be overridden. The problem that emerges is obvious. Is this philosophy shared by those members of society presently deprived of material, as distinguished from theoretical, benefits, and thus deprived of decent food, shelter, health care and job opportunities? If these persons had their druthers, would they reject all these creature comforts for abstract freedoms of speech, assembly and religion, and other tangible aspects of liberty? As I inquired earlier, are these strictly middle class values, or are they universally shared? In this context, the clash between adherents to the benefit and rights theories, rather than the simplistic labels of "liberal," "conservative" or "moderate," characterizes much of our present constitutional law litigation.

Perhaps more obvious are the strident clangs in criminal procedure that loudly broadcast divergent philosophies on how to balance properly the interests set forth in the Bill of Rights. Herbert Packer suggested that judges appear to adopt one of two theoretical positions. He called the first position the "crime control" model. The goal of this model is to streamline the arrest and processing of offenders so that crime is deterred through efficient enforcement. The second category, the "due process" model, places special emphasis on the need to control governmental interference in individuals' lives. This model contends that abuse is frequent in law enforcement, thus necessitating tight guidelines regulating the use of confessions and the conduct of searches and arrests, providing for the availability of counsel, and protecting against self-incrimination. Certainly, the so-called "conservatives" seem to adhere to the "crime control" model, and the "liberals" to the "due process" model.

Recourse to universal principles inclines a judge's decision one way or another, depending upon the jurisprudential temperament of the judge, but this recourse cannot demean the importance of precedents. Judges always use precedents in the publicly stated reasoned elaboration set forth to justify their constitutional decisions. The reliance on precedent is a process that is as delicate as it is fraught with responsibility, because in recent years settled disciplines of state law have been superseded by newly fashioned constitutional precepts. This paradigm of judicial creativity churns out new jurisprudence in which the temperament of the judge draws upon a subjective legal philosophy to declare what the law ought to be. If I were to attempt to generalize, I should say that the major question in the controversial constitutional law cases is not new. It is that posed by Heraclitus: "The major problem of human society is to combine that degree of liberty without which law is tyranny, with that degree of law without which liberty becomes license."

D. Public Opinion

At any given time a body of beliefs exists, convictions, sentiments, accepted principles or firmly-rooted prejudices, which, taken together, make up the public opinion of an era, or what may be called the reigning or predominating current of opinion. Sir Robert Peel was more cynical than accurate in 1820 when he described public opinion as "the tone of England—of that great compound of folly, weakness, prejudice, wrong feeling, right feeling, obstinacy, and newspaper paragraphs...." As the public has opinions and beliefs, so do judges. Moreover, the whole body of beliefs existing at any given time generally may be traced to certain fundamental assumptions that, whether they are true or false, are believed by judges (and the public) to be true with such confidence that these beliefs hardly appear to bear the character of assumptions.

These currents that influence both court decisions and legislation acquire their force and volume only by degrees, and are in their turn liable to be checked or superseded by other and adverse currents, which themselves gain strength only after a lapse of time. We, however, cannot talk of a prevalent belief or opinion as "being in the air" or "brooding in the sky." Rarely does a widespread conviction spring up spontaneously among the multitude. John Stuart Mill was absolutely right, I think, when he said: "The initiation of all wise and noble things, comes and must come, from individuals; generally at first from some one individual." The discoverer of the new conception, or some follower who has embraced it with enthusiasm, preaches it to his friends or disciples, often in a classroom, or expresses it either in a professional or popular journal, and they who hear and read become impressed with its importance and its truth, and gradually a whole new school accepts a new creed. When the apostles are either persons endowed with special ability or, what is quite as likely, are persons who are deemed free of a bias, whether moral or intellectual, they loom in fashioning public opinion and influencing judicial decisions. We have seen this phenomenon in many branches of substantive law—Samuel Williston influencing contract law, William Prosser with torts, Joseph Beale and later Willis Reese and Robert Leflar formulating conflicts of law theories, and Charles Alan Wright, Bernard Ward, Herbert Wechsler and Henry Hart developing procedures and court jurisdiction concepts, to name but a few.

When constitutional law is involved, this phenomenon assumes *a fortiori* proportions. An entire school of constitutional law philosophy that has emerged essentially from articles published in the Ivy League law reviews and books has settled successfully in federal court opinions. Whatever we may do in cases involving other legal disciplines, when it comes to constitutional law, I do not think we follow the example of Rabelais' famed Judge Bridlegoose:

> [H]aving well and exactly seen, surveyed, overlooked, reviewed, recognized, read and read over again, turned and tossed about, seriously perused and examined the preparatories, productions, evidences, proofs, allegations, depositions, cross, speeches, contradictions ... and other such confects and spiceries, both at the one and the other side, as a good judge ought to do, I posit on the end of the table in my closet all the pokes and bags of the defendant—that being done I thereafter lay down upon the other end of the same table the bags and satchels of the plaintiff [and then I roll the dice,] little small dice [when

there are many bags and] other large, great dice, fair and goodly ones
[when there are fewer bags.]

On the contrary, I believe that with decision-making in constitutional law every
rule of conduct must, whether or not the judge perceives the fact, rest on some
general universal principle—some moral principle, personally and subjec-
tively held by the judge; some conception of proper community moral standards, if you will—about which he feels strongly enough to reduce that
conception to constitutional efficacy. It is more often than not a phenomenon
of "Have opinion, need case."

E. "Federal Courtization" of Society

At times new waves of belief or opinion drown the substantive law previously established by court decision or by the legislature, in most cases, the
state legislature, but occasionally Congress. In the process, the jurisprudence,
whether termed positive or substantive law, is replaced with newly-minted
constitutional dogma. This process properly can be called the modern "federal courtization," the "constitutionalization" or "the Fourteenth Amendmen-
tization" of our society. A case can be made that the extent to which this
federalization occurs varies proportionately with the judges' personal beliefs
or opinions relating to the trust or distrust of the public, of state and federal
officials, and state and federal legislators. Implicated here are several interrelated universal principles of political science and general philosophy.

The most primitive of these principles, and perhaps the most anchored in
the political science bedrock, is the centuries-old clash between the Hamil-
tonian and Jeffersonian views of democracy. Thomas Jefferson unquestion-
ably lost this battle in the federal courts in the past fifty, if not one hundred,
years. With one major exception, the trend has been toward federal domination over states' rights either by determinations that Congress has pre-empted
a field of activity through the commerce clause or, more recently, by reliance
on section five of the Fourteenth Amendment, or by determinations that particular state action somehow violates the Constitution. The sop to states' rights
occurred in 1938 with *Erie Railroad Co. v. Tompkins*, in which the Supreme
Court declared that substantive state law should control in diversity cases.

I find in many of us the "philosopher king" syndrome to which Learned
Hand once made reference. A philosopher king is akin to what Joseph Epstein
described as a "virtucrat": "The virtucrat is certain he has virtue on his side.
The virtue being laid claim to is public virtue; it is the virtue that comes from
the certainty that one's own opinions are the only correct opinions. The vir-

tucrat is a prig, but a prig in the realm of opinion." I find this attitude somewhat pervasive among federal judges and content myself with only reporting
its existence without either endorsing it or disapproving it. We must recall
what the distinguished political scientist, Robert Dahl, has said: "After twenty-
five centuries, almost the only people who seem to be convinced of the advantage of being ruled by philosopher-kings are ... a few philosophers." Yet the
philosopher-king mentality has an extremely respectable pedigree. For example, we can trace the mentality to Plato, who taught that in the state three
classes are distinguished: that of the wise, destined to dominate; that of the
warriors, who must defend the social order; and that of the artisans and farmers, who must feed society. I hasten to add that most federal judges do not
consider themselves warriors, artisans, or farmers. In ancient times, in the
Orient, the supreme object of intellectual activity was religion; in Greece, it
was philosophy; and in Rome, it was law. Federal judges seem to be more
philosophers than lawyers, to use a kind expression; more autocrats of the intellect, to be unkind. Some examples of this tendency follow.

F. Distrust of State Institutions

Reflected in the opinions of certain federal judges, I see a philosophy of
hauteur, if not deep distrust of state law, state courts, state government and state
and locally elected officials. In discussing the Burger Court in 1978, John Hart
Ely commented:

> The current Court's constitutional jurisprudence is ... not content
> with limiting its intervention to disputes with respect to which there
> exist special reasons for supposing that elected officials cannot be
> trusted—those involving the constriction of the political process or
> the victimization of politically defenseless minorities. Instead, it im-
> portantly involves the Court in the merits of the policy or ethical judg-
> ment sought to be overturned, measuring those merits against some
> set of "fundamental" value judgments. This is not by any means an
> orientation original to the Burger Court. It plainly marked the work
> of the Court that decided *Lochner* v. *New York* and its 200-case prog-
> eny.

I neither endorse nor inveigh against this concept of political science. I state
only that this attitude of personal-concepts-of-ethics-equals-constitutional-
law not only does exist, but is extremely alive and flourishing.

This is a classic example of the nonapplicability of the labels "liberal" and
"conservative." As a result, although the federal courts are charged with the

evolution and application of society's fundamental principles, the major problem is to decide what elevates a garden variety, run-of-the-mill value or principle to the exalted status of "fundamental." Ely suggested, and I agree completely, that although the judge or commentator in question may be talking in terms of some "objective," non-personal method of identification, what he is likely really to be "discovering," whether or not he is fully aware of it, are his own values. In any event, I do not think you can be a true liberal or populist, in the traditional political sense, and decry the presence of politics in the basic schema of the republic. Traditionally, the call of the liberal has been "The people, yes!" Yet under the guise of the First Amendment, some judges seem hell-bent on taking politics out of politics.

For example, in *Elrod v. Burns*, the Court found to be taboo the 200-year-old practice of firing by the victorious party those political supporters of the losers. Society long has recognized that patronage in employment played a significant role in democratizing American politics and that before such practice fully developed, an "aristocratic" class dominated political affairs, a tendency that persisted in areas where patronage did not become prevalent. Yet notwithstanding Holmes' admonition that "[i]f a thing has been practised for two hundred years by common consent, it will need a strong case for the Fourteenth Amendment to affect it," certain judges obviously adhered to the philosophy that the lifeblood of political party strength is very tainted and that the First Amendment will cleanse it all. Former Chief Justice of the West Virginia Supreme Court Richard Neely has commented:

> In elected politics, the legislature and executive take idealistic, energetic, ambitious young men and turn them into whores in five years; the judiciary takes good, old, tired, experienced whores and turns them into virgins in five years. The men are not the source of either transformation—they are of the same type, particularly since judges are either graduates or rejects of politics. The decisive factor is the institution—whether the exact same creatures are quartered in the local house of ill fame or in the Temple of the Vestal Virgins.

As a result, the philosophy "To the victor belongs the spoils" has given way to "If you are independently wealthy or can muscle enough Political Action Committee money to buy TV time and street workers, you, too, can be the victor."

I think that the same philosophy, to a reduced extent, underlies the demise of the law of defamation as to public persons. The Court discarded more than 200 years of protecting either a property or a liberty interest, as the case may be, in one's reputation in *New York Times v. Sullivan*. The formidable scholarship that underlies these two landmark cases was not drawn from orthodox

American jurisprudence. The decisions emerged from first principles of philosophical universality as expressed in personal values.

Similarly, the demeaning of state legal remedies caused by an expansive stretch of constitutional dogma in cases brought under 42 U.S.C. § 1983 has occurred. The Court has elevated the traditional tort concepts of assault and battery and at least gross, if not ordinary, negligence to a constitutional dimension when state action is found. Notwithstanding that many of such cases ordinarily would have been brought in state small claims courts, they now are elevated to the exalted level of "federal cases" and enjoy the full panoply of judge, jury and ceremony instead of the more traditional atmosphere of television's Judge Judy.

G. Civil Law/Criminal Law Dichotomy

Yet the personal beliefs and opinions of individual judges reflect an intricacy much more sophisticated than a mere distrust of states. It is more than a simple antipathy toward, to use the pejorative, "states' rights." It goes further than a preference for individual rights as against the state. The problem is much more complex. Over the years in my own court, I have seen judges who will stretch the Fourteenth Amendment to its outer limits in order to grant relief to a plaintiff in a civil action against state officials. I find in these colleagues an antipathy toward the school boards, university and college administrators, hospital superintendents, wardens, governors, mayors and other local, county and state officials. I use the word "antipathy" purposely because in many cases these judges do not evaluate the case on the basis that the plaintiff has met his burden; they proceed to decide in favor of the individual against the social order on little more than a prima facie case. These judges are willing to "constitutionalize" the most mundane aspect of government administration simply because they disagree with the administrative action taken by the official. Often, in essence, these judges merely disagree with the exercise of broad administrative discretion. The disagreement should not be the test for a Fourteenth Amendment violation, yet the annotations to 42 U.S.C. § 1983 show hundreds of cases where this has occurred. These civil cases are examples of the judges' jurisprudential temperaments disclosing a highly developed Platonic complex.

Yet some of these same judges hold different philosophical beliefs and opinions in criminal cases involving the interaction between the Fourteenth Amendment and the defendant. These judges who insist that government officials dot every i and cross every t in the civil administration of justice do not seem to hold police, district attorneys, government prosecutors, and trial judges to the same exacting standards in criminal cases. Perhaps the reasons can be found in the background and experience of federal judges. Many previously served as government prosecutors. Many emerge from law firms that never have represented defendants in criminal cases. Many are very concerned about crime in the streets (often the sidewalks and streets surrounding a federal courthouse located in a metropolitan area are not safe after nightfall). Whatever the reasons, many judicial "libertarians" in civil cases are to the far right of old Justice McReynolds in criminal cases. This, of course, is another reason why simplistic labels of "liberal" or "conservative" should not be attached to federal judges.

Conclusion

I end as I began. As a long time judge-watcher, I believe that attaching one word labels to federal judges is a mighty inexact pastime. Ninety percent of the cases that come before us are rather simple matters implicating issues where the law and its application alike are plain or where the rule of law is certain and the application alone doubtful. Precepts of logical analogy unerringly control these cases. The particular jurisprudential temperament of the judge and his or her legal philosophy do not figure largely in affecting the outcome because the sole inquiry is whether the facts in the compared case are similar or dissimilar with the case at bar. It is merely a matter of comparing one particular with another particular. In the remaining ten percent of the cases, in Cardozo's words, a decision one way or the other "will count for the future, will advance or retard, sometimes much, sometimes little, the development of the law." It is in these cases where the judge's complex personality comes under examination and dissection. Perhaps two anecdotes relating to games show the mix of legal philosophy, jurisprudence and jurisprudential temperament that I have been discussing in these pages. The first comes from Professor Maurice Rosenberg, himself a long time judge-watcher:

> [There is] the well-known fable that has three baseball umpires arguing about how they distinguish balls from strikes during the game. The first one says: "It's simple. I call 'em as I see 'em." The second one snorts: "Huh! I call 'em as they are!" And the third one ends the debate with: "They ain't nothin' til I call 'em!"

The other anecdote comes from Learned Hand:

> Remember what Justice Holmes said about "justice." I don't know what you think about him, but on the whole he was to me the master craftsman certainly of our time; and he said: "I hate justice," which

he didn't quite mean. What he did mean was this. I remember I was once with him; it was a Saturday when the Court was to confer. It was before we had a motor car, and we jogged along in an old coupe. When we got down to the Capitol, I wanted to provoke a response, so as he walked off, I said to him: "Well, sir, goodbye. Do justice!" He turned quite sharply and he said: "Come here, come here." I answered: "Oh, I know, I know." He replied: "That is not my job. My job is to play the game according to the rules."

Our judges run the gamut from playing the game according to the rules to making up the rules as we play the game.

CHAPTER FOURTEEN

MAKING THE DECISION

Author's Note: *This chapter first appeared as text in my book,* The Judicial Process: Text, Materials and Cases, *548–550, 555–557, 572–575, 610–613 (2d ed. West 1996). These are three of a series labeled "Overview" that introduced particular sections of the book. They are reprinted here with permission. This chapter highlights the critical—but often overlooked—step in the judicial process of actually making the decision, an awareness of which will allow the lawyer to better understand how to convince judges and how to win a case.*

"The Why" and "The How"

If courts are not judicial slot machines, some accommodation must be sought between the objectivity of theoretical decision making and the subjectivity that is prevalent in the actual process. To do this, it is important to recognize that the judicial resolution of a legal dispute implicates two separate processes: (1) deciding, or the process of discovering the conclusion, and (2) justifying, or the process of the public explanation of that conclusion.

The anatomy of the decision making process reveals the acquisition of an initial tentative disposition, followed by testing or retesting of that disposition to determine whether it should prevail. Thus, even with the most objective of decision makers, lay and juridical, there is always a risk that an initially acquired disposition will prevail over a later view. H.H. Price characterized this phenomenon as the "preferential character" of the "initial assent." Implicated in the initial disposition and its subsequent testing processes are the judge's personal sympathies and antipathies, his or her political, economic, moral and social prejudices. To recognize this is not to exaggerate its importance because, in the words of Felix Cohen, "actual experience does reveal a significant body of predictable uniformity in the behavior of courts. Law is not a mass of unrelated decisions nor a product of judicial bellyaches."

Nevertheless, if we are to have a complete and accurate understanding of the judicial process, we must be acquainted with personality profiles of those who

judge in order to ascertain the "maturity of the motive," to discern "the intellectual method," and to probe "behind the decision of the forces which it reflects." This more searching analysis may be as important as knowing the naked
holding of the case or its supporting rationale. The lawyer who discovers "why"
the decision was made is the consummate investigator and will probably be
the successful advocate. The lawyer who understands at least that a distinction
does exist between "how" a decision was reached and "why" it was reached is
on the way to becoming a good lawyer. That lawyer has learned that two
processes abide within the judicial process—first, discovering the decision and
second, justifying it—and moreover, how to cope with them.

Putting aside the judge's biography and the external stimuli which contributed
to fashioning his or her total personality, a valuable study of a judge may be
gleaned from the written opinions he or she writes. The substantive law set forth
in the *ratio decidendi* constitutes the "how" of the conclusion, specifically, the reasoning supporting it. Publicly stated procedures of inquiry constitute the "performative utterances" of a court. If properly analyzed, however, the methodologies
that opinion writers use may reveal much more. As we have emphasized, an
identification of the interests that have affected the opinion writer, positively or
negatively, may provide insight into the motivation for the conclusion, or the
"why" of the case. Such study, then, is the earnest work of accomplished advocates, who become true legal scientists. They identify and isolate, one by one,
the tools of decision making used by a given judge, or by the judges of a multi-
member court before which they practice. Having identified, isolated and col-
lated, the advocates relate their findings to the cause at hand. They translate
forensic data into arguments that reflect the methodologies to which the court
is hospitable and that will, therefore, be effective and probably persuasive.

On the other side of the bench, judges who epitomize intellectual honesty
always will equate the publicly stated reasons for their decisions with their true
motivation in reaching them. Yet even as to such judges, Herman Oliphant re-
assures us that "[a] study with more stress on their *non-vocal behavior, i.e.,*
what the judges actually do when stimulated by the facts of the case before
them, is the approach indispensable to exploiting scientifically the wealth of material in the cases." A classic example of a Supreme Court case that did not
publicly express the process of discovery, the motivation for the decision, is
Fay v. Noia. The unexpressed motivation, "the why," for the case: a distrust of
state court fact-finding and a lack of confidence that state courts would vindicate the constitutional rights of unpopular litigants, to-wit, those convicted
of crime. Fourteen years were to pass until the Court made an oblique reference to the true reason for *Fay.* In *Stone v. Powell,* the majority inserted a very
significant footnote:

The policy arguments that respondents marshal in support of the view that federal habeas corpus review is necessary to effectuate the Fourth Amendment stem from a basic mistrust of the state courts as fair and competent forums for the adjudication of federal constitutional rights. The argument is that state courts cannot be trusted to effectuate Fourth Amendment values through fair application of the rule, and the oversight jurisdiction of this Court on certiorari is an inadequate safeguard. The principal rationale for this view emphasizes the broad differences in the respective institutional settings within which federal judges and state judges operate. Despite differences in institutional environment and the unsympathetic attitude to federal constitutional claims of some state judges in years past, we are unwilling to assume that there now exists a general lack of appropriate sensitivity to constitutional rights in the trial and appellate courts of the several States. State courts, like federal courts, have a constitutional obligation to safeguard personal liberties and to uphold federal law. *Martin v. Hunter's Lessee*, 1 Wheat. 304, 341–344 (1816). Moreover, the argument that federal judges are more expert in applying federal constitutional law is especially unpersuasive in the context of search-and-seizure claims, since they are dealt with on a daily basis by trial level judges in both systems. In sum, there is "no intrinsic reason why the fact that a man is a federal judge should make him more competent, or conscientious, or learned with respect to the [consideration of Fourth Amendment claims] than his neighbor in the state courthouse."

Justice Brennan, author of *Fay v. Noia*, responded in dissent:

Enforcement of federal constitutional rights that redress constitutional violations directed against the "guilty" is a particular function of federal habeas review, lest judges trying the "morally unworthy" be tempted not to execute the supreme law of the land. State judges popularly elected may have difficulty resisting popular pressures not experienced by federal judges given lifetime tenure designed to immunize them from such influences, and the federal habeas statutes reflect the congressional judgment that such detached federal review is a salutary safeguard against any detention of an individual "in violation of the Constitution or laws ... of the United States."

Considering Holmes' definition of law as "the prophecies of what the courts will do in fact and nothing more pretentious," how can lawyers "predict" if publicly stated reasons given to justify a court's decision do not square with the true reasons for reaching it? The answer lies in the ultimate integrity of the judge in expressing in the public opinion, the unpublished original, actual reasons for the decision.

What Is Expected from Our Judges

What we should expect from our judges, at a minimum, is a willingness to *consider* alternative solutions to a problem. A "resulted-oriented" judge, in the sense condemned, is one who consistently resists the act of considering arguments that may be contrary to an initial impression, to the conscious or unconscious initial assent to a given proposition. We cannot expect judicial minds, just as we cannot expect any reflective thinker, to be completely divorced from an initial assent to a proposition in the evaluating process.

What we can expect, however, is that the initial assent to a proposition, giving it a preferential character, will be fluid enough to yield to later impressions. What we can expect is that a judge be sufficiently intellectually interested to respect and consider competing arguments and arrive at an outcome based on sound reason. We can demand that judges channel their interest by means of inquiry and reflection to reach a value judgment as to what the law ought to be, and then to tell us why in clearly understood language.

People do take judicial reasoning seriously, Professor Charles H. Miller observes, and "they are not fools nor being fooled in doing so, at least no more than in other forms of communication or with respect to other strands that form the web of a political culture." Legal reasoning must not be esoteric or artificial. It must be capable of public comprehension and not a ritual understandable only to an elite legal priesthood.

At bottom, we ask our judges to have wisdom, and to have had an education or experience in history, letters, poetry, philosophy, science and the arts. Responding to a young man who had requested advice as to how he should prepare for a law career, Justice Frankfurter once wrote: "No one can be a truly competent lawyer unless he is a cultivated man.... The best way to prepare for the law is to come to the study of the law as a well-read person." He recommended a "truly liberal education" in order to acquire "habits of good thinking" and "the capacity to use the English language on paper and in speech." He also wrote: "No less important for a lawyer is the cultivation of the imaginative faculties by reading poetry, seeing great paintings, in the original or in easily available reproductions, and listening to great music. Stock your mind with the deposit of much good reading, and widen and deepen your feelings by expe-

riencing vicariously as much as possible the wonderful mysteries of the universe."
Learned Hand also fashioned a statement of inspiration:

> I venture to believe that it is as important to a judge called upon to pass
> on a question of constitutional law, to have a bowing acquaintance
> with Acton and Maitland, with Thucydides, Gibbon and Carlyle, with
> Homer, Dante, Shakespeare and Milton, with Machiavelli, Montaigne,
> and Rabelais, with Plato, Bacon, Hume, and Kant as with books which
> have been specifically written on the subject. For in such matters every-
> thing turns upon the spirit in which he approaches the questions be-
> fore him. The words he must construe are empty vessels into which
> he can pour nearly everything he will. Men do not gather figs of this-
> tles, nor supply institutions from judges whose outlook is limited by
> parish or class. They must be aware that there are before them more
> than verbal problems; more than final solutions cast in generaliza-
> tions of universal applicability. They must be aware of the changing
> social tensions in every society which make it an organism; which de-
> mand new schemata of adaptation; which will disrupt it, if rigidly
> confined.

But assuming wisdom in our judges, we are brought to what Harry W. Jones
calls the final and showdown question: if judges are to reach their decisions by way
of a genuinely informed evaluation of the probable consequences on the quality
of human life in society, where do they get the data they need to accomplish that
design? This is especially true in the judicial declaration of public policy. Certainly in the traditional fields of law, the judge may turn to sources of legal scholarship such as treatises, studies, case books and law reviews where a thoughtful
answer may be readily available. At other times, only a vague hint is discernible
to form the proper guidepost; at still other times, there simply is no answer.

But even the great Cardozo, when pressed with the question of where a
judge is to get the social data he needs to know when one interest outweighs
another, gave an answer that at once said it all, and still said nothing: "[H]e must
get his knowledge ... from experience and study and reflection; in brief, from
life itself." Then, too, Professor White noted:

> As legal scholars of the 1950s grew increasingly convinced of the im-
> portance of judicial rationalization, they came to criticize its con-
> temporary manifestations and to formulate a new set of ideals and
> standards for judicial decision making. Reasoned Elaboration, a catch
> phrase coined by Henry Hart and Albert Sacks in 1958, came to sum-
> marize those ideals and standards. The phrase, as applied to the U.S.

Supreme Court, demanded first, that judges give reasons for their decisions; second, that the reasons be set forth in a detailed and coherent manner; third, that they exemplify what Hart called "the maturing of collective thought"; and fourth, that the Court adequately demonstrate that its decisions, in the area of constitutional law, were vehicles for the expression of the ultimate social preferences of contemporary society.

Finally, what is expected from our judges is to protect the solemnity and importance of the judicial process. This is especially important in high profile trials. The trial judge must never become a prisoner of the media and permit extra-judicial versions of the litigation to be described in sidewalk press conferences. A trial is a search for the truth, and the dog of undue controversial advocacy, especially outside the courtroom in an era of sound-bite journalism, must never wag the high noble purpose of a court's quest for the true facts in the cause. The judge is the public's trustee and by his or her oath is sworn to preserve respect for court traditions; the judge must never permit a circus-like peripheral atmosphere to deface or disfigure the public's perception of our judicial system. At a minimum the trial judge must possess an expert's knowledge of the law of evidence and at the end of pre-trial proceedings must be totally familiar with the substantive law of the particular case to avoid delays in the conduct of the trial. Judges and attorneys are officers of the court, but they are not of equal rank. Judges are superior commissioned officers and possess broad discretionary powers to preserve the propriety and decorum of the judicial process.

Factors that Alter Reflective Thinking

In 1922, Charles C. Haines set forth certain categories of factors likely to influence decisions. In the category of remote and indirect factors, he listed general and legal education, family and personal associates, wealth and social position. For direct factors, he listed legal and political experience, political affiliation and opinions, and intellectual and temperamental traits. These factors do affect judicial thinking to some extent. Judges inevitably come to their robes with the stigmata of their past experience. The difficult question is the degree to which any one experiential factor exerts a meaningful influence. For attorneys who appear before the judges, the important consideration is to what extent a given judge's decision will be predictable on the basis of these factors.

A judge's track record on the bench is more likely to furnish indicia to predictability than pre- or extra-judicial experience. New judges from certain geographical and psychological environments that might have suggested the judge would decide social and civil rights matters one way, have adjudicated those cases in a different manner. Court-watching disciplines of journalism, political science and sociology often prove to be wrong. Former prosecutors have become staunch defenders of individual rights in criminal cases. Former plaintiff lawyers in personal injuries actions have become extremely defense-oriented on the bench. Former criminal defense lawyers have become prosecution-oriented. And minority judges and Justices who may have benefitted from affirmative action prove themselves opposed to it once installed on the bench.

With sufficient bench experience, especially on a court that requires opinion writing, a judge's jurisprudential personality may be detected. Moreover, after proper analysis, a certain predictability of approach may be ascertained. More often than not, this requires an identification of the individual, public and societal interests implicated in the litigation, and a determination of the circumstances in which an identifiable interest receives approbation or reprobation.

The media and the academy's favorite labels of "liberal" and "conservative" are of little value. Sheldon Goldman suggests that a more accurate analysis would be an understanding of a judge's position in (1) criminal cases: for the claims of criminal defendants or prisoners, excluding white collar crimes; (2) civil rights cases: for the claims of blacks, women and identifiable minority groups who lack political clout in a given context; (3) labor: for the claims of employees and unions in labor-management cases; (4) private economic cases: for the claims of the insured as opposed to the insurance company; for small businesses when opposed by a large business; for the tenant in landlord-tenant cases; for the debtor or the bankrupt; for the buyer as opposed to the seller; for the stockholder in stockholder suits; against alleged antitrust violators; (5) injured persons: for the claims of injured workers; for the injured or deceased's estate in automobile or other accidents; for the injured in federal tort cases. Professor Goldman intimates that one voting in favor of the foregoing positions is a "political liberal" or an "economic liberal," and that one who votes in favor of the governmental agency in regulation of business cases is also an "economic liberal."

A quality of relative anonymity generally is associated with a judge's activity notwithstanding the fragility of tenure due to political selection processes. State judges who seek reelection, who have either received the approval of the bar or, more important, have not incurred its wrath, usually have no difficulty in being re-elected. Where a volatile political climate is present, the judge is more inclined to conduct him or herself in a manner that seeks the approbation of the bar and the media than to placate identifiable political elements. Where the political climate is more stable, where the judge's political party dominates or where the jurisdiction has a modified Missouri plan in which one runs against no opponent but only against one's record, political considerations are minimized.

"The process of judging, so the psychologists tell us, seldom begins with a premise from which a conclusion is subsequently worked out," Jerome Frank noted. "Judging begins rather the other way around—with a conclusion more or less vaguely formed; a man ordinarily starts with such a conclusion and afterwards tries to find premises which will substantiate it. If he cannot, to his satisfaction, find proper arguments to link up his conclusion with premises which he finds acceptable, he will, unless he is arbitrary or mad, reject the conclusion and seek another." John Dewey instructed that reflective thinking "involves (1) a state of doubt, hesitation, perplexity, mental difficulty, in which thinking originates, and (2) an act of searching, hunting, inquiry, to find material that will resolve the doubt, settle and dispose of the perplexity."

The conscientious judicial decision maker will recognize this and understand that forming tentative conclusions is all part of the reflective thinking process. Experienced appellate judges begin with some general conclusion, or at least alternative conclusions, and then look around for principles and data which will substantiate it or which will enable them to choose intelligently between rival conclusions. But being aware that appellate judges form tentative impressions is not enough. We must be careful not to fall in love with initial conclusions. H.H. Price has explained the danger of the initial assent to any proposition:

> Believing a proposition is, I think, a disposition and not an occurrence or "mental act," though the disposition is not necessarily a very long-lived one and may last only a few seconds.... There is a characteristic sort of mental occurrence which we sometime notice when we are in the process of *acquiring* such a disposition. I am going to call this occurrence "assenting" to the proposition.... When our belief is a reasonable one, this assenting, and especially the initial assent, has a *preferential* character.
>
> Now because of this preferential element in it, assent may look like voluntary choice. But the appearance is deceptive. It is not a free choice at all, but a forced one. If you are in a reasonable frame of mind ... you cannot help preferring the proposition which *your* evidence favors, the evidence *you* are at the moment attending to, though the evidence which other people have may of course be different.... It just is not in your power to avoid assenting to the proposition which [your evidence] favors, or to assent instead to some other proposition when [your evidence] is manifestly unfavorable to it.

Human experience has demonstrated that when there is a lack of disinterestedness there is not likely to be independence of judgment. Lord Chancellor Birkenhead said that the judge

> must purge his mind not only of partiality to persons, but partiality to arguments, a much more subtle matter, for every legal mind is apt to have an innate susceptibility to particular classes of argument. Hume Brown used to say that "a man cannot jump off his own shadow, but the judge must try his best to do so."

Intellectual disinterestedness in a judge, in the words of Harvard Dean and Solicitor General Erwin Griswold, "is a price, achieved only by continual care and striving."

Subtle Extra Judicial Factors

Additional and subtle extra-judicial factors affecting judicial decision makers include a lack of "judicial confidence," slothful work habits and psychological barriers to decision making not present in other professions or other aspects of the legal profession. These factors undermine the quality of the judicial process and, regrettably, there has been little exposure of this problem to public analysis. Unfortunately, I have had experience with several judges, including a U.S. Circuit Judge, who agonized to the detriment of their health when faced with making a decision. To them decision making was constant psychological trauma. This was a genuine affliction that caused them to depart eventually.

Some judges simply lack judicial confidence, stemming from either an actual lack of basic decision making experience as a lawyer or a strongly held feeling that they lack basic intelligence or intellectual strength. This lack is manifested in several ways. One is to adjudicate strictly on the basis of precedent, to articulate no original or reasoned elaboration for a given decision, but simply to note the existence of conflicting precedents, to select one with the unreflective justification that "This is the better reasoned view" without adequate explanation of why it is better. To this judge there is nothing new in the law; decisions must be based on cases that have been pre-digested and pre-packaged by other judges in earlier cases. This is the process condemned by Cardozo in 1921 when he stated that some judges decide cases in accordance with precedents that plainly fit, in a process of search, comparison and little more: "Their notion of their duty is to match the colors of many sample cases spread out upon their desk. The sample nearest in shade supplies the applicable rule."

Another manifestation of lack of judicial confidence is a relatively new phenomenon: an undue reliance on law clerks for the actual decisional process. Over-awed by impressive credentials of law review editors, especially those from the top 15 law schools, and members of the Order of the Coif, a number of judges yield too much responsibility to these judicial assistants. Often this is illustrated by a change in the judge's jural philosophy as law clerks come and go, or at least a change in the judge's opinion writing style which makes it difficult for students of the opinions of these judges to identify the societal, individual or public interests that really have influenced the judge. A leading U.S. Supreme Court Justice, now of happy memory, fit this description. Undue reliance upon law clerks by appellate judges, especially in the highest federal and state appellate levels, is a more serious problem than legal literature and public discussions reveal. It is one thing for a judge to use the clerk as a research and writing assistant; it is quite another thing to abdicate to the clerk the dominating role in both the decision making and opinion writing process.

Another aspect of lack of judicial confidence relates to a felt awareness of personal unworthiness to make final evaluations. To recognize the awesome responsibility in meeting the challenge of "crisis" cases is one thing; to run and to duck the issue to be decided is quite another. Often a judge simply cannot explain "why" a decision is reached, as is evidenced by Holmes' "can't help" formulation: "When I say a thing is true, I mean that I can't help believing it." To decide, and to acknowledge that the responsibility goes with the robe, requires a steadfastness of spirit described by Harry W. Jones as "attributes of judicial greatness fully as important as the attributes of reason." Professor Jones makes these thoughtful observations:

> Is there any reason for jurisprudence to suppress or underplay the known fact that moral courage and integrity are as important as intelligence as qualifications for judicial office? This is not to abandon one's faith in law's rationality but to insist that intellect and character are factors of equal significance in legal decision making. I think that Marshall, Holmes or Cardozo could have written the following:
>> Certainly the relation of faith is no book of rules which can be looked up to discover what is to be done now, in this very hour.... I give the word of my answer by accomplishing among the actions possible that which seems to my devoted insight to be the right one. With my choice and decision and action — committing or omitting, acting or preserving — I answer the word, however inadequately, yet properly: I answer for my hour.

Another factor generally ignored in the writings is, bluntly speaking, the lazy judge. Judging today is hard work. It often is intensive, demanding and taxing, requiring the judge to be a self-starter, to face up to the rigors of a calendar and not to put off until tomorrow what can be done today. Or, unfortunately, not to put off until next month or six months hence what should be done today. Often members of the bar complain, with justification, that judicial sloth is more to be disdained than incorrect decisions. Work habits of individual judges constitute a more important factor in the decisional process than the writings and studies reveal.

Herbert Simon describes management decisions in industry: "Making non-programmed decisions depends upon psychological processes that, until recently, have not been understood at all. Because we have not understood them, our theories about non-programmed decision making have been rather empty and our practical advice only moderately helpful." Often we hear that these non-programmed decisions are made by good judgment, insight and experience. But saying this is not saying much. Simon refers to a scene in *La Malade Imaginaire* in which the physician is asked why opium puts people to sleep. "Because it possesses a dormitive faculty," he replies triumphantly. Saying that good personal decisions are made by exercising good judgment names the phenomenon, but does not explain it. It does not help one who does not make decisions well but does not know why.

A possible reason why we may have difficulty in understanding this problem may be that no single educational discipline, no single college or university department, treats all dimensions of the decisional process. Mathematicians, psychologists, political scientists, military strategists and management analysts approach the subject from different perspectives. Decisional theory also attracts the attention of philosophers, economists, anthropologists and psychiatrists, and these specialists, too, have addressed the problem from specialized points of view. Leon Festinger pointedly observes in his book, *Conflict, Decision and Dissonance*, that, after much theorizing, experimenting and studying, much of the psychology of decision making is still not well understood:

How do human beings make decisions? This seemingly simple question has been a major concern of psychologists for many decades and of philosophers for centuries. In the eighteenth century, for example, an argument raged as to whether or not the fact that human beings could, and did, make choices implied a free will which contradicted the idea of determinism. If a human being could voluntarily decide which of several possible courses of action he would pursue, then clearly he had free will and a deterministic philosophy was untenable. The success of this argument, of course, depended upon the assumption that the process of making a choice, of making a decision, was inevitably surrounded with mystery.

Knowing it is desirable in judicial decision making that careful thought should precede every choice selection, the problem is that ordinary problems present sophisticated nuances. Again, in the words of Professor Festinger:

> The answer is very simple if the choice is merely between something the person likes and something he dislikes. Some doubts arise when the choice is more difficult, as when it is between two things which the individual likes and his preference is very slight. The question becomes difficult and interesting when the alternatives offered are complex, each involving some pleasant and some unpleasant aspects, or where the person chooses without being certain as to the outcome he will receive.

But any help to a judge with pre-decision jitters must start by eradicating a threshold barrier—the emotional trauma generated by the mere prospect of making the decision. Often, it is not the choosing itself that causes the problem; it is the specter that the prospective decider sees down the road. To this judge it is a lion roaring in the distance. That at decision time it turns out to be a pussycat makes no difference. The afflicted judge already has suffered. His or her pre-decision jitters, in most instances, are unnecessary. What causes the fear is the judge's unfamiliarity with the rudiments of the decisional process. In the words of President Franklin D. Roosevelt, "The only thing we have to fear is fear itself." I have known judges like this—two on state trial courts in Pittsburgh and the third, a U.S. Circuit Judge—and every one of them had very little experience as a trial or transaction lawyer and had not undergone substantial experience in the daily routine of decision making under pressure.

The common verbalization "I just don't know where to begin!" is real and signifies actual anguish. This distress then feeds on itself, causes frustrations to multiply in intensity, often climaxing in anger and aggression or withdrawal, but always causing a deterioration of performance. Pre-decision jitters magnify the dimensions of the actual problem and create mental clutter at the very time when the judge should be making up his or her mind effectively and efficiently. Professor Robert Heilbroner, in *How to Make an Intelligent Decision*, perceptively observes that, faced with a choice, we often *allow* our thought to fly around and our emotional generators to overheat rather than try to bring our energies to bear as systematically as we can. The problem is not new. The French schoolman, Buridan, posed the problem five centuries ago. He argued that a hungry ass placed equidistant from two bales of hay would starve to death. Why? Because the attraction of the two bales being equal and opposite, the ass would never make a choice. But Festinger suggests that the problem is not which pile of food is chosen: "The real problem concerns the process by which the organism evaluates the alternatives and does make a choice."

But whatever be the idiosyncratic aspects of judicial decision making—be they hunching or pre- and extra-judicial subjective factors—actual experience reveals a significant body of predictable uniformity in the behavior of a court. The great majority of cases are adjudicated in accordance with time-tested precepts of substantive and procedural law, applied fairly and justly in orthodox and professional form. The exceptional case which is decided because of the state of a judge's digestion is just that—exceptional. Notwithstanding the excitement of a large body of lay and professional literature that attempts to "psyche out" a court and to show how many extra-judicial factors go into decision making, one must not forget the high percentage of cases which could not, with semblance of reason, be decided in any way but one.

Conclusion

Overall, direct, indirect and—quite simply—human factors may affect how judges decide the disputes before them. Notwithstanding the variety and potential unpredictability of these factors, however, the studious lawyer may learn to identify the likely approach of a particular judge. Through examination of the judge's jurisprudence alongside an awareness of the direct and indirect factors that affect decision making, the lawyer may more effectively advance a position, especially in that set of cases where neither the law nor the application of it to the facts are clear.

CHAPTER FIFTEEN

JUSTIFYING THE DECISION

Author's Note: This material first appeared as text in my book, The Judicial Process: Text, Materials and Cases, *200–201, 208–210, 213–214, 604–610, 612–616, 625–626, 653–654 (2d ed. West 1996). It is reprinted here with permission. From this chapter, the lawyer can learn how to approach and address cases where no precedent controls and the law is not clear. To effectively persuade a judge in such a case, the lawyer must understand the judicial process culminating in the public justification of a decision—from selecting the material facts to choosing or finding the law to interpreting the legal precept to applying that precept to the facts. So informed and, consequently, so armed, the lawyer can present a case that will allow the judge to craft a durable and fully justified opinion in the lawyer's favor.*

When one asked Pound whether a recent Supreme Court decision was a "good" decision or a "bad" one, the old gentleman—for so I remember him with gratitude and considerable awe—had a way of answering not in terms of the correctness or incorrectness of the Court's application of constitutional precedents or doctrine but in terms of how thoughtfully and disinterestedly the Court had weighed the conflicting social interests involved in the case and how fair and durable its adjustment of the interest-conflicts promised to be.
—Professor Harry W. Jones

We learned that two processes inhere in the judicial function: first, reaching the decision and second, justifying it. It is to the second part of this analysis that we now turn.

Some judges will deny that such a dichotomy exists, insisting that decisions are the results only of their stated reasons. Sometimes this contention is true, often it is not. Surely the most desirable jurisprudential climate occurs when the motivation of the decision—the "why"—coincides with the public exposition justifying it—the "how." That reasons given in justification may coincide with reasons leading to the decision does not disprove the existence of two separate processes. Rather, the reality that the public justification often does not coincide with the actual motivation tends to prove that there is a dichotomy.

William James succinctly articulated why many judges fail to recognize the distinction: "The completed decision wipes off memory's slate most of the process of its attainment." When judges read their public exposition (the court's opinion) a year or so after decision, they may incorrectly but honestly believe that what was stated coincides precisely with that which went into the making of the decision. Another reason for not recognizing the distinction is a reluctance to admit publicly that decisions are made sometimes for extra-legal, even political, populist or pro- or anti-business reasons. Sometimes, they are made for purely personal, if not petty, motivations. Sometimes, they are made for overriding considerations which cannot, or so it is felt, be publicly stated.

For purposes of our study, many of the previous observations relating to the process of decision making apply as well to the process of justification. Similarly, what follows relates primarily to the justifying process, although it may also be considered in the context of decision making. In this chapter we focus on justification—a public explanation for the decision, a statement of norms which contains an exposition of stated rules and principles of law, a statement that originates with the judge's choice of a legal precept, through the interpretation of that choice, and finally to its application to the cause at hand. The several phases of the process are intimately interrelated and no doubt often occur simultaneously. With this qualification in mind, and also recognizing that value judgments inhere throughout, we must accord this aspect of the judicial process careful attention and analysis.

The Purpose of the Opinion

It is critical that the private reasons for the decision be the same as those publicly stated justifying it. This is most critical because those to be affected by the decision must have the benefit of the true motivation and explanation in order for there to be "predictability" in the Holmes formulation or, in Karl Llewellyn's words, "reckonability."

Piero Calamandrei, the Italian jurisprudent, explains in *Processo e Democrazia* (*Process and Democracy*):

> Naturally, if in the actual process of judging, the reasoning follows the decision and is an explanation of it rather than a preparation for it, the reasoning may become a screen to hide the real factors on which the judgment is based, covering with plausible reasoning the true mo-

tives for the decision, which cannot be admitted.... The legal scholar
with little experience in the courtroom reading the intricate reasoning of a decision as reported in a law review may often suspect, from
the dialectical contortions and subtleties that the judge uses to justify
his decision, that not even he was fully convinced by what he was writing, and that those arguments, couched in legal language, serve merely
as a façade to hide from view the intrigue or partiality that was the
true motivating factor of the decision.

Although the process of discovery—making or reaching the decision—is
locked in the thought processes of the judge, the process of justification is public and discernible; it manifests itself in the opinion of the court. Perhaps some
elementary definitions from Professor John Dewey are in order for a basic understanding of the process of justification:

Considerations which have weight in reaching the conclusion as to
what is to be done, or which are to be employed to justify it when it
is questioned are called "reasons." If they are stated in sufficiently general terms they are "principles." When the operation is formulated in
a compact way the decision is called a conclusion, and the considerations which led up to it are called the premises.

These "considerations" form the anatomy of a judicial opinion. A judicial
opinion may be defined as a reasoned elaboration, publicly stated, that justifies the court's conclusion or decision. Its purpose is to set forth an explanation for a decision that adjudicates a live case or a controversy that has been
presented before a court. This explanatory function of the opinion is paramount. In the common law tradition, the court's ability to develop case law finds
legitimacy and acceptance only because the decision is accompanied by a publicly recorded statement of reasons.

Announcing a rule of law of the case is solely a by-product of the court's adjudicative function. It is acceptable only because the public explanation sets
forth the grounds for the decision. Without this explanation, the court's decision would merely resolve that particular dispute presented by parties to the
court. Thus, in our tradition the critical by-product of the decision survives
long after the dispute between the litigants has been resolved. That by-product promulgates a legal rule describing the legal consequence that flows from
the adjudicative facts set forth in the opinion. It forms the bedrock of the common law doctrine of *stare decisis* because the consequence attached to the relevant or material facts becomes case law, which is binding on all future cases
that come before the court containing identical or similar material facts. Case

law possesses the same power and force as a legislative act until or unless subsequently changed by the court or modified by the legislature.

The judicial opinion is much more than a naked statement. To use J.L. Austin's phrase, it becomes a "performative utterance" because the *decision* that it explains performs as a declaration of law. We have chosen the word "decision" deliberately. It is not the "opinion" that performs; it is the "decision." Only the decision declared in the opinion has the force of law. The doctrine we respect is *stare decisis*; it is not *stare rationibus decidendi* or *stare rationes dictis*. Our tradition, elegantly stated, is *stare decisis et non quieta movere* (to stand by the decisions and not to disturb that which is settled).

Because courts tend to overwrite opinions (and this is particularly true in the U.S. Supreme Court), it often may be said that the "discussion outran the decision." It should be understood, therefore, that the decision of the case will be measured by the precise adjudicative facts that give rise to the rule of the case. As Henry Black states, "Two cases or decisions which are alike in all material aspects and precisely similar in all the circumstances affecting their determination, are said to be or run on all fours with each other, or, in the more ancient language of the law, the one is said to 'run upon four feet' with the other." To be sure, case law may survive and endure when the decision reflects desirable current public opinion or is congruent with contemporary community moral standards even though, upon analysis, the case's stated reasons may prove to have been fallacious or the reasons prove to be valid because societal changes have intervened. Even recognizing this, it is necessary to emphasize that the acceptability and vitality of the decision are usually measured by the quality of the reasons that originally supported it.

The public explanation for the decision is the public's insurance policy against decision by judicial fiat. As Justice Frankfurter once observed, a court is "not a tribunal unbounded by rules. We do not sit like a kadi under a tree dispensing justice according to considerations of individual expediency." This occurs in cases which are not clearly controlled by precedent or statute, yet the court acts without stating a reason or utters cryptic non-reasons such as "reasons and authority support the decision" or "utility and justice require this result."

Public expression of judicial reasoning is a necessary concomitant of what is generally conceded to be the dual function of any appellate court—settling the dispute between the parties and institutionalizing the law. Dispute-settling can be described as reviewing the trial record for the errors asserted in a particular case; it is a review for correctness. The review process may also serve as a vehicle for stating and applying constitutional principles, for authoritatively interpreting statutes, for formulating and expressing policy on legal issues, for developing the common law, and for supervising the levels of the judicial hierarchy below the appellate courts. This set of tasks is called the institutional function of the court.

The stated reasons constitute the critical support for the decision. The quality of a decision is commensurate with the quality and logical force of the reasons that support it. Even so, two other necessary ingredients go into the mix: the narration of adjudicative facts and the statement of the issue or issues framing the case for decision.

Adjudicative facts are those selected from the gross facts found by the fact-finder from the congeries of record evidence. They are facts deemed necessary, relevant and material to the particular issue(s) presented for decision. There is an important reason why the facts set forth in an opinion should be selected with care, a reason that goes to the heart of *stare decisis*: like cases should be treated alike. And because our tradition is fact-specific, it is critical that the concept of "like cases" should refer to cases that contain like material or relevant facts. The decision that emanates from the opinion, the law of the case, is used to inform, guide and govern future private and public transactions. This future use of the decision is absolutely necessary if we accept Holmes's definition that law is nothing more pretentious than a prediction of what the courts will do in fact. Thus perceived, a quality opinion will predict how similar factual scenarios will be treated.

The purpose of a judicial opinion is to tell the participants in the lawsuit why the court acted the way it did. Drawing upon an analogy to marketing strategy, the opinion should first address a primary market. There are two discrete sectors of the primary market for appellate opinions. One sector consists of the actual participants before the appellate court—the appellant or petitioner, the appellee or respondent, and the tribunal of the first instance whose judgment or order is being criticized or upheld. These participants have an all-pervasive interest in the case, an interest in the error-correcting activity of the appellate court. The other sector is the appellate court as an institution. Although always concerned with error-correcting, the reviewing court must at all times consider the effect the opinion will have on itself as an institution charged with responsibilities for setting precedent and for defining law. These two sectors—one, the litigants and the trial court, the other, the appellate court itself—form the audience in the primary market. Writing should be directed to them. The opinion writer must focus on these mutually interested primary readers at all times in order to make as certain as possible that they understand the contents of the written communication precisely as the writer intends. What the receiver receives should be exactly what the sender has sent.

The lay parties to the lawsuit should understand what is being said. "Lay parties" does not mean the public at large. The broad spectrum of society may often be unfamiliar with the context, the terms of art, usages or customs of the transaction that gave rise to the litigation. The lay parties to the litigation, however, understand those elements. They will understand the decision if the explanation is clear and logical. All is lost if the parties do not know why the court did what it did. It is one thing to lose a case; not to understand why compounds the loss. Mehler summed it up: "[T]he gulf that often separates sender and receiver [of communications], spanned at best by a bridge of signs and symbols, is sought to be narrowed yet further so that ultimately the intended communication may have the same meaning, or approximately the same meaning, for those on the left bank as those on the right." If the explanation is clear to "lay parties," it should be clear to all members of the court.

Important secondary markets also exist for judicial opinions. Although they ought not be ignored, their interests are subordinate to those of primary market consumers. These markets may be far removed in space and time from the instant case, but if the opinion is written well enough for the primary consumers, the secondary ones will also reap the same cognitive benefits. These secondary consumers vary. Some are institutions in the same judicial hierarchy, some at a higher rung, some lower. The highest court of the jurisdiction may be called upon to examine carefully the explanations of trial and intermediate court decisions. The court or agency in which the litigation originates studies them for future direction and seeks materials that will form the grounds for future decisions. Other secondary markets include lawyers, who generally look for predictions as to the course of future decisions. Still others represent the persons and institutions in the court's jurisdiction who seek reasonable guidance for conducting themselves in accordance with the demands of the social, political and economic order.

Law school faculties and students seek the opinions as study tools and research materials. Depending on the subject matter, so do state legislators and academics, among them, political scientists, philosophers, sociologists, behaviorists and historians. In addition, representatives of the print and electronic media are among the instant readers. When the media does report opinions, the courts' statements are subject to merciless editing or compressed to 60-second TV or radio sound bites. Ultimate consumers also may be the bench and bar of other jurisdictions, the committees, the council and assembly of the American Law Institute, committees of federal and state legislators and authors of popular and professional commentary.

We can say that a court's public performance in reaching a conclusion is at least as important as the conclusion. If we evaluate a decision in terms not of "right" or "wrong," nor of subjective agreement or disagreement with the result, but rather in terms of thoughtful and disinterested weighing of conflicting social interests, it becomes critical that the "performative utterance" include a socially acceptable explanation.

Although reasoned exposition traditionally takes the form of a logical syllogism, there is much more to the judicial process than dry logical progression. We have recognized that judges do not necessarily use formal logic to select or formulate legal premises. Professor John Wisdom suggests that this selection process "becomes a matter of weighing the cumulative effect of one group of severally inconclusive items against the cumulative effect of another group of severally inclusive items." In exercising this choice, courts do not necessarily appeal to any rational or objective criteria; essentially they exercise a value judgment and should be recognized flatly as doing so. Moreover, because courts have the power to alter the content of rules, no immutability attaches to their major or beginning premises. The desirability of *elegantia juris*, with its concomitant stability and reckonability, is often subordinate to the desirability of rule revision in the light of claims, demands or desires asserted in the public interest.

Once the controlling rule or principle has been selected or modified, however, there is an insistence, that the public exposition—the process of justification—follow the canons of logic with respect to formal correctness. The process requires formal consistency of concepts with one another. The logic of justification is concerned with the relations between propositions rather than the content of the propositions themselves. Thus, the reasoning process dictates formal correctness, rather than material desirability. This process of justification and reasoning, considered in depth in the next part, becomes paramount in situations in which no precedent controls and the law is not clear.

Where No Precedent Controls and the Law Is Not Clear

Of all the cases that come before the court in which I sit, a majority, I think, could not, with semblance of reason, be decided in any way but one. The law and its application alike are plain. Such cases are predestined, so to speak, to affirmance without opinion. In another and considerable percentage, the rule of law is certain, and the application alone doubtful. A complicated record must be dissected, the narratives of witnesses, more or less incoherent and unintelligible, must be analyzed, to determine whether a given situation comes within one district or another upon the chart of rights and wrongs. . . . Often these cases and others like them provoke difference of opinion among judges. Jurisprudence remains untouched, however, regardless of outcome. Finally there is a percentage, not large indeed, and yet not so small to be negligible, where a decision one way or the other, will count for the future, will advance or retard,

sometimes much, sometimes little, the development of the law. These are the cases where the creative element in the judicial process finds its opportunity and power.
—Benjamin N. Cardozo

It is the third category of Cardozo's analysis that is the subject of the following pages—where the law is not clear, and *a fortiori*, there can be no application of facts to any legal precept. For guidance we turn to Dean Roscoe Pound:

> Analysis of the judicial process ... distinguishes as the functions which are involved in the decision of a case according to law: (1) finding the facts, *i.e.* ascertaining the state of facts to which legal precepts are to be applied in order to reach a determination; (2) finding the law, *i.e.* ascertaining the legal precept or precepts applicable to the facts found, (3) interpreting the precept or precepts to be applied, *i.e.* ascertaining their meaning by genuine interpretation, and (4) applying the precept or precepts so found and interpreted to the case at hand.

Once the facts are established by the fact finder, the general judicial function follows the above procedure. At the onset, a judge will evaluate the facts to determine which are material to settlement of a dispute. Selection of the relevant law then envelopes these facts in a particular arena of competing legal precepts or competing analogies. I draw a distinction between choosing (or selecting) the law and finding the law. When it comes to choice, the judge has the option of choosing between or among competing principles of law. The next step, interpretation, may be clear-cut, as with some precepts of property, contract or tort law, or it may involve broad principles subject to disparate analyses, particularly in the realm of statutory construction. Reasoned elaboration should support the application of the precepts, so found and so interpreted, to the facts at hand.

A. Choosing the Law

It may be useful to recall first what Jerome Frank has observed:

> It is sometimes said that part of the judge's function is to pick out the relevant facts. Not infrequently this means that in writing his opinion he stresses (to himself as well as to those who will read the opinion) those facts which are relevant to his conclusion—in other words, he unconsciously selects those facts which, in combination with the rules of law which he considers to be pertinent, will make "logical"

his decision. A judge, eager to give a decision which will square with his sense of what is fair, but unwilling to break with the traditional rules, will often view the evidence in such a way that the "facts reported by him," combined with those traditional rules, will justify the result which he announces.

If this were done deliberately, one might call it dishonest, but one should remember that with judges this process is usually unconscious and that, however unwise it may be, upright men in other fields employ it, and sometimes knowingly.

When it comes to choice, the judicial function in this context may be viewed also from the perspective of the relations between logical propositions. To choose the law is to select the major premise of a categorical deductive syllogism. Accordingly, if one accepts the value judgment inherent in the major premise and if the minor premise is valid, then, logically, one must accept the conclusion. But we know that it is not always that neat, for the reverse process often takes place. One may accept a conclusion as a valid legal norm and seek to use it as a precedent, and purposely omit the major and minor premises (the logicians call such omissions "enthymemes"). This conclusion may be considered as a precedent but, lacking logical support, it is merely judicial fiat and will not be considered as a precedent with a strong bite. In the words of Karl Llewellyn, "Where stops the reason, there stops the rule," the old common law maxim of *cessante ratione legis, cessat et ipsa legit.*

Legal reasoning is subject to more scrutiny than any aspect of the judicial process. Forming the very fiber of argument and persuasion, it is the heart of the written brief, the essence of the process of justification. It constitutes the foundation of the case system by which law students are trained. Criticism of the "reasoning" of courts seems, at times, to form the *raison d'etre* for many law review publications. Yet in these publications there is little analysis of reasoning *qua* reasoning. Often an alleged attack on the "reasoning" of a court is really a disagreement with the value judgment implicit in the court's choice of a major premise—a disagreement with the selection and interpretation of the legal precept. This difference is actually a quarrel with the value judgment that accepted a particular legal norm rather than a disaffection with the reasoning process. Criticism of court opinions would be more professional, briefs more clear, points of friction between litigants earlier identified and accommodated with more fairness and durability, if resort to the cosmos of "reasoning" were minimized, and attention directed instead to the precise components of that cosmos. It is not too much to ask whether one disagrees with the choice of the "authoritative starting point" and, if so, why; or whether the quarrel is with formal correctness of the syllogism used and, if so, where. It is not too much to ask if it is contended that facts in the minor premise are not properly subsumed in the major, or the conclusion lacks elements common to the major and minor premises.

From the trial memoranda or briefs submitted by counsel, or from experience and independent research, judges begin the process of justification by making a value judgment in the form of a choice. They select from competing legal precepts or competing analogies presented by counsel in the adversary process. Often, however, these suggestions offered by counsel are inadequate or inappropriate.

Two guidelines may aid both the choice or the formulation and its ultimate acceptance: the judge should avoid arbitrary or aleatory choices and the judge has a duty of "reasoned elaboration in law-finding." Julius Stone says this is necessary so that the choice seems to the entire legal profession, "if not right, then as right as possible. The duty of elaboration indicates that reasons cannot be merely ritualistic formulae or diversionary sleight of hand."

Because a value judgment inheres in finding the law, how can a judge arrive at this threshold decision yet avoid being arbitrary? Sometimes the exercise of the value judgment involves forthright line-drawing. The Supreme Court, in *Burch v. Louisiana*, acknowledged this in 1979 in deciding that although a six-person jury satisfied the Sixth and Fourteenth Amendments, a jury of five did not: "[W]e do not pretend the ability to discern *a priori* a bright line below which the number of jurors participating in the trial or in the verdict would not permit the jury to function in the manner required by our prior cases ... [, but] it is inevitable that lines must be drawn somewhere.... This line-drawing process, 'although essential, cannot be wholly satisfactory, for it requires attaching different consequences to events which, when they lie near the line, actually differ very little.'" Roger Traynor reminded us that

> one entrusted with decision, traditionally above base prejudices, must also rise above the vanity of stubborn preconceptions, sometimes euphemistically called the courage of one's convictions. He knows well enough that he must severely discount his own predilections, of however high grade he regards them, which is to say he must bring to his intellectual labors a cleansing doubt of his omniscience, indeed even of his perception.

B. Finding the Law

Where no clear rule is present, it is necessary to draw upon the experience of the judiciary to fashion a proper major premise from existing legal rules, and specific holdings of other cases. This is done by inductive reasoning, which moves from the particular to the general, or from the particular to the particular. In the law, the method of arriving at a general or universal proposition (a principle or doctrine) from the particular facts of experience (legal rules or holdings of cases) is called inductive generalization. This is reasoning from the particular to the general.

Inductive generalization is used in all aspects of the legal profession—in studying law, in practicing law and in judging cases. Thus, it looms large in the common law tradition in the development of legal precepts in the case by case experience.

Instance 1 of fact A is accompanied by legal consequence B.
Instance 2 of fact A is accompanied by legal consequence B.
Instance 3 of fact A is accompanied by legal consequence B.
...
<u>Instance 25 of fact A is accompanied by legal consequence B.</u>
Therefore, every instance of fact A is accompanied by legal consequence B.

Apply this to a precise example in the law:

A's oral conveyance of real estate is invalid.
B's oral conveyance of real estate is invalid.
C's oral conveyance of real estate is invalid.
...
<u>Z's oral conveyance of real estate is invalid.</u>
Therefore, all oral conveyances of land are invalid.

Inferences proceed on the assumption that the new instances will resemble the old one in all material circumstances. This is purely hypothetical, and sometimes we discover we are mistaken. Thus, for years the Europeans proceeded along the following induction:

A is a swan and it is white.
B is a swan and it is white.
C is a swan and it is white.
...
<u>Z is a swan and it is white.</u>
Therefore, all swans are white.

But then explorers discovered Australia and it was learned that there are swans that are black.

Inductive generalization underlies the development of the common law. From many specific case holdings, we reach a generalized proposition. From many cases deciding that individual oral conveyances of real estate were invalid, we reached the conclusion that all such conveyances were invalid. We arrived at that point by what Lord Diplock described as "the cumulative experience of the judiciary." In generalization by enumeration, we can say that the larger the number of specific instances, the more certain is the resulting generalization. This simply bodes fealty to the concept of probability. It is the common law tradition of creating a principle by connecting the dots.

We now have chosen or found the law. The next step is to decide what it means.

C. Interpreting the Legal Precept

As value judgments inhere in finding or choosing the law, so do they also loom large in interpreting the legal precept selected. Interpretation may occur after choosing the precept or simultaneously with the choice. Some rules or principles—particularly in orthodox fields of static law, such as contract or property law and most statutes—admit to but one, clear interpretation. In other sectors of the law, such as constitutional law, principles are "rubbery," possessed of what H.L.A. Hart calls "open texture," and subject to disparate interpretations.

As with the choice of a precept, the interpreting process can be intellectually disinterested. Usually, however, some degree of orientation is present that leads to a desired result, albeit a rational and respectable one. As with the choice or formulation, reasoned elaboration, not naked conclusion, should support judicial interpretations. Absent such elaboration, determining whether the ultimate decision is "as right as possible" or "good" is a difficult, if not impossible, task.

Interpreting case law and legal documents is the subject of various methodologies. Comparison of the material facts of the cases must be made to determine controlling precedents and the presence of proper analogies under the teachings of inductive reasoning. The meaning of legal instruments, especially contracts, brings into play two related but distinct concepts, with different standards of appellate review: "contract interpretation" and "contract construction." The distinction between interpretation and construction is not always easy. Professor Corbin described the distinction:

> By "interpretation of language" we determine what ideas that language induces in other persons. By "construction of the contract," as that term will be used here, we determine its legal operation—its effect upon the action of courts and administrative officials. If we make this

distinction, then the construction of a contract starts with the interpretation of its language but does not end with it; while the process of interpretation stops wholly short of a determination of the legal relations of the parties. When a court gives a construction to the contract as that is affected by events subsequent to its making and not foreseen by the parties, it is departing very far from mere interpretation of their symbols of expression, although even then it may claim somewhat erroneously to be giving effect to the "intention" of the parties.

Professor Patterson makes the same point:

Construction, which may be usefully distinguished from interpretation, is a process by which legal consequences are made to follow from the terms of the contract and its more or less immediate context, and from a legal policy or policies that are applicable to the situation.

Thus, we often are presented with the question of "interpreting the fact" of language and the related question of "interpreting law," or as the nice distinction appears in the law of contracts, "construction" of the legal aspects of the instrument. This brings into play Pound's definition of legal rules: "These are precepts attaching a definite detailed legal consequence to a definite, detailed state of facts." In construing, explaining or comprehending case law, it does make a difference whether one is describing the factual or legal component of the legal precept.

Statutory construction is a chief example of the interpreting process. Evolving from the English Rules of statutory construction are numerous methods and techniques used by American courts to interpret statutes. The cumulative experience of the judiciary furnishes no absolute rules for guidance. We are treated to abstract expressions: "If the statute is clear and unambiguous, that is the end of the matter, for the court must give effect to the unambiguously expressed intent of Congress," or, "in determining the scope of a statute, we first look at its language. In the case before us, the language is plain and unambiguous. We will apply it." But that is not always the end of the matter. The reports are filled with cases where "clear and unambiguous language" is shunted in a quest for legislative intention or purpose. The task of interpretation begins, however, only after recognizing three separate problems present in the analytical process:

1. The problem of language analysis in the strict sense—the presence of an unclear norm;
2. The problem of lacunae—the nonexistent norm; and

3. The problem of evolution—the norm whose meaning changes while its text remains constant, thus bringing into tension the original intent and the ongoing history theories of interpretation.

The reader may wish to determine for himself the difference, if any, between interpreting statutes and judge-made rules. A modicum of truth probably resides in the tongue-in-cheek statement: "When the legislative history is ambiguous, we look to the language of the statute."

1. The Unclear Norm

Most methods of statutory construction come into play when the statutory norm is unclear. This approach assumes that the legislature intended to address the relevant factual scenario at issue, but did so in unclear language. It is then the necessary task of the court to construe the statute and clarify the norm. To interpret ambiguities, judges (and some legislatures) created "canons of construction" to apply to statutory precepts but not to judicially-created precepts. We understand the reason why judicial precepts were fashioned because judicial opinions are required to include a *rationes decidendi*, a reason for the decision. Statutes, unlike case law, usually have neither a factual scenario nor a statement of reasons to assist in interpretations. Thus, "canons of constructions" were invented.

For example, Judges have played with the Mischief Rule of *Heydon's Case*, the Golden Rule and the Literal Rule. Judges have dallied with what American jurisprudence has called the "Plain Meaning Rule" as stated in the 1917 case of *Caminetti v. United States*:

> It is elementary that the meaning of a statute must, in the first instance, be sought in the language in which the act is framed, and if that is plain, and if the law is within the constitutional authority of the law-making body which passed it, the sole function of the courts is to enforce it according to its terms. Where the language is plain and admits of no more than one meaning the duty of interpretation does not arise and the rules which are to aid doubtful meanings need no discussion.

The problem is that every stated canon seems to spawn an antonym. By 1950, most canons were so enervated by contradictions that Karl Llewellyn's taxonomic treatment deftly devitalized them. For every court that says, "A statute cannot go beyond its text," another court may say, "To effect its purpose a statute may be implemented beyond its text." Similarly, we see juxtaposed: "If language is plain and unambiguous it must be given effect" with "Not when literal interpretation would lead to absurd or mischievous consequences or thwart manifest purpose"; "Every word and clause must be given effect" with "If inadvertently inserted or if repugnant to the rest of the statute, they may be rejected as surplusage"; and, finally, "Expression of one thing excludes another" with "The language may fairly comprehend many different cases when some only are expressly mentioned by way of example." Judge Richard Posner goes further: "I think Llewellyn's criticism is correct, but I also think that most of the canons are just plain wrong."

Recourse to legislative history is a relatively new concept technique to discern the drafter's intent (Justice Antonin Scalia has not been one of its converts). In 1899, Holmes lamented that courts did not inquire what the legislature meant but only what the statute meant. He would not voice this complaint today, for although contemporary courts are fond of stating that "[t]he starting point in every case involving the construction of a statute is the language itself," current approaches seem to abjure a strictly semantic approach.

2. The Lacunae or Nonexistent Norm

A separate interpretive problem occurs when the legal issue arises in an area covered by the statute but in a context that clearly did not occur to the legislature at the time of the statute's enactment. This problem is not the problem of the unclear norm, but the problem of the lacunae, of the nonexistent norm.

Decades ago John Chipman Gray recognized the lacunae as a very serious problem:

> The fact is that the difficulties of so-called interpretation arise when the legislation has had no meaning at all; when the question which is raised in the statute never occurred to it; when the question is not to determine what the Legislature did mean on a point which was present to its mind, but to guess what it would have intended on a point not present to its mind, if the point had been present.

Plowden, in his note in *Eyston v. Studd* in 1574, made an observation that is in striking anticipation of modern principles of discerning the meaning of a statute:

> And in order to form a right judgment when the letter of a statute is restrained, and when enlarged, by equity, it is a good way, when you peruse a statute, to suppose that the lawmaker is present, and that you have asked him the question you want to know touching the equity; then you must give yourself an answer as you imagine he would have done, if he had been present.... And if the lawmaker would have

followed the equity, notwithstanding the words of the law ... you may safely do the like.

Referring to Plowden, Lord Denning set forth a brilliant credo that should be understood by all lawyers and judges:

> Put into the homely metaphor it is this: A judge should ask himself the question: If the makers of the Act had themselves come across this muck in the texture of it, how would they have straightened it out? He must then do as they would have done. A judge must not alter the material of which it is woven but he can and should iron out the creases.

Experience in civil law jurisdictions assumes that situations will occur that were not contemplated by the legislative draftsmen, and that they made adequate provisions for these occurrences. Perhaps the most well known model is the Swiss Civil Code of 1907:

> Where no provision [in the Code] is applicable, the judge shall decide according to the existing Customary Law and, in default thereof, according to the rules which he would lay down if he had himself to act as legislator. Herein, he must be guided by approved legal doctrine and case law.

Still another dimension of this problem is where the court finds the lacuna when there is no evidence that Congress left the matter open. An example can be found in *J.I. Case Co. v. Borak*, and the relatively new practice of inventing implied causes of action where the statute is silent. This federal court innovation marks a drastic departure from the presumption that on the topic a statute is dealing with, Congress said all that it wanted to say. The discovery, if not the fabrication, of implied federal causes of action represents activity by judges described by Lord Devlin as "moths outside a lighted window, ... irresistibly attracted by what they see within as the vast unused potentiality of judicial lawmaking." In *Cort v. Ash*—a case in which the Supreme Court paraphrased an opinion I wrote in the Court of Appeals—the Supreme Court interpreted a federal criminal statute prohibiting corporations from making certain types of contributions in connection with a presidential election. The Court found that the language itself did not authorize, and Congress did not intend to so authorize, a shareholder to bring a private cause of action against a transgressing corporation. The Court developed factors to use in determining whether a statute authorizes such a cause of action.

Therein lies the problem. The factors identified by the Court leave more than enough maneuvering room for a judge to decide the issue either way, and the courts have done just that. There has not been much predictability to the cases. Some decisions have found no implied cause of action. Others have swung in the other direction. Relying on legislative history as an indication of whether a private cause of action is permitted once again involves all the dangers of drawing conclusions from bits and pieces of legislative history. The cases are in disarray, because the Supreme Court and other federal courts departed from traditional legal principles to achieve result-oriented conclusions.

Whether the problem arises either in the unclear or nonexistent norm, at bottom always is the task of divining the intent of the legislature. Learned Hand once observed:

> When a judge tries to find out what the government would have intended which it did not say, he puts into its mouth things which he thinks it ought to have said, and that is very close to substituting what he himself thinks right.... Nobody does this exactly right; great judges do it better than the rest of us. It is necessary that someone shall do it, if we are to realize the hope that we can collectively rule ourselves.

3. Changing Meaning of the Norm

From the unclear and the nonexistent norm we now turn to the norm whose meaning changes. This became the subject of much public controversy in 1985, when Attorney General Edwin Meese III publicly criticized Supreme Court justices for failing to interpret the Constitution in accordance with the intent of the drafters and instead substituting the judges' idiosyncratic political science and moral philosophies. Justices William J. Brennan, Jr., and John Paul Stevens leaped into public print arguing that judges were not required to rely on the original intent theory insofar as the Constitution was concerned. Attorney General Meese put his finger on the serious question of how federal judges should determine public policy when they refuse to consider the intent of the framers. Probably he was correct in suggesting that many constitutional law interpretations are at odds with the original intent of the drafters. The justices, however, were surely right in saying that insofar as interpreting the Constitution is concerned, unlike interpreting statutes and contracts, judges are not bound by the original intent theory of adjudication.

This is so because the Constitution is a moral statement more than a set of by-laws. Conditions in the nation that have occurred since its ratification should be relevant to its interpretation. These changing conditions allow federal judges to reject the original intent theory of interpretation and use a continuing or ongoing historical approach, thus permitting the Constitution to reflect the prevailing temperament of the country. In *Furman v. Georgia*, a widely-studied death penalty case, the various opinions relied on the ongoing history technique to demonstrate that the Eighth Amendment's proscription of cruel and unusual punishment "is not fastened to the obsolete but may acquire meaning as public opinion becomes enlightened by a humane justice," and "must draw its meaning from the evolving standards of decency that mark the progress of a maturing society." As Holmes reminded us:

> The life of the law has not been logic; it has been experience. The felt necessities of the times, the prevalent moral and political theories, intuitions of public policy, avowed or unconscious, even the prejudices which judges share with their fellow meant, have had a good deal more to do than the syllogism in determining the rules by which men should be governed.

D. Applying the Law to the Facts

From choosing the law and interpreting it, we come now to applying the law to the facts found by the fact finder. This is the third of the methodologies described under this chapter's general rubric, "Justifying the Decision." It also is the third of the flash points of controversy between the litigants.

In the difficult case, usually one of first impression, the courts will have expended much thought in the earlier processes: finding the law, or making a choice among competing legal precepts. After the choice is made, efforts must then be directed toward interpreting the law. Once the law is chosen and then interpreted, courts are ready for the final process—applying the law to the facts. Because all three processes have been utilized, this is the paradigm case that uses all three methodologies.

Often, however, the first step is not involved because there is no question of choice, but instead the question is one of interpretation, usually in the form of statutory construction. After the question of interpretation is resolved, the court then must apply the law as interpreted to the facts.

Most cases, however, do not involve the questions of choice or interpretation. In the overwhelming percentage of litigation the law is settled and its interpretation equally clear, and the sole issue for the decision is the application of the law to the facts. Here the court may be faced with a "slam dunk" case, where the law and its application alike are plain, or alternatively, a dispute in which the law is plain and the sole issue is its application to the facts.

Clearly, the process of justification always requires application of a legal precept to a fact situation. The application may be, and usually is, purely mechanical. If the material facts at hand are substantially similar to those present in an earlier case announcing a rule of law, the doctrine of precedent becomes operative and the case is quickly decided and easily justified. Where there is no quarrel over the choice or interpretation of the legal precept, the root controversy, as we have emphasized in the discussion of precedents, is traced to the value judgment of whether there is similarity between the fact situations under comparison. Professor Edward Levi explains that "the scope of a rule of law, and therefore its meaning, depends upon a determination of what facts will be considered similar to those present when the rule was first announced. The finding of similarity or difference is the key step in the legal process." Predicting a court's action in a precept-application controversy, therefore, requires a prediction of which facts in the compared cases a given court at a given time will deem either material or insignificant. The facts considered material are, in the words of Hart and Sacks, "adjudicative" facts, or "facts relevant in deciding whether a given general proposition is or is not applicable to a particular situation."

Conclusion

The effective advocate must understand this entire judicial process in cases in which there is no controlling precedent and the law is not clear. By formulating and presenting an argument that addresses all aspects of the process—finding or choosing the law, interpreting the legal precept and applying the precept to the facts—the lawyer greatly improves his or her chance of persuading the judge. Under the common law tradition of precedent, it is the judge's duty to publicly justify the opinion in a thorough, honest and durable manner. Presented with arguments that walk the judge down that path, counsel stands ready to reap the benefits of proper preparation and understanding.

AN AFTERWORD

I was 90 years old when I started to write this book. I was, as now, a very busy senior judge on the U.S. Court of Appeals for the Third Circuit hearing appeals from Delaware, New Jersey, Pennsylvania and the U.S. Virgin Islands. I had been on this court for 42 years, and had been entitled to retire at full salary since 1984, but instead decided to take senior status in 1987 and work on a reduced, but nevertheless, substantial caseload. This is because I love doing what I do; when that Last Great Day comes, it will be with my robe on. I enjoy what I do on the court—studying briefs, deciding cases, writing opinions, reading drafts of my colleagues' opinions—as well as my satellite activities—writing books and articles on the law. I do all this because I have an unabashed love affair with the law.

The love affair started in September, 1941, when I began my study of the law, three months before December 7 and Pearl Harbor. That the Japanese attacked us came as a surprise; eventually going to war was not. In my senior year as an undergraduate at the University of Pittsburgh I was Editor-in-Chief of *The Pitt News*, the student thrice-weekly newspaper. *A year before* Pearl Harbor, on December 6, 1940, the main editorial that I wrote began, "We are, of course, at war." All of us who enrolled in law school the following September knew that our three-year studies were going to be interrupted. The only question was when.

Yet, I was so excited by the study of law that I hit the books more intensely in those first three months than in my entire last year as an undergraduate. I refer to those early law school days because I enlisted in the U.S. Marine Corps on Monday, the day after Pearl Harbor, and during my second semester, I studied more about the War than my law school curriculum, and conjectured how well I would survive the rigorous Marine Corps life. I was appalled at our Nation's lack of preparedness, as evidenced by the debacle in Hawaii. At the same time, I was amazed at the kindness of the Marine recruiters to delay my call to active duty from March until I finished my law school year in May. I contemplated my future life in the Marine Corps more than I concentrated on contracts, torts, property and criminal law.

After the war I returned to law school at Pitt in February, 1946, for the start of the spring semester. I immediately became a very serious student among a coterie of returning vets who made life very difficult for the professoriat because we were not interested in the philosophy of law, the Socratic method or its nuances. Time and again us vets let our professors know that we wanted only one thing: what's the Pennsylvania rule and would it be on the bar exam. We looked at the next two years as only a cram course for the bar exam.

The law school had an accelerated program with year-round classes for those of us who were in a hurry to get on with our lives. After taking the spring semester in 1946, I continued that summer, then took a complete year beginning in September and, to get my degree, had to finish in the summer of 1947. It was toward the end of that last full year that five of us returning vets gradually organized a serious study group. The Pennsylvania bar examinations were scheduled for the second week in August, 1947, and my group of five guys took our final law school exams on Monday and Tuesday and then the Pennsylvania bar exams on Thursday and Friday of the same week.

For the next four months I roamed Pittsburgh courtrooms while serving my Pennsylvania preceptorship, a system in which law school graduates had to clerk with a lawyer—without pay—two months before the bar exam and four months afterwards before they could be admitted to the bar. As a courtesy to vets, we were required to serve only four months. Upon advice of my preceptor, I religiously followed the most popular Pittsburgh trial lawyers, especially two outstanding ones—James P. McArdle and Charles J. Margiotti. Both of them tried civil and criminal cases. I would watch a case from the opening statements to the completion of the trial judge's charge to the jury. Then move on to another case.

I was admitted to the bar on the morning of Monday, December 8, 1947. In the afternoon I had my first court trial as court-appointed counsel for a man who pleaded guilty of forgery, before Judge Sammy Weiss, a friend of my father. When I concluded my remarks, Judge Weiss thanked me for a job well done, but added, "Mr. Aldisert, don't take any checks as a fee from this man." Fourteen years later I became a judicial colleague of Judge Weiss.

I described those days in my book, *Road to the Robes: A Federal Judge Recollects Young Years and Early Times*, 253–255 (AuthorHouse 2005):

> Dad was a special friend of Jack, the Chief Crier in Criminal Court, whose job it was to recruit pro bono lawyers for defendants who could not afford counsel and whom the Legal Aid Society people could not represent because of overloads or conflicts of interest.
>
> Long before the U.S. Supreme Court made it mandatory, every defendant in Allegheny County, Pennsylvania, had to be represented by counsel, whether the offense was a felony or misdemeanor, and whether

the plea was guilty or not guilty. Jack promised my father: "John, I'll keep him busy every day of the week, if he wants it."

I wanted it. And I was kept busy for the better part of my first 18 months of practice, and as a result, I became a very experienced trial lawyer.

Sure, I floundered at first, and made mistakes. Lots of them. I got outmaneuvered by experienced D.A.s and got suckered by police witnesses who held back testimony on direct examination only to release damaging evidence against my client through my clumsy cross-examination. At first, sometimes hearsay evidence rolled past me when I was too inept to block its admission. But I learned by making mistakes, and when you learn this way you usually don't make the same mistake twice, and certainly not three times. I made too many objections and got slammed around by the judges. At first I was too intense and too emotional and sometimes got tongue tied when I should have been calm and urbane. To the jury I looked worried instead of putting on the lawyer's show of utmost confidence. But I learned. Oh, how I learned! The pedagogues say that one learns by two techniques: (1) reading and listening and (2) practical experience. I got the giant economy size dose of both.

When I walked into a courtroom, or perhaps it was strutting when I got the hang of it, every day during that early period of my life at the bar, I acquired trial experience that many lawyers never get today. Every morning, five days a week, I showed up in a criminal courtroom and soon I stopped getting my head bashed in. I stopped leaving my own blood on the courtroom floors. Soon I started to receive the top accolade—praise from the court attachés: "You're getting real good, Rugi!"

After the Chief Crier would assign me a case, I'd enter my appearance, sign papers for a plea of not guilty and demand a jury trial. Sure, there was not much time to prepare, but what made the system work was that the assistant D.A. got the case even later than I did; moreover I had the advantage of sitting through the prosecution's case and learning the details at about the same time as the prosecutor. Thus, I jumped into the world of robbery, rape, burglary, breaking and entering, larceny, receiving stolen goods, aggravated and simple assault and battery, attempted murder, drunk driving, involuntary manslaughter, vehicular homicide, fornication and bastardy, forgery and embezzlement.

I mastered the elements and nuances of each crime and soon gleaned the strategies used by the prosecution to establish its cases. I learned the routine of police work and the courtroom mannerisms of individual prosecutors. I knew what to expect from the few who were good prosecutors and how to tap dance around those who were not. I learned sentencing proclivities of the various judges and assimilated their idiosyncrasies in the conduct of a trial. I grasped what annoyed them, and what pleased them, judge by judge.

I learned how to deal and plead. Because my main objective was to polish professional skills of a litigator by trying a case from opening speech to jury verdict, my clients got the best of both worlds—trying a case or pleading it. I was not courtroom shy, like most lawyers were then and still are today. I was not afraid to face jurors and gradually became very comfortable in relationships with them and the judges. The police and the D.A.s no longer intimidated me. Nevertheless, if in the midst of a case, I determined that I could work out a good deal for my client, I did not hesitate to plea bargain.

During 1949, my second full year of practice, I defended a number of murder cases. No moment in the practice of law is more disquieting, worrisome or fraught with apprehension than to sit at counsel table with your client and hear the prosecutor in his opening statement to the jury intone these sink-in-the-pit-of-the-stomach words: "Ladies and gentlemen of the jury, we are asking the death penalty in this case."

Compared to this, all other moments of courtroom drama—even detrimental surprises, unlucky and devastating, that come rushing in the midst of a trial and threaten large-scale financial stakes in a high profile civil case—all these are serendipitous encounters by comparison. You grow up in a hurry when you defend in a case where the state asks the death penalty, though their only reason is to intimidate you into making a plea bargain. Professionally speaking, I matured rapidly between 1948 and 1950.

You can't become a good trial lawyer without experience, and yet this trial opportunity is not readily available today. Clients for defendants, insurance companies or corporations are unwilling to pay fees for second seaters, as was the case in the late Forties and Fifties, and lawyers for individual plaintiffs too often cave in and settle cases because they are papered to death by financially secure defendants in discovery matters—interrogatories and depositions—the illegitimate offspring of notice pleadings. Nevertheless, I offer one suggestion that I learned when I was co-counsel with Edward Bennett Williams, without question one of the finest trial lawyers in the Nation. He died at an early age but his firm, Williams & Connelly LLP, carries on the traditions of its founder. It represented President Clinton in his Whitewater and impeachment proceedings. Ed was a sole practitioner when we first got together.

What I learned from him was not to have a solitary file for a case; instead prepare a file for every potential witness—yours and your opponent's. When opened on one side, have a typed statement setting forth the facts expected to be forthcoming from the witness. On the other side, display a mini-brief setting forth the relevant law on evidence governing the expected facts. This always required some research before trial because the Federal Rules of Evidence did not take effect until about 20 years later on July 1, 1975.

The advantage of this preparation is that you can always have the law at your fingertips if there is an objection to the testimony of your witness, or to support your objection to an opponent.

When I came to the bar I was astonished that with the exception of the largest law firms, very few law offices had comprehensive libraries. To be sure, some of the sole practitioners serving as specialists had treatises in their office, but, for the most part, the great majority of lawyers and small firms depended on the Allegheny County Law Library for their research; as a result, very little research was conducted for the average trial. I decided otherwise when I began my practice. For example, my preceptor had no books in his office, and most of the offices I had visited were the same. In my meanderings around town, I met Ignacio Baca from Puerto Rico, the Western Pennsylvania representative of West Publishing Company, and he found me a very willing customer—with one problem; I did not have a nickel in my jeans. We eventually worked out a deal. I would install a full service library in my office, with no money down, no installment payment schedule and no interest.

When I began my practice, I had a night office with a real estate broker in my hometown of Carnegie, which I used four nights a week at first, and after a year cut down to three nights until 1952 when I got married. At first I shared a daytime office with five other lawyers who all had other full time, law-related functions—two were assistant district attorneys, another was a member of the Board of Viewers (an agency of the Common Pleas Court that processed eminent domain claims), the fourth a retired lawyer who seldom appeared but was active in preparing and distributing Pittsburgh City maps, and finally Louis L. Kaufman, one of Pittsburgh's first radio news reporters in the Twenties who still had one broadcast a day. His practice was limited to family law, largely from women who listened to his broadcasts. I shared my own office with one of the assistant district attorneys who used the office only after 4 p.m. I paid him one half of his share of the rent, and one half of his share of paying the secretary.

With this as a background, in a few weeks my library arrived: *Atlantic 2d Reporter* (containing, *inter alia*, Pennsylvania Supreme Court and Superior Court cases), *Vale's Pennsylvania Digest*, *Corpus Juris Secundum* and the United States

Code Annotated. In addition, somehow I came into possession, without any expense to me, of a set of old Pennsylvania Supreme Court Reports from 1900 to the advent of Atlantic 2d. I purchased some metal shelves, and my library soon filled the walls of the generous reception room of Suite 600, Jones Law Building.

I used the books immediately in my unpaid public defender capacity; in so doing I soon earned the respect of the assistant D.A.s, but especially the respect of the trial judges in matters of evidence, substantive law and jury instructions. From my own 14-year practice of law, my advice is loud and clear: whether through books or online materials, prepare your case better than your opponent. There's no other way.

The law is far more complicated today than it was during the late 1940s and the 1950s when I worked as a sole practitioner. During my 18-month introduction to the courtroom as an unpaid public defender, I was able to develop a private practice in my home town, Carnegie, Penn. In the years following World War II, retuning G.I.s purchased lots and existing houses in townships and boroughs, many of which were former coal mining camps. I soon was able to create a thriving real estate practice representing purchasers. In Greater Pittsburgh, the commercial real estate title companies had not yet developed the monopoly they enjoy today. In representing purchasers, more often than not, lawyers also searched titles. Within a few years I was able to develop a personal abstract of titles going back as far as William Penn and extending to relatively recent development tracts. These were my bread-and-butter clients who paid my Pittsburgh office and secretarial expenses. As the local boy who "done good" becoming a Marine Corps officer during the war and then literally hanging out his shingle in the home town, my practice as a "country lawyer" in the big city gradually expanded to representing families in all aspects of family law— writing wills and real estate agreements, representing decedent's estates or parties in neighborhood disputes, getting their children out of jail in the middle of the night, representing small businesses such as restaurants, building contractors, bars and saloons, groceries, and yes, doing their federal income tax returns. I soon became one of the organizers of the local Kiwanis Club and an officer of the local chamber of commerce.

As I became active in fraternal and charitable organizations in Western Pennsylvania, my clientele expanded substantially beyond my original hometown base to a corps of large construction and land development businesses, including builders and operators of shopping centers, and commercial and school construction builders. I found a loophole in the Pennsylvania hospital law and was able to acquire a charter for a hospital for osteopathic physicians who had been denied access to Western Pennsylvania hospitals. I served as its counsel and officer and board member until 1961 when I was elected judge of the Common Pleas Court of Allegheny County.

Additionally, during this time, I had become a very successful personal injuries lawyer, having acquired excellent courtroom skills during my early days in criminal court. The insurance companies soon learned that I would go to court rather than accept a small settlement offer, and in time, I had referrals from other plaintiffs lawyers to try cases for them.

On balance I had an excellent and successful 14 years as a sole general practitioner.

My next observation is to not be intimidated by the reputation of strength or righteousness of your opponent, whether it be the federal or state governments or corporations represented by huge law firms. A classic example was my five-year *pro bono* representation of Aldo ("Ike") Icardi, who in World War II had been an agent of the OSS, the precursor to the CIA. He was a friend of long standing. When we were undergraduates at the University of Pittsburgh, he was a year behind me, serving as catcher of the varsity baseball team and as head cheerleader during football season; after the war he was also a year behind me when we were in law school at Pitt.

Ike returned from the war a decorated hero, and by the summer of 1951 he was married and had two children (delivered by my brother, Caesar, an obstetrician and gynecologist). Ike was beginning a career in New York City as an in-house counsel for Panagra, the airline jointly owned by Pan-American Airlines and Grace Steamship Lines, which operated between the United States and Central and South America. He was splendidly suited for this position because after receiving his degree from the School of Law of the University of Pittsburgh, he had pursued additional law studies at the Catholic University of Lima, Peru. He was trilingual, fluent in Italian and Spanish as well as English.

On the evening of August 15, 1951, his world caved in.

After dinner he had been scanning a newspaper while his wife was clearing the dinner table. The radio had been broadcasting a music program as a prelude to the evening news. The news came on with a lead story:

> Aldo Icardi, New York lawyer, has been accused by the Defense Department of ordering the murder of his commanding officer when they were on an espionage mission for the OSS behind German lines in Northern Italy in December, 1944.

There was no indictment. No initiation of prosecution. Only a press release from the Department of Defense's Office of Public Information making the accusation.

Here are the events that led to the press release. On September 26, 1944, then an Army first lieutenant assigned to the OSS, Icardi parachuted into enemy territory in Northern Italy as a member of a small, special intelligence mission headed by Major William V. Holohan. The men had been dropped in the midst of Nazi garrisons and Italian fascists on a mountain known as the Mottarone, which separated Lake Maggiore and Lake Orta. From the time of the initial drop, its members had been constantly on the move to avoid detection. On the night of December 6, Major Holohan disappeared. Seven years after Icardi had received the Legion of Merit Award for his activities in espionage and sabotage working with Italian partisan fighters behind enemy lines, and had been honorably discharged, the Defense Department made the accusations in the form of a press release.

Two days after the thunderbolt, Icardi returned with his wife and children to his parents' Pittsburgh home. He had just started his job in New York, had borrowed money from his parents to move his family from South America where he had completed his graduate work, and had paid the initial rent for a house in New Jersey. He was 31 years old and flat broke.

He telephoned me the day after he arrived and we made arrangements to meet that evening in the privacy of my home. We were to be joined by another law school classmate, Samuel L. Rodgers of nearby Washington County. Ike told us:

> I am not guilty of any crime. I had nothing to do with Holohan's disappearance. The OSS investigated the case while I was still in the service. They even asked me to take a lie detector test. I did so willingly and came through with flying colors. They told me, "We are absolutely convinced that you are telling the truth." Now, I'm now being shafted. My career is ruined. I have a wife and two kids and no money. I've returned to Pittsburgh and my parents have given us a roof over our head. I'm turning to you guys as my friends. I want your advice and, God, I need your help.

From August 14, 1951, to June 17, 1956, I extended the best of my professional services, sometimes working night and day, in Pittsburgh, Buffalo, New York and Washington, D.C., without even a thought of compensation, and at a substantial personal expense. I did it for three reasons:

- I was convinced that he was innocent.
- I felt strongly that he was a victim of two sinister circumstances totally beyond his control—the anti-Communist McCarthy era in which it was easy to accuse one of being a Communist or siding with them, and a po-

litical damage control reaction in which the Defense Department set into motion a series of events originally designed to protect it against accusations made in a sensational magazine story.

- He was my friend. I had to help him. It's trite to say but, "That's what friends are for."

In *Road to the Robes*, I described at length the factual background and legal investigation, preparation and argument—worthy of a Hollywood blockbuster—around which this case revolved. As a solo practitioner acting on a pro bono basis, and with the help of others, including Edward Bennett Williams, I participated actively in complex, arduous and exhausting court proceedings:

- Defeating an attempt by the Republic of Italy in the U.S. District Court for the Western District of New York to extradite him to stand trial for murder.
- Preparing and filing documents in the Italian court system challenging its right to try him for murder *in absentia*.
- Assisting in the successful defense of charges in the U.S. District Court for the District of Columbia where he was indicted in six counts of perjury for saying six times under oath before a Congressional committee that he was an innocent man.

Icardi was finally acquitted of the perjury case in the U.S. District Court for the District of Columbia, and my five year representation of a friend was the most important case in my 14 years as a lawyer. And I did all of it *pro bono publico*. As a sole practitioner I was up against the powerhouse lawyers of the State Department, the Defense Department and later, the Justice Department. I never faltered and I was never afraid because of one reason: I researched the law—intricate law, private and public international law, military law, the law of international extradition, the law governing the limitations of committees of Congress. And throughout this experience I was confident that I learned the law better than the government lawyers on the other side. Then, too, I worked side by side with Ed Williams from whom I learned sophisticated trial skills that I utilized successfully in the years that would follow as a trial lawyer, that is, until I became a Pennsylvania trial judge.

In this Afterword I have offered but a few suggestions—have a folder with facts expected from every witness, yours and your opponent's, and the relevant law of evidence; spend time in a library (tangible or digital); and heed the call of professional representation regardless of the adversary. The astute reader will note that a common kernel of these suggestions revolves around research and preparation. These suggestions are but a gloss on the preceding material of this book, which examined our common law tradition and offered nuts-and-bolts tips for practitioners. It is my hope that as you close these pages, you will carry with you some of the knowledge and insights gained from my seven-decade vantage point of experience in the law. All of this experience compels me to say to my readers that ours is an adversarial system: researching the law and knowing its intricacies—from the macro to the micro, from the common law system to the inductive generalization—better than your opponent is the best way to become a compleat lawyer.

THE END

A Lawyer's Response

Bobby R. Burchfield, Esq.

Author's Note: *I have asked for a response to this book from Bobby R. Burchfield, a prominent "compleat lawyer" and a former law clerk of mine from 1979–1981.*

He is a partner in the law firm of McDermott Will & Emery LLP based in the Firm's Washington, D.C., office. Bobby serves on the Firm's Management Committee and as co-partner-in-charge of the Firm's Washington, D.C., office.

He has practiced in the area of complex corporate litigation since 1981. He has been named three times as one of the top 500 lawyers in America by LawDragon, *as one of the top 261 commercial litigators in the United States by* Who's Who Legal: USA; *as one of the top 100 lawyers in the D.C. area by* Super Lawyers; *and as one of the top trial lawyers in the D.C. area (*Legal Times, *June 16, 2003). He has been listed in all recent editions of* Best Lawyers in America, *and is highly rated by* Chambers USA. *He served in 1992 as General Counsel of President George H. W. Bush's re-election campaign. By appointment of President George W. Bush, he served on the Antitrust Modernization Commission, which issued its Report and Recommendations on April 7, 2007. At The George Washington University Law School, Bobby was Editor-in-Chief of the Law Review.*

On a lovely Santa Barbara evening on August 15, 2009, Judge Ruggero J. Aldisert and his beautiful wife Agatha joined me for dinner at the Biltmore Hotel. Over the course of dinner, Judge Aldisert ruminated about a book he was composing in his head. The book would pass to current and future judges, lawyers, and law students his accumulated wisdom from fifty years on the bench and over a decade in private practice. It would draw upon several decades of writings by this thoughtful and experienced man about the essence of the American legal system. This is that book.

For the thirty-three years I have known him, Judge Aldisert has always been passionate about these topics. His passion was undiminished that evening, even as he approached his 90th birthday. Whether as an instantaneous thought or a considered plan, he suddenly asked me to write a "real world lawyer's reaction" to the ideas he was articulating. The invitation was both flattering and humbling, but I immediately agreed. This chapter is the result.

From 1979 to 1981, I was one of Judge Aldisert's three law clerks while he served as an active judge on the United States Court of Appeals for the Third Circuit. It was an exciting time to be in Pittsburgh, with the Steelers winning Super Bowls and the Pirates winning the 1979 World Series. We worked efficiently and hard; like his colleagues, Judge Aldisert was justifiably proud of the Third Circuit's reputation as the fastest of the federal courts of appeals to decide cases. It was the rare case not decided within four months of argument, and most were resolved even more quickly.

But more was occurring within those chambers than resolution of federal appeals. In addition to his judging, Judge Aldisert maintained a schedule of teaching, speaking, and writing that would have kept most mortals fully occupied. And central to these endeavors was his study of the judicial process. By occupation judges decide cases, and Judge Aldisert has a well-earned reputation as a wise and decisive judge. Rare among jurists, however, Judge Aldisert was fascinated with the manner in which judges make decisions.

As his books and many articles show, he has studied the common law tradition, and how law has evolved over the centuries. He reflects on the importance as well as the limits of logic and precedent in the law, and how great jurists have avoided "mechanical jurisprudence" and "slot machine justice." Judge Aldisert has participated in the decision of many thousands of cases in his tenure as a state court trial judge in Pennsylvania and as an appellate judge on the Third Circuit, and knows from firsthand experience how he and his many colleagues over the years go about deciding cases, from their initial inclinations through the final written decision. Practicing lawyers will note that he has read tens of thousands of briefs and observed thousands of lawyers at the lectern. He knows what works and what doesn't, what persuades and what doesn't, and what wins and what doesn't.

Few judges in the nation's history have had such a rich experience, and fewer still have undertaken to distill that wisdom and pass it forward. In concept, this work is an ambitious undertaking. For the jurist, it will assist in self-understanding and honing the craft of judging. For the academic, it will provide a rare glimpse at the intersection of the theory and reality of decision making. For the practitioner, it is both a warning and opportunity: a warning that advocacy may not be meeting the standard that it should meet, and an opportunity to learn how to improve and adapt advocacy to the wants and needs of the decision maker.

Against this ambitious background, my task seems relatively simple. It was my objective to draw upon the insights from Judge Aldisert and explain how those insights can best be applied by the practicing lawyer. Although enthusiastic about this task, I feel in many ways ill-equipped to perform it. After thirty years of practicing at the trial and appellate level in courts throughout the United States, I am certain the judges before whom I appear would say that I still have a lot to learn. So I come to this task with more caution and humility than wisdom, and hope that the thoughts that follow will at least trigger reflection and discussion among my colleagues at the Bar.

I.

Judges are generalists. In a recent appearance before the United States Court of Appeals for the Third Circuit, my antitrust class action was preceded by a case involving the Digital Millennium Copyright Act, one presenting evidentiary issues in a criminal case, and another presenting an international jurisdictional dispute. Similarly, in a recent appearance before the California Court of Appeals, argument in my California False Claims Act case was preceded by arguments concerning a drug possession case, a bail bond dispute, and the issue of damages in a residential real estate matter. In each case, questioning from the judges demonstrated their thorough preparation and understanding of the central issues presented. The facility of our trial and appellate judges to move within minutes from one complex legal issue to another completely unrelated legal issue should be a source of great pride for our profession.

As private practitioners, however, many of us lose sight of the fact that judges are generalists. In pursuit of our interests and by force of modern economics, we often become expert in a legal specialty. We practice in an area for years or decades, become thoroughly familiar with the law and lore in the area, and engage in highly sophisticated oral and written conversations with peers in the specialty about the hot issues of the day. This intense focus is certainly beneficial to clients seeking efficient and effective representation. It is also important to the development of the law. As Judge Aldisert makes clear, busy judges typically have little time to engage in lengthy and rigorous analysis of the most difficult issues confronting each field of law. Rather, they rely upon specialists in private practice and academicians to work their way through those complexities and then present the carefully considered issue as advocates in a concrete and understandable way. This extra-judicial analysis of difficult issues allows the courts to move the law forward.

Because each judge is juggling scores or even hundreds of cases presenting unique facts in different areas of the law, it is not possible for our judges to spend as much time mastering the facts or the law of an individual case as the attorneys presenting the case. By the time a complex case is presented for decision in the trial or appellate court, the lawyers will have spent hundreds or thousands of hours marshalling the facts, researching and analyzing the law, and constructing their arguments. Courts are neither designed nor intended to duplicate that effort. But we must also recognize that judges are highly intelligent beings, committed to doing justice. So how does a lawyer prominent in his or her specialty present a highly complex matter to a generalist judge in a way that is understandable and persuasive without appearing to patronize the jurist?

There is wisdom in Winston Churchill's observation that "Out of intense complexities intense simplicities emerge." For my money, this is one of the great challenges of private practice today. But our best contemporary advocates meet this challenge. Lawyers who do—such as Seth Waxman and Ted Olson at the appellate level and Phil Beck and Ted Wells at the trial level—move from case to case and subject area to subject area while communicating effectively and most often successfully with courts about some of the nation's most complex and difficult issues.

It is best left to those advocates to describe how they do it, but certain common traits can be observed. First, as brilliant as these lawyers are, they are able to cut to the essence of the issue and focus the court's attention on the decisive points without undue distraction by collateral matters. They develop a sense of what is important to the court, and they address it head-on. They determine the focal point, the pivotal issue, of the case, and carefully reason through it. Second, they communicate in straightforward and common language. They avoid jargon. They are less concerned with appearing erudite than being clear. As discussed below, when used well, common language is eloquent and effective. Third, they are realistic about their cases and candid with the courts. This trait allows them to anticipate and prepare for weaknesses in their positions, and rarely if ever to be caught unprepared to address those weaknesses. And finally, they maintain clarity in their thinking, writing, and oral advocacy. I have found through many years of law practice and before that years of competitive debate that whenever an argument gets confused, I tend to lose. Maintaining simplicity, clarity, and candor dramatically enhances the prospects for success.

Of course, not all attorneys are courtroom lawyers, and not all courtroom lawyers limit themselves to advocacy. Many lawyers are counselors. If to a hammer everything looks like a nail, a legal specialist must avoid seeing every issue as one within his or her specialty. When I think of the legendary "wise men" of Washington law, such as Clark Clifford, Lloyd Cutler, and Charlie Horsky, I see them foremost as counselors whose legal judgment was sought for the most difficult issues facing clients and the Nation. Their judgment was informed not necessarily by expertise in a particular legal specialty, but by a panorama of experience in the law, in public service, and in life.

As our profession and our clients push younger lawyers to earlier and narrower specializations, we must ask ourselves where the next generation of wise men and women will come from. This is not to say that lawyers should not specialize, but it is to say that lawyers should maintain an intellectual curiosity about legal topics outside their normal daily fare, and should be bold in seeking out and taking on new challenges—inside and outside the law—throughout their careers. This too is part of being a "compleat lawyer."

II.

The written word is a lawyer's stock in trade. Appellate courts are requesting oral argument in a smaller and smaller portion of cases. At the trial level, a smaller percentage of cases go to trial, and judges seem to request oral argument on a smaller portion of motions. As a result, the written word is often the only chance an advocate has to present the client's case. Even when the trial or appellate court entertains oral argument, the briefs frame the issues and dispose the court on how to rule. Against these truths, our profession must be concerned when pre-eminent jurists criticize the state of our legal writing.

Criticism of contemporary legal writing is not new, but appears to be increasing. Whether it is because the 21st century lawyer has received less rigorous training in English composition than his or her predecessors, or because the sheer volume of written work thrust upon our courts has made bad writing much more painful, or because the profession (and our clients) simply place less value on careful, precise writing than in the past, the alarms are too constant and loud to be ignored.

In parallel with these criticisms, almost all lawyers believe they are great writers. For my part, I will die aspiring to be a great writer. That aspiration, I hope, is an incentive to be constantly attentive to my own written work and that of my colleagues, and to improve the skills over time.

So what is great legal writing? I will venture a few observations from the perspective of a senior partner at a large law firm.

Great legal writing is more Hemingway than Faulkner, more muscle than flowers, and more conversational than pedantic. For example, Strunk and White teach use of the active voice. Many critical readers view flowery prose, or prose laden with adjectives and adverbs, with skepticism. And for good reason: Adjectives and adverbs tend to be subjective. Heavily qualified statements, dependent clauses, and compound sentences are difficult to follow. Well-reasoned directness sells.

We must also remember that the English language naturally provides points of emphasis. The opening sentence of a brief has the potential to grab the reader's attention and draw him or her into the argument on the author's terms. Why, then, do so many briefs start with "This is an appeal from the United States District Court of New Jersey from an order entered July 1, 2011," or "Plaintiff ABC Company through counsel, hereby responds to Defendant XYZ Company's motion to dismiss"? If we assume the brief has a caption and a heading, and that the judge or clerk has not picked it up randomly, these sentences tell the reader nothing. Not only has the author wasted a sentence, he has lost the only opportunity to make a memorable first impression. The introductory sentence should be a strong, concise statement of why your client should win. Alternatively, it should lure the reader into the argument on terms that set the stage for winning. But it should not just tell the court what it already knows. In brief writing as in life, you have only one chance to make a good first impression.

A brief should lead with its strongest argument. Rarely if ever should a brief present more than three arguments. Argument headings should be declarative statements. Within each argument, propositions should be stated directly and in a logical order, with appropriate use, but not overuse, of subheadings.

The topic sentence of each paragraph can carry emphasis, and should introduce the paragraph. Among other uses, topic sentences can set forth direct propositions to be proved in the paragraph, or state the issue to be addressed. Topic sentences are important; be attentive to topic sentences.

Each sentence has points of emphasis at the beginning and the end; do not bury a key thought in the middle of a long sentence. Short, declarative sentences are virtuous. Long, unwieldy sentences are frequently mischievous.

With regard to word choice, Winston Churchill said it well: "Short words are best, and the old words when short are best of all." A lawyer eager to win his case is less interested in testing the judge's vocabulary than in plainly making a compelling point. This is not to say, however, that fancy words have no place in legal writing. Years ago, I recall a senior partner, Roberts B. Owen, adding the word "*eleemosynary*" to an antitrust brief, sending associates, junior partners, and senior partners at several law firms, and doubtless the judge and his law clerks, scrambling for the dictionary. Owen drove home—in a way memorable twenty years later—precisely the point that our client was not in business for a *charitable* purpose. That was effective. But use of fancy words merely to convey personal erudition typically is not. Use big words purposely.

As we write, we would do well to recall "Dirty Harry" Callahan's admonition: "A man must know his limitations." If you know you are an eloquent writer whose elegant prose can persuade the unpersuadable, be eloquent. You are in a rare class. On the other hand, if (like me) you lack that facility, write simply.

Another important precept to great writing is that of my mentor, Judge Aldisert: "There is no such thing as *good writing*; there is only *good rewriting*." With the advent of personal computers, and now a generation of lawyers who compose at the keyboard, lawyers often claim to "edit as I go." This seems to mean that the author corrects misspellings, makes word substitutions, and perhaps occasionally changes organization while composing. When the final period is placed on the final page, the document is saved and then sent. This is not editing.

Editing consists of carefully going through the document numerous times (my average for a brief is about eight or ten times), beginning to end, reading each argument, paragraph, sentence, and word for precision, conciseness, and flow, rewriting heavily at first and more lightly with each pass; then seeking comment from colleagues; and then, at the end of this process, carefully proofreading the document before sending it on its way. Spellchecking programs, though handy, are no substitute for careful proofreading because they do not detect logical leaps, noun and verb disagreements, omissions of words, errors of syntax, or other problems.

The old saying bears repeating: a brief should be *brief*. Page and word limits set forth maxima, not requisites. Careful organization, tight reasoning, studied use of adjectives and adverbs, and careful editing all make briefs shorter. It would not be possible to state a one-size-fits-all length for every brief. We can, however, gain insight from Abraham Lincoln's response when asked how long a man's legs should be: "just long enough to reach the ground."

To test whether these precepts can really produce good writing, I surveyed a number of colleagues about their favorite quotations in the English language. A small sampling follows:

"To be or not to be? That is the question."
   —William Shakespeare

"Discretion is the better part of valor."
   —William Shakespeare

"Hope is necessary in every condition."
   —Samuel Johnson

"I have nothing to offer but blood, toil, tears and sweat."
   —Winston Churchill

"Never was so much owed by so many to so few."
—Winston Churchill

"I have a dream that my four little children will one day live in a nation where they will not be judged by the color of their skin but by the content of their character."
—Martin Luther King, Jr.

"Four score and seven years ago our fathers brought forth on this continent a new nation, conceived in liberty, and dedicated to the proposition that all men are created equal."
—Abraham Lincoln

"Do unto others as you would have them do unto you."
—The Golden Rule

These memorable phrases, and others we all know, have common traits. They use short, every day words in simple sentence structure. Yet they are both compelling and memorable.

Out here in the real world, we can respond to Judge Aldisert's observation that courts are overworked and over-briefed by making our writing more succinct, more direct, and simpler. I am newly pledged to take this advice.

III.

Judge Aldisert reminds us of the common law tradition. The common law evolves case by case, with each decision addressing the particular set of facts before the court, and the court following precedent under the doctrine of *stare decisis*. The holding of a case, and the precedent it sets, is limited to the court's actual decision of the legal issue based upon the particular facts in front of it. Language used by the court in its opinion is *dicta*, not precedent, and cannot bind later courts. Reliance upon quotations rather than holdings is, in Judge Aldisert's phrase, "*stare dictis*" rather than *stare decisis*.

No doubt lawyers have long relied upon *dicta* rather than holdings in making their arguments. Often, in a case of first impression, *dicta* from an earlier decision is the best guidance the lawyer has of a court's leanings on an issue. Yet, under the common law tradition the holdings of prior cases, not the *dicta*, control future cases.

Overreliance on *dicta* may be more pervasive now than in the past. Computer research tools such as LexisNexis® and Westlaw® teach lawyers to conduct legal research by using phrases to find pertinent cases. Led to particular passages in the court opinion that match the word search, many a young lawyer can believe that the task is completed by simply adding language from the matching passage to the brief. A capable lawyer using modern legal research tools can readily support almost any argument by stringing together quotations from cases, some of which might have little or nothing to do with the actual holdings of the cases being quoted. Discerning courts are not persuaded by strings of *quotations*. Rather, as Judge Aldisert notes, courts rely on actual precedent— *holdings*—aided by logic.

Determining the court's holding is more difficult than extracting quotations, but it is far more important. We learned to distinguish holding from *dicta* in the first week of law school. This distinction is a basic part of the common law tradition. Yet, it is often overlooked.

Part of the fun and challenge of practicing law is addressing novel issues. In those situations, we may have no true precedent to guide us. In those circumstances, reasoning from precedent and using logic to fill in the gaps can be a more persuasive way to make an argument than reliance on *dicta*. An argument reasoned from precedent, combined with pertinent, well-considered quotations from related decisions, can be powerful in persuading a court to resolve an open issue in the desired way.

IV.

In his effort define the "compleat lawyer," Judge Aldisert alludes to the importance of lawyers being complete people. Intellectual curiosity beyond the law, broad reading, and public service are certainly attributes of a "compleat lawyer."

Although lawyers are the butt of jokes and poorly regarded in every public survey of professions, they are at the same time a subject of immense fascination to the public. Books, television shows, and movies about lawyers are legion. Lawyers are well if not over represented in positions of governance: 26 of our 44 presidents have been lawyers, as were 24 of 56 signers of the Declaration of Independence, and 22 of 40 signers of the Constitution. In any community, people look to lawyers as leaders.

The "compleat lawyer" is a creature not only of the profession, but of the community as well. And so it should be. The issues lawyers are called upon to advocate touch the lives of clients, but also affect whole communities and even the Nation. Public policy and common good are integral to the decisions courts are called upon to make, and to the issues lawyers are called upon to advocate. Not every lawyer will devote time to government service (although many do), and not every lawyer will argue important issues of public policy in court or before agencies (although many do), but a "compleat lawyer" must have an active curiosity about public policy. Whether liberal or conservative, Democrat or Republican, activist or originalist, the compleat lawyer should not and cannot ignore the ongoing debate.

———————

As I write, I reflect upon how my approach to being a lawyer has been molded by my long association with Judge Ruggero Aldisert. It is my hope that readers of his book will have occasion over the course of their careers as lawyers, or as people who know lawyers, to reflect on the more noble aspects of this wonderful profession.

Appendix

References

Chapter 1

Ruggero J. Aldisert, *On Being Civil to Younger*, 11 Conn. L. Rev. 181 (1979).

Thomas G. Barnes, Introduction to W. Blackstone, Commentaries on the Laws of England (1983).

Jacques Barzun, *Behind the Blue Pencil*, 54 Am. Scholar 385 (1985).

William Blackstone, Commentaries on the Laws of England (1765–1769).

John D. Calamari & Joseph M. Perillo, Contracts (2d ed. 1977).

Benjamin N. Cardozo, The Nature of the Judicial Process (1921).

Arthur L. Corbin, Corbin on Contracts § 992 (1964).

Alfred Denning, The Family Story (1981).

Alfred Denning, What Next in the Law (1982).

Deuteronomy 23:20.

John H. Ely, *The Supreme Court 1977 Term, Foreword: On Discovering Fundamental Values*, 92 Marv. L. Rev. 5 (1978).

Ralph W. Emerson, Society and Solitude (1870).

Exodus, 22:5–6, 9.

Genesis 38:7–11.

Hugo Grotius, The Law of War and Peace (1646).

Laird Kirkpatrick, *Defining a Constitutional Tort Under Section 1983: The State of Mind Requirement*, 46 U. Cin. L. Rev. 45 (1977).

Thomas B. Macaulay, The History of England from the Accession of James II (1914).

Henry S. Maine, Ancient Law: Its Connection with the Early History of Society, and Its Relation to Modern Ideas (John Murray, 1861).

Charles T. McCormick, Handbook on the Law of Damages (1935).

SIR FREDERICK POLLOCK & FREDRICK W. MAITLAND, THE HISTORY OF THE ENGLISH LAW, XXXVIII (2d ed. 1899).

Roscoe Pound, *Hierarchy of Sources and Forms in Different Systems of Law*, 7 TUL. L. REV. 475 (1933).

Fred Rodell, *Goodbye to Law Reviews*, 23 VA. L. REV. 38 (1936).

Eugene Rostow, *The Democratic Character of Judicial Review*, 66 HARV. L. REV. 193 (1952).

SAMUEL P. SCOTT, THE VISIGOTHIC CODE (1910).

JOSEPH A.C. THOMAS, THE INSTITUTES OF JUSTINIAN, TEXT, TRANSLATION AND COMMENTARY (1975).

JOSEPH A.C. THOMAS, TEXTBOOK OF ROMAN LAW (1976).

RICHARD THOMSON, AN HISTORICAL ESSAY ON THE MAGNA CHARTA OF KING JOHN (1829).

Barbara Tuchman, *An Author's Mail*, 54 AM. SCHOLAR 313 (1985).

SAMUEL WILLISTON, A TREATISE ON THE LAW OF CONTRACTS (W. Jaeger 3d ed. 1968).

Cases

Abraham v. Pekarski, 728 F.2d 167 (3d Cir. 1984).

Allgeyer v. Louisiana, 165 U.S. 578 (1897).

Cantwell v. Connecticut, 310 U.S. 296 (1940).

General Elec. Co. v. Gilbert, 429 U.S. 125 (1976).

Goldberg v. Kelly, 397 U.S. 254 (1970).

Griffin v. Breckenridge, 403 U.S. 88 (1971).

Hampton v. Mow Sun Wong, 426 U.S. 88 (1976).

Ingraham v. Wright, 430 U.S. 651 (1977).

Lemon v. Kurtzman, 403 U.S. 602 (1971).

Levy v. Louisiana, 391 U.S. 68 (1968).

Meachum v. Fano, 427 U.S. 215 (1976).

Meyer v. Nebraska, 262 U.S. 390, 399 (1923).

Monell v. New York City Dep't of Social Servs., 436 U.S. 658 (1978).

New York Times Co. v. Sullivan, 376 U.S. 254 (1964).

Roe v. Wade, 410 U.S. 113 (1973).

Sedima, S.P.R.L. v. Imrex Co., 473 U.S. 479 (1985).

Smith v. Wade, 461 U.S. 30 (1983).

Trimble v. Gordon, 430 U.S. 762 (1977).

Statutes

U.C.C. § 1–106 (1976).

8 U.S.C. § 224.

8 U.S.C. § 1081.

8 U.S.C. § 1201.

8 U.S.C. § 1341.

8 U.S.C. § 1953.

8 U.S.C. § 2113.

8 U.S.C. § 2312.

8 U.S.C. § 2421.

18 U.S.C. § 371.

18 U.S.C. § 1951.

18 U.S.C. §§ 1961–1968 (1982).

21 U.S.C. § 801.

42 U.S.C. § 1983 (1982).

Civil Rights Act of 1964, 42 U.S.C. § 2000a (1982).

Chapter 2

Ruggero J. Aldisert, *Judicial Expansion of Federal Jurisdiction: A Federal Judge's Thoughts on Section 1983, Comity and the Federal Caseload*, 1973 ARIZ. ST. U. L.J. 557 (1973).

JOHN L. AUSTIN, PHILOSOPHICAL PAPERS (1961).

BACON'S ESSAYS (1900 ed.).

John Barton, *Behind the Legal Explosion*, 27 STAN. L. REV. 567 (1975).

Hugo Black, *Book Review of A. Cox, The Role of the Supreme Court in American Government*, in N.Y. TIMES, Feb. 29, 1976.

1 WILLIAM BLACKSTONE, COMMENTARIES ON THE LAWS OF ENGLAND (1769).

BENJAMIN N. CARDOZO, THE NATURE OF THE JUDICIAL PROCESS (1921).

SIR RUPERT CROSS, PRECEDENT IN ENGLISH LAW (2d ed. 1968).

PATRICK DEVLIN, SAMPLES OF LAWMAKING (1962).

Thomas Ehrlich, *Legal Pollution*, N.Y. TIMES, Feb. 8, 1976 (Magazine).

Felix Frankfurter, *Some Reflections on the Reading of Statutes*, 47 COLUM. L. REV. 527 (1947).

Charles Fried, *Two Concepts of Interests: Some Reflections on the Supreme Court's Balancing Test*, 76 HARV. L. REV. 755 (1963).

Wolfgang Friedmann, *Legal Philosophy and Judicial Lawmaking*, 61 COLUM. L. REV. 821 (1961).

Henry J. Friendly, *The Gap in Lawmaking—Judges Who Can't and Legislators Who Won't*, 63 COLUM. L. REV. 787 (1963).

JOHN C. GRAY, THE NATURE AND SOURCES OF THE LAW (2d ed. 1921).

JEROME HALL, FOUNDATIONS OF JURISPRUDENCE (1973).

LEARNED HAND, THE CONTRIBUTION OF AN INDEPENDENT JUDICIARY TO CIVILIZATION (1942).

LEARNED HAND, THE SPIRIT OF LIBERTY (2d ed. 1954).

John Hanna, *The Role of Precedent in Judicial Decision*, 2 VILL. L. REV. 367 (1957).

WILLIAM SEARLE HOLDSWORTH, A HISTORY OF ENGLISH LAW (1903).

Oliver Wendell Holmes, Jr., *The Path of the Law*, 10 HARV. L. REV. 457 (1897).

James D. Hopkins, *Fictions and the Judicial Process: A Preliminary Theory of Decision*, 33 BROOKLYN L. REV. 1 (1966).

Shirley M. Hufstedler, *New Blocks for Old Pyramids: Reshaping the Judicial System*, 445 CAL. L. REV. 901 (1971).

Harry W. Jones, *An Invitation to Jurisprudence*, 74 COLUM. L. REV. 1023 (1974).

Harry W. Jones, *Our Uncommon Common Law*, 42 TENN. L. REV. 443 (1975).

HERMAN KAHN, 1965–1975: A DECADE OF MALAISE (1976).

Robert E. Keeton, *Judicial Law Reform—A Perspective on the Performance of Appellate Courts*, 44 TEXAS L. REV. 1254 (1966).

JOSEPH H. KOFFLER & ALISON REPPY, HANDBOOK OF COMMON LAW PLEADING (1969).

Robert A. Leflar, *Sources of Judge-Made Law*, 24 Okla. L. Rev. 319 (1971).

Karl Llewellyn, *A Realistic Jurisprudence—The Next Step*, 30 COLUM. L. REV. 431 (1930).

Karl Llewellyn, *Remarks on the Theory of Appellate Decision and the Rules or Canons About How Statutes Are to Be Construed*, 3 VAND. L. REV. 395 (1950).

CARL McGOWAN, CONGRESS AND THE COURTS (1976).

Roscoe Pound, *Address to the American Bar Association*, Aug. 29, 1906, *in* 40 AM. L. REV. 729 (1906).

Roscoe Pound, *Hierarchy of Sources and Forms in Different Systems of Law*, 7 TUL. L. REV. 475 (1933).

Roscoe Pound, *Mechanical Jurisprudence*, 8 COLUM. L. REV. 605 (1908).

Roscoe Pound, *A Survey of Social Interests*, 57 HARV. L. REV. 1 (1943).

William L. Prosser, *The Fall of the Citadel (Strict Liability to the Consumer)*, 50 MINN. L. REV. 791 (1966).

Elliott L. Richardson, *Freedom of Expression and the Function of Courts*, 65 HARV. L. REV. 1 (1951).

ROBERTS' DIGEST (2d ed. 1847).

Eugene Rostow, *The Democratic Character of Judicial Review*, 66 HARV. L. REV. 193 (1952).

Kenneth E. Scott, *Two Models of the Civil Process*, 27 STAN. L. REV. 937 (1975).

Harlan F. Stone, *The Common Law in the United States*, 50 HARV. L. REV. 4 (1936).

Roger J. Traynor, *Reasoning in a Circle of Law*, 56 VA. L. REV. 739 (1970).

CHARLES E. WVZANSKI, WHEREAS—A JUDGE'S PREMISES (1964).

John M. Zane, *German Legal Philosophy*, 16 MICH. L. REV. 287 (1918).

Cases

Caminetti v. United States, 242 U.S. 470 (1917) (Day, J.).

Fay v. Noia, 372 U.S. 319 (1963).

Ferguson v. Skrupa, 372 U.S. 726 (1963).

Gaudette v. Webb, 284 N.E.2d 222 (Mass. 1972).

Hamilton v. Rathbone, 175 U.S. 414 (1899) (Brown, J.).

Hoffman v. Jones, 280 So. 2d 431 (Fla. 1973).

Li v. Yellow Cab Co., 13 Cal. 3d 804, 532 P.2d 1226 (1975).

Lowden v. Northwestern Nat'l Bank & Trust Co., 298 U.S. 160 (1936).

Marbury v. Madison, 5 U.S. (1 Cranch) 137 (1803).

Moragne v. States Marine Lines, Inc., 398 U.S. 375 (1970).

River Wear Commissioners v. Adamson, 2 App. Cas. 743 (1877) (Lord Blackburn).

Roe v. Wade, 410 U.S. 113 (1973).

Southern Pacific Co. v. Jensen, 244 U.S. 205 (1917) (Holmes, J., dissenting).

Towne v. Eisner, 245 U.S. 418 (1918).

Vacher & Sons, Ltd. v. London Society of Compositors, (1913) A.C. 107 (Lord Atkinson).

Chapter 3

RUGGERO J. ALDISERT, LOGIC FOR LAWYERS: A GUIDE TO CLEAR LEGAL THINKING (1989).

HUGO BLACK, LAW OF JUDICIAL PRECEDENTS (1912).

BLACK'S LAW DICTIONARY 1261 (5th ed. 1979).

1 WILLIAM BLACKSTONE, COMMENTARIES ON THE LAWS OF ENGLAND (1769).

JESSE F. BRUMBAUGH, LEGAL REASONING AND BRIEFING (1917).

BENJAMIN N. CARDOZO, THE NATURE OF THE JUDICIAL PROCESS (1921).

Thomas S. Currier, *Time and Change in Judge-Made Law: Prospective Overruling*, 51 VA. L. REV. 201 (1965).

JOHN DEWEY, HOW WE THINK (2d ed. 1933).

THE FEDERALIST No. 78 (A. Hamilton) (H. Lodge ed. 1888).

Arthur L. Goodhart, *Determining the Ratio Decidendi of a Case*, 40 YALE L.J. 161 (1930).

OLIVER WENDELL HOLMES, JR., THE COMMON LAW (1881).

Oliver Wendell Holmes, Jr., *The Path of the Law*, 10 HARV. L. REV. 457 (1897).

COURTNEY S. KENNY, A SELECTION OF CASES ILLUSTRATIVE OF THE ENGLISH LAW OF TORT (5th ed. 1928).

JAMES KENT, COMMENTARIES ON AMERICAN LAW (12th ed. 1896).

RICHARD KLUGER, SIMPLE JUSTICE (1975).

Andrew Lang, *The Lady Dragonissa*, *in* A CAVALCADE OF DRAGONS (R. Green ed. 1970).

KARL LLEWELLYN, THE BRAMBLE BUSH: ON OUR LAW AND ITS STUDY (7th printing 1981).

Dennis Lloyd, *Reason and Logic in the Common Law*, 64 L.Q. REV. 468 (1948).

Herman Oliphant, *A Return to Stare Decisis*, 14 A.B.A. J. 71 (1928).

Roscoe Pound, *The Theory of Judicial Decision II*, 36 HARV. L. REV. 802 (1923).

WILLIAM LLOYD PROSSER, W. PAGE KEETON, DAN B. DOBBS, ROBERT E. KEETON, DAVID G. OWEN, PROSSER AND KEETON ON TORTS (5th ed. 1984).

RABELAIS, BK. III.

RESTATEMENT (SECOND) OF TORTS (1966).

Walter V. Schaefer, *Precedent and Policy*, 34 U. CHI. L. REV. 3 (1966).

Roger J. Traynor, *La Rude Vita, La Dolce Giustizia; Or Hard Cases Can Make Good Law*, 29 U. CHI. L. REV. 223 (1962).

Roger J. Traynor, *Reasoning in a Circle of Law*, 56 VA. L. REV. 739 (1970).

Cases

Allegheny County Gen. Hosp. v. NLRB, 608 F.2d 965 (3d Cir. 1979).

Andrews v. Styrap, 26 L.T.R. (N.S.) 704, 706 (Ex. 1872).

Bair v. American Motors Corp., 535 F.2d 249 (3d Cir. 1976).

Beckwith v. United States, 425 U.S. 341 (1976).

Berkebile v. Brantly Helicopter Corp., 462 Pa. 83, 337 A.2d 893 (1975).

Boy's Markets, Inc. v. Retail Clerks Union, Local 770, 398 U.S. 235 (1970) (Stewart, J., concurring).

Brown v. Board of Ed., 347 U.S. 483 (1954).

Cohens v. Virginia, 19 U.S. (6 Wheat.) 264 (1821).

Com. v. Little, 432 Pa. 256, 248 A.2d 32 (1968).

Coolidge v. New Hampshire, 403 U.S. 443 (1971).

Dillon v. Legg, 68 Cal. 2d 728, 441 P.2d 912 (1968).

Duckworth v. Eagan, 492 U.S. 195 (1989).

Finberg v. Sullivan, 634 F.2d 50 (3d Cir. 1980).

Harris v. New York, 401 U.S. 222 (1971).

Horton v. California, 493 U.S. 889 (1989).

Illinois Elections Bd. v. Socialist Workers Party, 440 U.S. 173 (1979).

Leong v. Takasaki, 55 Haw. 398, 520 P.2d 758 (1974).

MacPherson v. Buick Motor Co., 217 N.Y. 382, 111 N.E. 1050 (1916).

McGrath v. Kristensen, 340 U.S. 162 (1950) (Jackson, J., concurring).

Michigan v. Mosley, 423 U.S. 96 (1975).

Miranda v. Arizona, 384 U.S. 436 (1966).

Monell v. New York City Dept. of Social Servs., 436 U.S. 658 (1978).

Moragne v. States Marine Lines, Inc., 398 U.S. 375 (1970).

Moran v. Burbine, 475 U.S. 412 (1986).

Patterson v. McClean Credit Union, 491 U.S. 164 (1989)

People v. Miller, 196 Cal. App. 3d 846 (1987).

Rumsey v. New York & N.E.R.R., 133 N.Y. 79, 30 N.E. 654 (1892).

Spicer v. Spicer, 79 Eng. Rep. 451 (K.B. 1620).

Strotman v. K.C. Summers Buick, Inc., 141 Ill. App. 3d 8, 489 N.E.2d 1148 (1986).

United States v. Carver, 260 U.S. 482 (1923).

Vasquez v. Hillery, 474 U.S. 254 (1986).

Webb v. Zern, 422 Pa. 424, 220 A.2d 853 (1966).

Statutes

5 U.S.C. §7324(a)(2) (1982).

28 U.S.C. §§2244, 2254 (1982).

Chapter 4

JOSEPH GERARD BRENNAN, A HANDBOOK OF LOGIC (1957).

JOHN C. COOLEY, A PRIMER OF FORMAL LOGIC (1942).

IRVING M. COPI, INTRODUCTION TO LOGIC (7th ed. 1986).

JOHN DEWEY, HOW WE THINK (2d ed. 1933).

Nicholas F. Lucas, Comment, *Logic and Law*, 3 MARQ. L. REV. 204 (1919).

JOHN STUART MILL, A SYSTEM OF LOGIC RATIOCINATIVE AND INDUCTIVE (8th ed. 1916).

L.S. STEBBING, A MODERN INTRODUCTION TO LOGIC (6th ed. 1948).

Cases

Tose v. First Pa. Bank, N.A., 648 F.2d 879 (3d Cir. 1981).

Chapter 5

BENJAMIN N. CARDOZO, THE NATURE OF THE JUDICIAL PROCESS (1921).

IRVING M. COPI & KEITH BURGESS-JACKSON, INFORMAL LOGIC (1996).

S. MORRIS ENGEL, WITH GOOD REASON: AN INTRODUCTION TO INFORMAL FALLACIES (6th ed. 2000).

Jack L. Landau, *Logic for Lawyers*, 13 PAC. L.J. 59 (1981).

GOTTFRIED WILHELM LEIBNITZ, NEW ESSAYS CONCERNING HUMAN UNDERSTANDING (Alfred Gideon Langley trans., 1916).

EDWARD H. LEVI, AN INTRODUCTION TO LEGAL REASONING (1949).

John Stuart Mill, A System of Logic Ratiocinative and Inductive (8th ed. 1916).

The Paper Chase (Twentieth Century Fox 1973).

Cases

Brown v. Board of Education, 347 U.S. 483 (1954).

Dred Scott v. Sandford, 60 U.S. (19 How.) 393 (1856).

Estate of Stinchcomb, 674 P.2d 26 (Okla. 1983).

Griswold v. Connecticut, 381 U.S. 479 (1965).

Home Office v. Dorset Yacht Co., [1970] A.C. 1004 (H.L.).

In re Linerboard Antitrust Litig., 305 F.3d 145 (3d Cir. 2002).

Marbury v. Madison, 5 U.S. (1 Cranch) 137 (1803).

Newton v. Merrill Lynch, 259 F.3d 154 (3d Cir. 2001).

O'Conner v. Commonwealth Edison Co., 807 F. Supp. 1376 (C.D. Ill. 1992).

Roe v. Wade, 410 U.S. 113 (1973).

United States v. Jannotti, 673 F.2d 579 (3d Cir. 1982).

Youngstown Sheet & Tube Co. v. Sawyer, 343 U.S. 579 (1952).

Chapter 6

Ruggero J. Aldisert, Logic for Lawyers: A Guide to Clear Legal Thinking (3d ed. 1997).

I The Works of Aristotle, De Sophisticis Elenchis (W.D. Ross trans. 1928).

John Dewey, How We Think (2d ed. 1933).

Ralph M. Eaton, General Logic (1931).

William S. & Mabel Lewis Sahakian, Ideas of the Great Philosophers (1966).

Chapter 7

Paul M. Bator, The State Courts and Federal Constitutional Litigation, 22 Wm. & Mary L. Rev. 605 (1981).

Benjamin Cardozo, The Nature of the Judicial Process (1921).

Robert M. Cover, The Uses of Jurisdictional Redundancy: Interest, Ideology, and Innovation, 22 Wm. & Mary L. Rev. 639 (1981).

Martha A. Field, The Uncertain Nature of Federal Jurisdiction, 22 Wm. & Mary L. Rev. 683 (1981).

Burt Neuborne, *Toward Procedural Parity in Constitutional Litigation*, 22 Wm. & Mary L. Rev. 725 (1981).

Chapter 8

Ruggero J. Aldisert, Winning on Appeal: Better Briefs and Oral Argument (NITA 2d ed. 2003) (1992).

Statistics on federal court filings and dispositions are published annually in Director of the Administrative Office of the United States Courts Annual Report, Annual Report of the Director.

Chapter 9

Ruggero J. Aldisert, *The House of the Law*, 19 Loy. L.A. L. Rev. 755 (1986).

Benjamin N. Cardozo, Growth of the Law (1924).

Benjamin N. Cardozo, The Nature of the Judicial Process (1921).

Shirley M. Hufstedler, *New Blocks for Old Pyramids: Reshaping the Judicial System*, 44 S. Cal. L. Rev. 901 (1971).

Thomas A. Marvel, *Abbreviated Appellate Procedure: An Evaluation of the New Mexico Summary Calendar*, 75 Judicature 86 (1991).

Thomas A. Reavley, *A Review of* Rationing Justice on Appeal: The Problems of the U.S. Courts of Appeals, 26 Tex. Tech L. Rev. 271 (1995).

Maurice Rosenberg, *Judicial Discretion of the Trial Court, Viewed from Above*, 22 Syracuse L. Rev. 635 (1971).

Cases

Martinez v. Court of Appeal of California, 528 U.S. 152 (2000).

McKane v. Durston, 153 U.S. 684 (1894).

Ross v. Moffitt, 417 U.S. 600 (1974).

Smith v. Robbins, 528 U.S. 259 (2000).

State v. Cooper, 498 A.2d 1209 (N.H. 1985).

Chapter 10

Administrative Office of the United States Courts, *United States Court of Appeals Judicial Caseload Profile*, at http://www.UScourts.gov/cgi-bin/cmsa 2002.pl.

Ruggero J. Aldisert, Logic for Lawyers: A Guide to Clear Legal Thinking (3d ed. 1997).

Ruggero J. Aldisert, Opinion Writing (1990).

Ruggero J. Aldisert, Winning on Appeal: Better Briefs and Oral Argument (NITA 2d ed. 2003) (1992).

Kenneth E. Andersen, Persuasion: Theory and Practice (1971).

Erwin P. Bettinghaus, Persuasive Communication (3d ed. 1980).

Myron H. Bright, *Appellate Briefwriting: Some "Golden" Rules,* 17 Creighton L. Rev. 1069 (1983).

Nicholas M. Cripe, *Fundamentals of Persuasive Oral Argument,* 20 Forum 342 (1985).

John W. Davis, *The Argument of an Appeal,* 26 A.B.A.J. 895 (1940).

John Dewey, How We Think (2d ed. 1933).

Robert J. Martineau, Appellate Justice in England and the United States: A Comparative Analysis (1990).

James L. Robertson, *Reality on Appeal,* 17 Litig. 3 (1990).

Joseph Story, Life and Letters II (William Wetmore Story, ed. 1851), *reprinted in* John M. Greaney, *Power of the Pen,* 38 Trial 48 (July 2002).

Chapter 11

Thomas Aquinas, II Basic Writings of St. Thomas Aquinas (A.C. Pegis ed. 1945).

Benjamin N. Cardozo, The Nature of the Judicial Process (1921).

Morris L. Cohen, Legal Research in a Nutshell (2d ed. 1971).

Ronald Dworkin, *The Model of Rules,* 35 U. Chi. L. Rev. 14 (1967).

Robert E. Keeton, Venturing to Do Justice (1969).

Edward H. Levi, *An Introduction to Legal Reasoning,* 15 U. Chi. L. Rev. 501 (1948).

Roscoe Pound, *Hierarchy of Sources and Forms in Different Systems of Law,* 7 Tul. L. Rev. 475 (1933).

Roscoe Pound, *Mechanical Jurisprudence,* 8 Colum. L. Rev. 605 (1908).

Roscoe Pound, *A Survey of Social Interests,* 57 Harv. L. Rev. 1 (1943).

William S. Sahakian & Mabel Lewis Sahakian, Ideas of a Great Philosopher (1966).

Philip Selznick, *Sociology and Natural Law,* 6 Nat. L.F. 84 (1961).

Harlan F. Stone, *The Common Law in the United States*, 50 HARV. L. REV. 4 (1936).

Herbert Wechsler, *Toward Neutral Principles of Constitutional Law*, 73 HARV. L. REV. 1 (1959).

Cases

Brown v. Allen, 344 U.S. 443 (1953) (Jackson, J., concurring).

Chapter 12

Ruggero J. Aldisert, *Introduction to the Third Circuit Review: Advice to Law Review Writers*, 30 VILL. L. REV. 828 (1985).

RUGGERO J. ALDISERT, LOGIC FOR LAWYERS: A GUIDE TO CLEAR LEGAL THINKING (3d ed. 1997).

Ruggero J. Aldisert, *Opinion Writers and Law Review Writers: A Community and Continuity of Approach*, 16 DUQ. L. REV. 139 (1977–78).

Harry W. Jones, *An Invitation to Jurisprudence*, 74 COLUM. L. REV. 1023 (1974).

Walter V. Schaefer, *Precedent and Policy*, 34 U. CHI. L. REV. 1 (1966).

HENRY WEIHOFEN, LEGAL WRITING STYLE (1961).

Chapter 13

JOHN AUSTIN, LECTURES ON JURISPRUDENCE (1945).

JEREMY BENTHAM, PRINCIPLES OF MORALS AND LEGISLATION (Haffner ed. 1970) (rev. ed. 1823).

ALEXANDER M. BICKEL, THE LEAST DANGEROUS BRANCH (1962).

ALEXANDER M. BICKEL, THE MORALITY OF CONSENT (1975).

BENJAMIN N. CARDOZO, THE NATURE OF THE JUDICIAL PROCESS (1921).

Felix Cohen, *Transcendental Nonsense and the Functional Approach*, 35 COLUM. L. REV. 809 (1935).

ROBERT DAHL, DEMOCRACY IN THE UNITED STATES (3d ed. 1967).

PATRICK DEVLIN, THE JUDGE (1974).

A.V. DICEY, LAW AND PUBLIC OPINION IN ENGLAND (1985).

RONALD DWORKIN, TAKING RIGHTS SERIOUSLY (1977).

John Hart Ely, *Foreword: On Discovering Fundamental Values*, 92 HARV. L. REV. 5 (1978).

Ralph Waldo Emerson, Society and Solitude (1870).

Joseph Epstein, *True Virtue*, N.Y. Times, Nov. 24, 1985, §6 (Magazine).

Charles Fried, *Correspondence: Author's Reply*, 86 Yale L.J. 573 (1977).

Learned Hand, The Bill of Rights (1958).

Learned Hand, *A Personal Confession*, Continuing Legal Education for Professional Competence and Responsibility (Report on the Arden House Conference, December 16–19, 1958), *reprinted in* Rugerro J. Aldisert, The Judicial Process (1976).

H.L.A. Hart, The Concept of Law (1961).

Thomas Hobbes, Leviathan (1651).

Harry W. Jones, *An Invitation to Jurisprudence*, 74 Colum. L. Rev. 1023 (1974).

Immanuel Kant, The Philosophy of Law (Kelley ed. 1974) (Hastie trans. 1887) (2d ed. 1798).

Jethro K. Lieberman, Milestones! (1976).

Karl Llewellyn, The Common Law Tradition (1960).

John Locke, Second Treatise on Civil Government (Everyman's ed. 1924).

John Stuart Mill, On Liberty (1849).

Richard Neely, How Courts Govern America (1981).

Robert Nozick, Anarchy, State, and Utopia (1974).

Herbert Packer, The Limits of the Criminal Sanction (1968).

Plato, The Republic, Bk. III.

Roscoe Pound, *Address Before the Pennsylvania Bar Association*, 22 Pa. Bar Ass'n Rep. 221 (1916).

Roscoe Pound, *Hierarchy of Sources and Forms in Different Systems of Law*, 7 Tul. L. Rev. 475 (1933).

Roscoe Pound, *The Theory of Judicial Decision*, 36 Harv. L. Rev. 641 (1923).

2 Francois Rabelais, Gargantua and Pantagruel (Everyman's ed. 1929) (1532).

John Rawls, A Theory of Justice (1971).

Maurice Rosenberg, *Judicial Discretion of the Trial Court, Viewed from Above*, 22 Syracuse L. Rev. 635 (1971).

Max Weber, On Law in Economy and Society (Rheinstein ed. 1954) (2d ed. 1925).

Cases

Brown v. Board of Education, 347 U.S. 483 (1954).

Brown v. Board of Education, 349 U.S. 294 (1955).

Cohens v. Virginia, 19 U.S. (6 Wheat.) 264 (1821).

Dartmouth College v. Woodward, 17 U.S. (4 Wheat.) 518 (1819).

Elrod v. Burns, 427 U.S. 347 (1976).

Erie Railroad Co. v. Tompkins, 304 U.S. 64 (1938).

Fletcher v. Peck, 10 U.S. (6 Cranch) 87 (1810).

Gibbons v. Ogden, 22 U.S. (9 Wheat.) 1 (1824).

Marbury v. Madison, 5 U.S. (1 Cranch) 137 (1803).

McCulloch v. Maryland, 17 U.S. (4 Wheat.) 316 (1819).

New York Times v. Sulllivan, 376 U.S. 254 (1964).

Osborn v. Bank of the United States, 22 U.S. (9 Wheat.) 738 (1824).

Chapter 14

Louis Blom-Cooper, The Language of the Law (1965).

Benjamin N. Cardozo, The Nature of the Judicial Process (1921).

Felix Cohen, *Transcendental Nonsense and the Functional Approach*, 35 Colum. L. Rev. 809 (1935).

John Dewey, How We Think (2d ed. 1933).

Leon Festinger, Conflict, Decision and Dissonance (1964).

Jerome Frank, Law and the Modern Mind (1930).

Sheldon Goldman, *Conflicts in the U.S. Courts of Appeals, 1965–1971: A Quantitative Analysis*, 42 U. Cin. L. Rev. 635 (1973).

Erwin N. Griswold, *Foreword: Of Time and Attitudes—Professor Hart and Judge Arnold*, 74 Harv. L. Rev. 81 (1960).

Charles C. Haines, *General Observations on the Effects of Personal, Political and Economic Influences on the Decision of Judges*, 17 Ill. L. Rev. 96 (1922).

Robert Heilbroner, *How to Make an Intelligent Decision*, Think Magazine (1960).

Oliver Wendell Holmes, Jr., *Ideas and Doubts*, 10 Ill. L. Rev. 1 (1915).

Harry W. Jones, *An Invitation to Jurisprudence*, 74 Colum. L. Rev. 1023 (1974).

Harry W. Jones, *Law and Morality in the Perspective of Legal Realism*, 61 Colum. L. Rev. 799 (1961).

Hugh P. MacMillan, *Lord Chancellor Birkenhead*, Law and Other Things (1937).

Charles H. Miller, The Supreme Court and the Uses of History (1969).

Herman Oliphant, *A Return to Stare Decisis*, 14 A.B.A.J. 71 (1928).

H.H. Price, *Relief and Will*, Proceedings of the Aristotelian Society, Vol. 28 (1954).

Herbert Simon, The New Science of Management Decision (1960).

G. Edward White, *The Evolution of Reasoned Elaboration: Jurisprudential Criticism and Social Change*, 50 Va. L. Rev. 279 (1973).

Cases
Fay v. Noia, 372 U.S. 391 (1963).

Stone v. Powell, 428 U.S. 465 (1976).

Chapter 15

J.L. Austin, Philosophical Papers (1961).

Henry Campbell Black, Handbook on the Law of Judicial Precedents (1912).

Piero Calamandrei, Processo e Democrazia (1956).

Benjamin N. Cardozo, The Nature of the Judicial Process (1921).

3 Arthur L. Corbin, Corbin on Contracts (1960).

Alfred Denning, The Discipline of the Law (1979).

Patrick Devlin, The Judge (1974).

John Dewey, *Logical Method and Law*, 10 Cornell L.Q. 17 (1929).

Jerome Frank, Law and the Modern Mind (1930).

Learned Hand, N.Y. Times, Nov. 28, 1954 (Magazine).

Henry M. Hart & Albert M. Sacks, The Legal Process: Basic Problems in the Making and Application of Law (1958).

Oliver Wendell Holmes, Jr., The Common Law (Howe ed. 1963) (1881).

Oliver Wendell Holmes, Jr., *The Path of the Law*, 10 Harv. L. Rev. 457 (1890).

William James, Principles of Psychology (1890).

Harry W. Jones, *An Invitation to Jurisprudence*, 74 Colum. L. Rev. 1023 (1974).

Edward Levi, *An Introduction to Legal Reasoning*, 15 U. Chi. L. Rev. 501 (1948).

Karl N. Llewellyn, *Remarks on the Theory of Appellate Decision and the Rules or Canons About How Statutes Are to Be Construed*, 3 Vand. L. Rev. 395 (1950).

Irving M. Mehler, Effective Legal Communication (1975).

Charles H. Miller, The Supreme Court and the Uses of History (1969).

Edwin W. Patterson, *The Interpretation and Construction of Contracts,* 64 Colum. L. Rev. 833 (1964).

4 Roscoe Pound, Jurisprudence (1959).

Richard Posner, *Statutory Interpretation—In the Classroom and in the Courtroom,* 50 U. Chi. L. Rev. 800 (1983).

Julius Stone, *Man and Machine in the Search for Justice,* 16 Stan. L. Rev. 515 (1964).

Roger Traynor, *Reasoning in a Circle of Law,* 56 Va. L. Rev. 739 (1970).

John Wisdom, Philosophy and Psycho-Analysis (1953).

Cases

Burch v. Louisiana, 441 U.S. 130 (1979).

Caminetti v. United States, 242 U.S. 470 (1917).

Cort v. Ash, 422 U.S. 66 (1975).

Eyston v. Studd, 2 Plowd (1574).

Furman v. Georgia, 408 U.S. 238 (1972).

Heydon's Case, 30 Co. 7a, 76 Eng. Rep. 637 (ex. 1584).

Home Office v. Dorset Yacht Co., [1970] A.C. 1004 (H.L.).

Teminiello v. Chicago, 337 U.S. 1 (1949).

Afterword

Ruggero J. Aldisert, Road to the Robes: A Federal Judge Recollects Young Years & Early Times (2005).

A Lawyer's Response

Ruggero J. Aldisert, The Judicial Process (2d ed. 1996).

Ruggero J. Aldisert, Winning on Appeal: Better Briefs and Oral Argument (2d ed. NITA 2003).

Gretchen Rubin, Forty Ways to Look at Winston Churchill (2004).

William Strunk, Jr. & E.B. White, The Elements of Style (4th ed. 2000).

About the Author

The following is a slightly modified version of the biography prepared by the
Legal Writing Institute on the occasion of presenting the author with the
Golden Pen Award of 2008.

Ruggero J. Aldisert, Senior U.S. Circuit Judge of the U.S. Court of Appeals
for the Third Circuit, received his B.A. and J.D. degrees from the University of
Pittsburgh. Following college, he served for four years on active duty during
World War II in the U.S. Marine Corps. His distinguished career on the bench
began in 1961, when he was elected a judge for the Court of Common Pleas
of Allegheny County, Pennsylvania. In 1968, he was nominated by President
Johnson to serve on the U.S. Court of Appeals for the Third Circuit, where he
served as Chief Judge from 1984 to 1986 and where he remains today. In addition to a distinguished career on the bench, Judge Aldisert has also written
several popular and influential books addressing legal writing issues.

For more than 20 years, from 1963 to 1986, Judge Aldisert was an adjunct professor at the University of Pittsburgh School of Law in Pittsburgh, Pennsylvania and he has been a longtime trustee of the University of Pittsburgh. He has
been a visiting professor at Arizona State University, New York University, the
University of Texas, the University of Virginia and Augsburg University in Germany. He has lectured throughout the United States, and throughout the world
in Canada, England, France, Germany, Italy, Poland, Croatia and Serbia. He
has also published more than 50 articles on the law.

The Legal Writing Institute honored him for his efforts to advance the cause
of better legal writing in his capacity as judge, educator and writer. With more
than 2000 members in the world, the Institute is an international organization dedicated to improving legal writing. Throughout a long career, Judge
Aldisert has demonstrated an unwavering commitment to promote the use of
clear language in his judicial opinions, in his books and in his teachings.

Not only has Judge Aldisert advanced the cause of better legal writing in his
capacity as judge, educator and writer, he has also earned the respect of some
of the most esteemed members of the legal community. In 2005, Aldisert be-

came the first recipient of the "Distinguished Appellate Jurist Award," bestowed by the American Bar Association's Council of Appellate Lawyers. He received that award for his outstanding efforts to educate appellate lawyers and judges, making significant contributions in the field of appellate jurisprudence, and consistently exhibiting the following attributes: fairness, objectivity, scholarship, clarity, mentoring, education and judicial temperament. On the occasion of his 90th birthday, the University of Pittsburgh honored Judge Aldisert with its highest alumni award, the Distinguished Alumni Fellow Award, in which it stated: "You are widely acclaimed as an accomplished jurist, gifted author, committed teacher, and dedicated community servant."